The Johannine Commandments

Theological Inquiries

*Studies in Contemporary
Biblical and Theological Problems*

General Editor
Lawrence Boadt, C. S. P.

PAULIST PRESS

The Johannine Commandments

1 John and the Struggle for the Johannine Tradition

Urban C. von Wahlde

PAULIST PRESS
New York • Mahwah

NOTE: All translations of New Testament passages are the author's own. Those from the OT are from the NAB. While it is the intention of the translator to render the text into gender neutral language when possible, where awkwardness or excessive paraphrasing would result, fidelity to the original text has required that the original gender specific language be employed even though such language would not be used in present day composition.

Library of Congress Cataloging-in-Publication Data

Von Wahlde, Urban C.
    The Johannine commandments: I John and the struggle for the Johannine tradition/by Urban C. von Wahlde.
        p.   cm.—(Theological inquiries)
    Includes bibliographical references.
    ISBN 0-8091-3061-0
    1. Bible.   N.T.   Epistle of John, 1st—Criticism, interpretation.
etc.   2. Johannine school.   I. Title.   II. Series.
    BS2805.2.V65   1990
    227'.9406—dc20   89-48604
                                                                CIP

Published by Paulist Press
997 Macarthur Boulevard
Mahwah, New Jersey 07430

Printed and bound in the
United States of America

CONTENTS

for
R.A.D., S.J.
and
C.A.D.

ACKNOWLEDGMENTS

I wish to express my gratitude for the support of a semester's paid leave of absence from Loyola University of Chicago which greatly aided in the writing of this book. I have profited considerably from the comments of three colleagues who have read the manuscript and offered valuable advice: Rev. Thomas Tobin, S.J., and Dr. John White, both of the Theology Department of Loyola University of Chicago and Dr. Fernando Segovia of Vanderbilt University. Rev. Prakash Mallavarapu, my graduate assistant, has prepared the indices and proofed much of the text. I thank him for his careful work.

Michael and Lisa have watched day after day as the work on this book has progressed. Their interest is always a great support of another kind. Finally, Rev. Raymond A. Dunne, S.J., early on in my career, taught me by his wise and prudent counsel to walk in the light, and my wife Carol has taught me by her daily example what it means to love. To them both this book is dedicated.

ABBREVIATIONS

BOOKS OF THE BIBLE

Gen	Genesis
Ex	Exodus
Lev	Leviticus
Dt	Deuteronomy
1Kgs	1 Kings
2Kgs	2 Kings
Ps	Psalms
Is	Isaiah
Jer	Jeremiah
Ez	Ezekiel
WisSol	Wisdom of Solomon
Dn	Daniel
Mt	Matthew
Mk	Mark
Lk	Luke
Jn	John
1Jn	First Letter of John
2Jn	Second Letter of John
3Jn	Third Letter of John

APOCRYPHA AND PSEUDEPIGRAPHA

T12P	Testaments of the Twelve Patriarchs
TAsh	Testament of Asher
TBenj	Testament of Benjamin

TGad	Testament of Gad
TIss	Testament of Issachar
TJos	Testament of Joseph
TLev	Testament of Levi
TNaph	Testament of Naphthali
TReu	Testament of Ruben
TSim	Testament of Simon

QUMRAN DOCUMENTS

CD	Cairo (Genizah text) *Damascus Document*
1Q, 2Q	Numbered Caves at Qumran
1QH	*Thanksgiving Hymns* Cave 1
1QS	*Manual of Discipline* or *Community Rule*
1QSer	Fragment from *Messianic Rule*

SERIAL AND PERIODICAL LITERATURE

AB	Anchor Bible
AnBib	Analecta Biblica
ANRW	Aufstieg und Niedergang der Romischen Welt
BAG	W. Bauer, W. F. Arndt and F. W. Gingrich, *Greek-English Lexicon of the NT*
BETL	Bibliotheca Ephemeridum Theologicarum Lovaniensium
BEvT	Beitrage sur evangelischen Theologie
BJRL	Bulletin of the John Rylands University Library, Manchester
BTB	*Biblical Theology Bulletin*
BU	Biblische Untersuchungen
CBQ	*Catholic Biblical Quarterly*
ConNT	*Coniectanea Neotestamentica*
DSSE	G. Vermes, ed., *Dead Sea Scrolls in English*
EspVie	*Esprit et Vie*
ETL	*Ephemerides Theologicae Lovaniensium*
EvT	*Evangelische Theologie*
ExpTim	*Expository Times*
FTS	Frankfurter theologische Studien

HNT	Handbuch zum Neuen Testament
HNTC	Harper's NT Commentaries
HTKNT	Herders theologischer Kommentar zum Neuen Testament
HTS	*Harvard Theological Studies*
JBL	*Journal of Biblical Literature*
KD	Kerygma und Dogma
LavTheolPhil	Laval Théologique et Philosophique
NAB	New American Bible
NCB	New Century Bible
NICNT	New International Commentary on the New Testament
NovT	*Novum Testamentum*
NovTSupp	Novum Testamentum Supplements
NRT	*Nouvelle Revue théologique*
NTM	New Testament Message
NTS	*New Testament Studies*
OTP	Old Testament Pseudepigrapha
OTS	Oudtestamentische Studien
RB	*Revue Biblique*
RevQ	*Revue de Qumran*
RSR	*Recherches de Science Religieuse*
SBLDS	Society of Biblical Literature Dissertation Series
SBLSBS	Society of Biblical Literature Sources for Biblical Study
SBT	Studies in Biblical Theology
SJLA	Studies in Judaism in Late Antiquity
SNTSMS	Society for New Testament Studies Monograph Series
TDNT	G. Kittle and G. Friedrich (eds.) *Theological Dictionary of the New Testament*
TLZ	*Theologische Literaturzeitung*
TS	*Theological Studies*
WBC	Word Bible Commentary
WMANT	Wissenschaftliche Monographien zum Alten und Neuen Testament

WUNT   Wissenschaftliche Untersuchungen zum
                 Neuen Testament
ZNW   *Zeitschrift fur die neutestamentliche*
                 Wissenschaft

OTHER

ET   English translation
Gk   Greek
LXX   Septuagint
UBS   United Bible Societies Greek New Testament
v(vv)   verse(s)

INTRODUCTION

It is one of the curious facts of the New Testament that the Johannine tradition, which today is so greatly admired for the profundity of its insight into the mystery and person of Jesus, could have had such a stormy beginning and such a turmoil-filled history. Certainly no New Testament community underwent more conflict and controversy than that founded on the Johannine tradition. For many of the members of the Johannine community, their belief in Jesus had led them first to the trauma of breaking with their parent religion of Judaism, with all of the emotional and intellectual agony that that must have involved, to find only later that they would be forced to undergo yet another trauma as their own Christian community split violently in two as controversy arose once again—this time among the members of the community themselves—over the meaning and identity of Jesus.

What is equally amazing to the serious student of the Johannine literature is the extent to which this series of contemporary crises is mirrored in the pages of the gospel and epistles. From the gospel we see constant signs of a group of Jewish Christians embattled in controversy with the parent synagogue. Their claims about Jesus are rejected violently by their Jewish brethren, and they are accused of not following the traditions of Moses, of perverting their faith, and of worshiping two gods. They are expelled from the synagogues for publicly confessing Jesus as the Christ, and some of them are even put to death by their fellow Jews thinking they are giving glory to God.

By the time of the first epistle, the conflict from without had eased. The Johannine group was now a thoroughly Christian com-

1

munity, independent of and distinct from Judaism. But what may have eventually proved to be an even greater tragedy awaited them. Now there was a violent division within their own ranks. The members of the community were divided about various aspects of their belief and apparently a large number of them had already left the ranks of the community. As the author of 1 John writes, he attempts to confirm the beliefs of the original group and to explain the basis for their steadfast opposition to the members of the radically progressive group. It is his message that the members must remain constant in a time of what must have seemed to be a veritable schizophrenia within their community. The crisis was clearly a major one, for the author refers to the situation as the "last hour"—and the opponents as antichrists! It was indeed a struggle for the very survival of the Johannine tradition as the author's community envisioned it.

This book deals with Johannine theology at the time of the second of these crises. And it views that crisis through the prism of the Johannine theology of commandment.

The Johannine theology of commandment is one of the least studied elements of Johannine theology. This is so in spite of the fact that the commandment of mutual love (the so-called "love commandment") is one of the most well known legacies not only of the Johannine community but of the New Testament as a whole. It is in fact the popularity of the love commandment that is responsible at least in part for the lack of interest in the larger dimensions of the Johannine commandment tradition and for the failure to conduct any full study of the concept within the Johannine tradition.

But there is also another reason for this lack of attention to the Johannine commandment tradition. For most scholars the love commandment is the *only* Johannine commandment. As we shall see in Chapter One even the most respected of Johannine scholars explicitly state that there is only one Johannine commandment. True, it has been the view of some others that there is a second commandment, which they define as "keeping the word of Jesus." But such a commandment is so general in nature, so "anemic," that there never has been an attempt to find a significant place for it within the larger context of Johannine theology.

The current study then tries to fill that void. As such it attempts to give a clearer answer to the most basic and essential of questions:

the number of commandments the tradition contains! But it also attempts, in addition to dealing with the other less basic questions involved, to address the larger dimensions of the commandment tradition within Johannine theology, the history-of-religions background of the term, the relation of the Johannine commandment tradition to the other commandment traditions within the New Testament, and finally its role within the historical situation of the community.

I shall argue that there are two Johannine commandments: to keep the word of Jesus and to love one another, and that these commandments were intended in their present formulation to refute the opinions of the author's opponents at the time of the schism of 1 John. The first commandment stressed fidelity to the word of Jesus as he had spoken it and as the community had heard it from the beginning. The second commandment stressed the necessity of actively demonstrating love for one another within the community in imitation of the love of Jesus for them.

Further I shall argue that the commandment texts within the gospel are not indigenous to the gospel but were added at the time of the schism of 1 John in order to clarify their understanding of what the message of Jesus had been.

A word is in order about the way the book proceeds.

In the first chapter, the concept of commandment within the gospel is studied. First, it becomes clear there are two commandments given to Jesus. But more importantly we find new evidence that, contrary to most current opinion, there are also two commandments given to the disciples and that these two are closely correlated with those given to Jesus.

But in the course of the study of the commandments given to Jesus a curious fact becomes evident. In the gospel, the concept of commandment functions as a theological conceptualization of the ministry of Jesus. But this relatively infrequent conceptualization of the ministry as commandment stands alongside another much more common conceptualization of the ministry as a "work" given to Jesus by the Father. These two conceptualizations are never harmonized, and there is no evidence that they are, or are intended to be, complementary of one another.

Chapter Two is devoted to a brief study of "work" as a conceptualization of the ministry in order to clarify the relationship between it and the ministry as commandment. The study confirms the previous suspicion that the two terms represent parallel independent versions of the ministry. In addition, "work," the dominant motif in the gospel, does not occur in the epistles, while "commandment," which had been a minor motif in the gospel, becomes a major one in the epistles. This pattern of occurrence in turn strongly suggests that the commandment texts within the gospel may be secondary, a claim which is then investigated more thoroughly in Chapter Four.

Chapter Three turns to a study of the commandments in the epistles. Within the epistles, even those who would otherwise claim that there is only one Johannine commandment admit that in one verse of the first epistle (3:23) a second commandment is clearly referred to. But further problems arise. In the gospel the commandments given to the disciples are described as "of Jesus," but in the epistles they are described not as "of Jesus," but as "of God." Although this is frequently noted, a satisfactory explanation has never been given for this change.

Chapter Four then returns to the question raised at the end of Chapter Two, that of the literary relationship between the commandment passages in the gospel and the rest of the gospel. This chapter concerns itself with a detailed examination of the literary features of each of the commandment passages in the gospel and concludes that in fact there is convincing evidence that the commandment passages (not only those which refer to the commandments given to Jesus but also those which refer to the commandments given to the disciples) are secondary additions to the major text of the gospel—the work of an editor.

The nature of the crisis that confronted the Johannine community at the time of the epistles is greatly disputed. Even after Raymond Brown's masterful commentary on the epistles, it is clear that questions remain about the nature of the problems which divided the Johannine group. In dialogue primarily with Brown's massive commentary on the epistles, Chapters Five and Six seek to address the question of the nature of the crisis. The analysis concludes that the crisis may be of a somewhat different character than Brown would have it. The opponents center their convictions on their possession of the Spirit and claim that Jesus' role in salvation was only to be

the agent of the eschatological outpouring of the Spirit and that therefore his role in salvation is not permanent. All of the prerogatives of
the Christian existence are derived from the Spirit rather than from
Jesus himself. Jesus is simply the agent by which the Spirit is given.
Both groups claim to base their position on the Johannine tradition
as it is found in the gospel.

In response to his opponents, the author of 1 John focuses his
attention on the two areas in which these different interpretations
most manifest themselves: the role of Jesus (particularly his word,
his death) and the role of conduct (does the eschatological possession
of the Spirit guarantee the fullness of life to such a degree that correct
conduct, manifest in love of the brethren, becomes irrelevant?). Specifically, the author of 1 John claims that opponents do not remain
rooted in the tradition which they have heard from the beginning in
the words of Jesus, but rather over-emphasize their possession of the
Spirit and go beyond the tradition's teaching. In addition, they do
not love the brethren because they think that such conduct is
irrelevant.

In the light of this analysis of the community's crisis, it becomes
clear that the two Johannine commandments are not simply an ab-
stract grouping of responsibilities but are designed to confront these
community issues directly. From this, the beginnings of a new understanding of the purpose of the commandment tradition emerges.
The concept of "commandment" emerges as the theological framework within which the author of 1 John defines the errors of the
opponents and exhorts his readers to correct belief and conduct.

Chapter Seven then turns to a reading of the first epistle to attempt to confirm this relation of commandment to crisis in a fuller
way. Three further elements of the epistle give convincing proof of
the relation of the Johannine commandments to the community's
crisis. First, a study of the structure of the epistle shows that the two
major divisions of the epistle center around the themes of "light" (as
a symbol of correct belief) and around "love" (as a symbol of the
correct conduct required). Second, the thought of the epistle in fact
follows this pattern, with a discussion of correct belief dominating
the first major division and discussion of love dominating the second,
a division paralleled in the distribution of the commandment texts

within the gospel. Finally within the first epistle *all the major disputed claims of both groups* are tested by the criteria defined in the commandments: correct belief and correct love.

Chapter Eight moves beyond the confines of the Johannine literature to discover the history of religions background of the Johannine use of commandment. The chapter is composed of three sections, the first of which is an examination of the background of "commandment" itself. Once again we find that there has been little study done of the topic. Surprisingly, aside from dictionary articles, only one article has been devoted to tracing the background of the Johannine use of commandment. A detailed study of the background in the materials from the intertestamental and apocalyptic literature, especially that of the Testaments of the Twelve Patriarchs and the Qumran literature, provides a fuller, more comprehensive background than that which is available from the canonical Hebrew scriptures alone. This literature joins the rich covenantal background of the term in the canonical scriptures with the modified dualism of sectarian Judaism.

The second part of the chapter compares the two Johannine commandments with other "two commandment" traditions in the Testaments of the Twelve Patriarchs and especially the two great commandments of the synoptic tradition to determine whether the Johannine commandments are that community's version of these attempts to summarize the law. This comparison attempts to show that the intent of the great commandment tradition is considerably different from that of the Johannine commandments.

However, within the Community Rule of Qumran (1QS), a "double scrutiny" is discovered in which the applicants for admission to the community are tested repeatedly regarding their "understanding" and their "deeds" with respect to the law. This parallel, studied in the third part of the chapter, provides a close parallel both in intention and in form to the Johannine commandments. In addition this provides a parallel to what may well have been one of the functions of the Johannine commandments: a scrutiny of Johannine converts associated with their entry into the community.

Chapter Nine, finally, is a detailed summary of the conclusions of the study and attempts to draw together the various elements of the study into a unified and coherent picture of the commandments and the crisis they confront.

Thus this investigation into the Johannine commandments hopes to provide a new understanding not only of the Johannine commandment tradition and of the crisis which divided that community but also of the way the commandment tradition, heretofore ill-defined and unrelated to the circumstances of the community, functioned as a theological tool for both the instruction of the community and the refutation of its opponents.

A NOTE ON THE LITERARY HISTORY
OF THE JOHANNINE TRADITION

This book is an attempt to define the Johannine commandments and to relate them to the crisis which divided the Johannine community. It is not intended to be a study of the literary process by which the gospel and epistles came to be. Nevertheless it is impossible to describe the commandment tradition adequately without some reference to the literary history of the Johannine corpus. It may be helpful therefore for me to present a brief outline of that literary history as I see it.

The Johannine gospel has experienced three stages of literary development. The first stage involved the writing of a narrative document focusing on the miracles ("signs") of Jesus and their importance for belief. This narrative began with the baptism of Jesus and extended to the post-resurrection appearances. In this gospel, the focus was on the belief of the disciples and of the common people as well as on the rejection of Jesus by the Jewish religious authorities. I have studied this stage of the gospel's development in detail in my *The Earliest Version of John's Gospel.*[1]

The second stage of the gospel considered the basis of belief to be much more complex. First, belief was based not just on miracles, but also on the words of Jesus, the scriptures and to a lesser extent the witness of John the Baptist. Second, belief in its most complete form is presented as coming about when one received and responded to the Holy Spirit. This stage of reflection on the mystery of Jesus clearly brought the Johannine literary tradition to a considerably more sophisticated understanding of both Jesus and the Christian life. It was this stage of the gospel's development which mirrored the community's struggle with "the Jews" and which witnessed to the community's expulsion from the synagogue. This stage of the community's theology, while it explained in a more detailed way both the basis for the community's belief and the reasons for rejection of Jesus, came to expression as a polemic against opposition from the "Jews." It was sufficiently ambiguous in its expression as to give rise to two divergent interpretations when viewed in other circumstances. These two interpretations of the tradition eventually led to the schism described in 1 John. 1 John was written to clarify the tradition and to confront that schism.

At the same (or almost the same) time as the writing of 1 John, additions were made to the (second) version of the gospel in order to make explicit in the text what had only been implicit at the time of the second edition. Thus there are many similarities in the theology and general approach taken by the author of 1 John and by the final redactor of the gospel.

To substantiate this view of the development of the Johannine tradition from a literary study of the documents is not possible here. In this book we will be looking at a number (but hardly all) of the theological features of both the second and third editions of the gospel in relation to the community's crisis. But it is hoped that some sense of my overall view of the tradition's development will enable the reader to relate the theological argument here to the overall history of the Johannine community and the Johannine literary tradition.

NOTES

1. U. C. von Wahlde, *The Earliest Version of John's Gospel* (Wilmington: M. Glazier, 1989).

Chapter One

IN THE JOHANNINE GOSPEL: THE FATHER'S COMMANDMENTS AND JESUS' COMMANDMENTS

The notion of "commandment" lies at the very heart of the Judaeo-Christian tradition. In the Hebrew scriptures, the ten "commandments" form the center of the Torah and express the essence of the covenant obligations of the Israelites.[1] Commandment evokes recollections of the majestic self-revelation of Yahweh at Sinai as he[2] revealed both himself and his will. The term reminds the hearer of the blessings and the curses which are attached to the fulfillment or neglect of the commandments. But commandment is linked in a particular way to the book of Deuteronomy where the association of commandment with Israel's election is emphasized, and where its fulfillment is so clearly identified as an expression of love for Yahweh.

The concept of commandment likewise colors the entire New Testament. Although the New Testament does not ever list the ten commandments as such, all of the commandments are mentioned individually in various places throughout the New Testament and their fulfillment is exhorted. When approached by the rich young man, Jesus tells him to "keep the commandments." There is also the repeated concern in the synoptics with the root and basis of all the commandments. In Luke the question is put to Jesus "Teacher, what must I do to inherit everlasting life?" (Lk 10:26); in Matthew and in Mark the question is "Which is the first of all the commandments?" (Mk 12:28). But in every case the answer is that the greatest of the commandments is that one should love God and the second is like it: that one should love one's neighbor. However there is never any doubt that the context of the discussion is the covenant tradition of Israel.

Although the synoptics speak of the commandments in general and of the "two great commandments," in the Johannine tradition there is a different emphasis. First, we find repeated exhortations that the disciples should keep the commandments that Jesus gives them, but curiously these occur exclusively within the last discourses (13: 31–17:26). Second, in spite of this mention of the commandments (plural), most commentators identify only one commandment as being mentioned in the Johannine tradition: the commandment that the disciples love one another. For example, recently Pheme Perkins has said in reference to John 15:7–17, "Though this section mentions commandments in the plural, the only commandment ever stated is the love commandment (similarly elsewhere in the Johannine tradition)."[3] Raymond Brown holds the same position: "for the Johannine tradition, to love is the only commandment explicitly mentioned . . ."[4] But then one could ask why the plural is used if there is in fact only one commandment.

On the other hand some would argue that there is another commandment, to "keep the word" of Jesus. However if this is so, there are still problems. In the Old Testament tradition, "word" can be a synonym of commandment itself, and it may be that the author is simply reaffirming what he had said previously: namely that they should keep the commandments. In addition, if there is a second commandment as some would affirm, the content of the commandment "to keep the word of Jesus" is so general that it would seem to have little or no importance for an understanding of Johannine theology.

From this it can be seen that there is much that is uncertain about the Johannine commandments. This is due in part to the fact that they are a generally neglected area of Johannine theology. The background of commandment has been studied in a scholarly article by M. J. O'Connell, and S. Pancaro examines the commandments briefly in his study of law in the fourth gospel.[5] Although the love commandment is frequently the object of attention, the whole complex of commandment texts in the gospel has never been the object of an extended, book-length study. It is hoped that this study can contribute in some way to a fuller understanding not only of the Johannine commandments but also of Johannine theology as a whole.

The starting point for our study of the commandments in the Johannine tradition is the gospel of John, since this is by common estimation the earliest of the documents of the Johannine community.[6] We will begin with some "statistics" of the appearance of the word in the gospel. In chapters one and three, we will examine all of the texts in the Johannine gospels and epistles which deal with the commandments. This analysis will be quite detailed, leading from the bare statistics to a gradually fuller view of the entire commandment tradition.

A. THE STATISTICS

The Greek word for commandment (*entolē*) appears eleven times in the gospel of John: 10:18; 11:57; 12:49,50; 13:34; 14:15,21,31; 15:10 [twice], 12. Of these all are pertinent to our discussion except 11:57 which states that the chief priests gave "orders" (*entolas*) that the people should provide information concerning the whereabouts of Jesus. Since our concern is only for the use of the term in its religious reference, this instance is not relevant for our study.

The verb (*entellomai*) appears three times in the gospel: 14:31; 15:14,17.[7] All of the verbal forms are significant for the study. Within these texts we find two broad classes of "commands": those given by the Father to Jesus and those given by Jesus to the disciples.

B. THE COMMANDMENTS GIVEN TO JESUS

In the gospel, there are four passages where there are references to the commands given to Jesus by the Father: 10:14–18; 12:44–50; 14:30–31; 15:10. We will begin by looking at each of these passages, calling attention to the various significant details, and then attempt to draw some general conclusions regarding the Johannine view of the commandments given to Jesus.

10:14–18

(14) I am the good shepherd. I know my sheep and mine know me, (15) just as the Father knows me and I know the

Father. And I lay down my life for the sheep. (16) I have other sheep which are not from this fold and I have to shepherd them also. They will hear my voice and there will be one flock, one shepherd. (17) My Father loves me because I lay down my life in order that I may take it up again. (18) No one takes it from me, but I lay it down of my own will. I have the power to lay it down, and I have the power to take it up again; this is the commandment I received from my Father.[8]

This passage forms part of the explanation of the parable of the good shepherd. It contains the first occurrence of the term "commandment" in the gospel. The commandment that Jesus has, he has received from the Father. The commandment requires that Jesus lay down his life "on behalf of his sheep" (v 15). The expression "on behalf of" (which in the translation I have rendered simply as "for") is noteworthy because it describes Jesus' coming death as a sacrifice of his life for his own. The phrase "on behalf of" is used other times in the gospel in this sacrificial sense (esp 15:13) and also is found elsewhere in the New Testament in a similar usage.[9]

The statement that the Father loves Jesus "for this reason: that he lays down his life" is striking because it implies a conditional quality in the love of the Father for Jesus. This conditionality is not usually associated with the relationship between God the Father and Jesus.[10] We will have reason to look at this feature in more detail later.

The Greek verb for love in v 17 is *agapan. Agapan, agapē* occurs thirty-four times in the gospel. Another word *philein*[11] is also used eleven times. Elsewhere in the New Testament there is a distinction frequently intended between the two terms,[12] and it is sometimes suggested that this difference is also operative in the gospel. However the use is not consistent enough in the gospel to warrant such a distinction.[13]

12:44–50

(44) Then Jesus cried out and said, "The one believing in me does not believe in me but in the one who sent me. (45) And the one who sees me sees the one who sent me. (46) I

have come into the world as the light in order that everyone who believes in me might not remain in darkness. (47) And if a person hears my words and does not keep them, I do not judge that person. For I did not come to judge the world but to save it. (48) The one who rejects me and who does not accept my words has a judge: the word which I spoke will judge him on the last day. (49) For I did not speak of my own authority; rather the Father who sent me has himself commanded me what to say and to speak. (50) And I know that his commandment is eternal life. Consequently those things which I say, I say just as the Father has told me."

This passage speaks of the second of the commandments given to Jesus by the Father: the commandment to say (to speak) what the Father has told him.[14] Throughout the passage there is depicted a Jesus who is dedicated to saying only what he has been commanded by the Father. In fact, belief in Jesus is said to be not in him for himself but through him to the Father. And the one who sees Jesus does not really see him but the Father.

Here we meet for the first time the concept of the "word" which Jesus is bidden to speak. The word *logos* is used in a theological sense to refer to the message of Jesus or to the message of the Father which Jesus is to speak.[15] This concept pervades the entire gospel. It is, however, most fully developed in chapter 8, where Jesus is said to witness to himself. Throughout the passages cited above, Jesus repeats the statement that his words are not his own but those of the Father. But 12:44–50 is important as describing this word as the object of a "commandment" given to Jesus by the Father!

In the passage the term "word" shifts from plural to singular. Such shifts also occur elsewhere in the gospel (compare 8:47 with 8: 43,51; 15:3 with 15:7, 17:8 with 17:6,14). This use is consistent in that the plural ("words," *logoi*) refers to the individual statements, pronouncements, etc. which go together to make up the overall "word" (*logos*).[16] In the Greek text, two terms occur for "word"— *rhēma* and *logos.* However there seems to be no distinction intended between them, although *rhēma* is never used to refer to the entirety of the message of Jesus.

The commandment is described in v 50 as "eternal life," that is, the obedience to this commandment will lead one to eternal life. The acceptance or the rejection of this word will be the judge of the person confronted by it "on the last day" (i.e. on the day of final eschatological judgment).[17]

In 10:17 it was said that the fulfillment of the commandment of the Father was related to continuance in love. As we shall see, the notion of love is closely connected with almost all of the commandment passages both in the gospel and in the epistles. It is curious, though not particularly significant, that in the present passage there is no mention of love.

14:30–31

> (30) I will not say many more things among you, for the ruler of the world is coming. He has no power over me, (31) but in order that the world might know that I love the Father, I act as the Father has commanded me. Rise; let us leave here.

This reference to commandment is very brief but significant, for it describes the entirety of Jesus' intention in the coming passion as being the fulfillment of the Father's commandment. The grammar of the last clause is made somewhat awkward by the presence of "and" (*kai*), but this is most likely an epexegetical use of *kai,* that is, specifying how the world will know that Jesus loves the Father.

The action referred to is of course Jesus' laying down of his life for his own, another (implicit) reference to his sacrificial death. Again we see that Jesus' love is manifest precisely in terms of keeping the commandments given him by the Father. Throughout the Johannine writings it is said that if one loves, one will keep the commandments; thus love must always be manifest in correct action. Keeping the commandments is a way of discerning *true* love of God/Jesus (cf 14: 15,21,23 (negatively in 24); 15:10,14; 1 Jn 2:5; 4:20; 5:2–3).

The fact that Jesus does what he does out of love for the Father is contrasted with the fact that "the ruler of the world" is coming. But Jesus affirms that the ruler "has no power over me." The term "ruler of the world" is an apocalyptic term. It reflects the dualistic conception of the world, partly controlled by the powers of evil.[18] It also occurs in 12:31 and 16:11.

This passage also speaks of the witness value in Jesus' actions. One of the purposes/results of Jesus' action will be that the world will see that he loves the Father. This same witness value is attributed to the disciples' love for one another in 13:35 below.

15:10

> (10) If you keep my commandments, you will abide in my love, just as I have kept the commandments of my Father and I abide in his love.

This reference to the commandments which Jesus has kept occurs within a description of the commandments given to the disciples. We will look at the larger context below but here want to focus on the reference to the commandment given to Jesus.

This reference confirms an element of the presentation regarding Jesus that we have seen before: by keeping the commandments of the Father, Jesus remains in the love of the Father. Again there is affirmation of the conditional element in the relationship between Jesus and the Father, and also between Jesus and his disciples.

C. CONCLUSIONS: THE COMMANDMENTS GIVEN TO JESUS

From our examination of the commandments given to Jesus in the gospel, it is clear that there are two commandments given to Jesus: what to say and what to do. In 10:17 we heard about the commandment what to "do": "This is why the Father loves me: because I lay down my life." V 18 then goes on to say: "No one takes it from me, but I put it down of my own accord. I have the power to put it down and the power to take it up again. This is the command I received (*Tautēn tēn entolēn elabon*) from the Father." Here the commandment is defined as one of action, specifically one of Jesus laying down his life "for his sheep" (v 15). This is also the case in 14:31.

In 12:49 we heard: "I do not speak on my own authority, but

the Father who sent me has given me a commandment (*entolēn de-dōken*) what to say and what to speak." Although the words of Jesus are repeatedly described as being from the Father, this is the only instance of them being described as the object of a commandment.

Thus it is clear that there are two commandments given to Jesus: to speak the word given him by the Father and to lay down his life on behalf of his own out of love for them. It was necessary for Jesus to fulfill these commandments in order to continue to be loved by the Father, and in fulfilling them he demonstrates the love which he in fact has for the Father also. The commandments provide both the content (the "what") and the motivation (the "why") of his earthly ministry. Thus for Jesus the "commandments" provide a theological framework within which his ministry is conceived and within which it is evaluated theologically.

D. THE COMMANDMENTS GIVEN TO THE DISCIPLES

The second group of commandment texts in the gospel deals with those commandments given by Jesus to the disciples. The presentation of this material on the commandment given to the disciples is found in three sections of the last discourses: (1) 13:34–35; (2) 14:15,21–24; (3) 15:9–17. Of these, the first is brief, but the second and third provide a more detailed treatment.

Again, we will look first at each of the passages in somewhat more detail, calling attention to various significant details and then draw more general conclusions.

13:34–35

(34) A new commandment I give you, that you love one another—that, just as I loved you, you love one another. (35) From this will all know that you are my disciples, if you have love for one another.

These verses form the first of the passages dealing with the commandments Jesus gives to his disciples in the gospel.

The verses have long been considered awkward in their present context. On one hand, they do not fit well with the statement of Jesus about his departure immediately before, and they do not figure in Peter's response in v 36 or in anything that follows (until perhaps 15:9–17 where the love commandment is again discussed). This had led several scholars to suggest that they are a later addition.[19] Whether they can legitimately be said to be secondary will be discussed in detail in chapter five. However from the point of view of the understanding of commandment, the verses provide little difficulty.

This is the first mention of the so-called Johannine love commandment, i.e. the disciples are commanded to love one another. This wording of the commandment is the typical one throughout the Johannine writings (except at 1 John 4:21, where the commandment is defined as "love of one's brother"). The verb for "loving" is in the present subjunctive; presumably this indicates that their love should be continuous.

The actual extent of the group to which Christian love is to be extended is an important topic but will be deferred until chapter eight, where the Johannine commandments are compared with the synoptic "great commandments." However it can be said at this point that throughout the Johannine writings, the consistent emphasis is on the love to be shown within the community, and it is likely that the love is also intended to be limited to the Christian community.

The commandment to love is referred to as "new." This same designation is applied to the commandment to keep the word of Jesus in 1 John 2:7–8 and in 2 John 5 (where the adjective "new" is denied for the commandment to remain faithful to Jesus' word). This "newness" is variously understood. Some would say that, as it is applied to the love commandment, it is new in that Jesus provides a new model of love: his own self-giving to the point of death. Others would say that both instances of newness refer to the eschatological newness of the commandments as given by Jesus. It is also suggested that the newness is evident in its being operative on an ongoing basis.[20] Each of these theories helps accentuate various aspects of the "newness." However it is clear that in 1 John 2:7 and 2 John 5, "new" is not intended in a way that might seem to affirm what his opponents affirm: that one is able to go beyond the "received tradition." In both of these instances, the author explicitly states that it is not new in the sense that it was not from the beginning. 1 John 2:8 provides a partial explanation: it is new as it finds its reality in the life of Jesus and in the life of the Christian.[21]

One final element of the passage is important: the love that the disciples have for one another is to have a witness value. The manifestation of this love will be an indication to the world that they are Jesus' disciples.

14:15

(15) If you love me, you will keep my commandments.

14:21-24

(21) "The one who has and keeps my commandments, that person is the one who loves me. And the one who loves me will be loved by my Father, and I will love and will manifest myself to that person." (22) Judas, not the Iscariot, said to him, "Lord, what has happened that you are about to manifest yourself to us but not to the world?" (23) Jesus answered and said to him, "If someone loves me, that person will keep my word, and my Father will love the person, and we will come and will make an abode with the person. (24) The one who does not love me does not keep my words, and the word which you hear is not mine but the word of the Father who sent me."

This commandment passage is unique in that the first of the verses (v 15) is separated from the remainder of the discussion of commandments by vv 16-20. The intervening verses contain the first of the Paraclete passages as well as material stating that Jesus himself will return and that the world will not recognize him but that the disciples will. Because that material is not directly pertinent to the commandment texts, it is not discussed here. However the material is important as will be seen later.[22]

In this passage, we find grouped together many of the elements scattered in the other passages dealing with the commandments given to Jesus. For example, love of Jesus is defined in terms of keeping his commandments; love of Jesus will mean that one is loved by God and by Jesus. In addition, it means that Jesus will manifest himself to the disciples. This statement of Jesus that he will manifest himself to the disciples (but not to the world as is said in v 22) is also unique. It clearly makes the self-revelation contingent upon obedience to the commandments. Still another promise of Jesus is made contingent upon obedience in v 23: Jesus and the Father will come and make their abode with that person.

What is commanded here is that disciples should "keep my word" (vv 23,24). It is also said that the one who does not love Jesus will not keep his words. Finally the words of Jesus are described as not his own but his who sent him, i.e. the Father's. There is considerable dispute about the meaning of "keep my word(s)" in these verses. Some would argue that it refers to the word of Jesus in the sense of his message; others would argue that word is a synonym for commandment and that the entire passage is simply a general exhortation. The meaning of this phrase is a central concern of our study, and the detailed examination of its meaning will be postponed until after the preliminary study of the second commandment in 15: 9–17. At that time I will also have some comments to make on the structure of this present section.

15:9–17

(9) As the Father loved me, I loved you. Remain in my love. (10) If you keep my commandments, you will remain in my love just as I have kept the commandments of my Father and I remain in his love. (11) I have said these things to you in order that my joy may be in you and that your joy may be fulfilled. (12) This is my commandment, that you love one another just as I loved you. (13) No one has greater love than this, that a person lay down one's life for one's friends. (14) You are my friends if you do what I command you. (15) I no longer call you slaves, because a slave does not know what the master is doing. I have called you friends, because I made known to you everything I heard from my Father. (16) You did not choose me, but I chose you and have ordained that you go and bear much

fruit and that your fruit remain, so that whatever you ask
from the Father in my name, he might give you. (17) This
I command you, that you love one another.

This passage describes the love commandment. Perhaps the most
obvious aspect of the passage is that, like the previous one, it begins
with a general exhortation to keep the commandments before it actually defines a commandment. It is not until v 12 that the "love
commandment" is actually mentioned. Previous to that there is general discussion. But several elements of the passage call for comment.

In v 9, "Remain in my love" is variously interpreted as either
Jesus' love for the disciples or the disciples' love for Jesus. Given the
conditional framework of love in the other passages as well as
throughout this one, it is most likely that the words are intended an
exhortation to continue being loved by Jesus.

In v 9, the use of the past tense (aorist) is somewhat unusual.
One would expect the present tense, which occurs in 3:35, 10:17, and
5:20. It has been suggested that the aorist is intended to indicate the
specific historical event of Jesus' death, but this is not completely
convincing.[23] In v 12, the commandment which the author has in
mind is identified: they are to love one another.

The death of Jesus for his own is given as the supreme example
of his love and also as an example of the love that the believer should
show to the other members of the community. The identification of
Jesus' death as an expression of love is also found in 1 John (e.g. ·.
16; 4:9–10). Nor is it restricted to the Johannine literature. For example, Romans 5:8 says: "God showed his love for us, in that when
we were still sinners, Christ died for us." Nevertheless, the theme of
the death of Jesus for his own is given the greatest emphasis in the
Johannine literature.

V 13 says: "Greater love than this no one has, than that he lay
down his life for his friends." In the context this is meant to describe
the importance of the death of Jesus as it is in 1 John 3:16. But in 1
John 3:16, it becomes clear that the believer is also intended to lay
down his own life for his brother. This does not seem to be intended
to be taken literally. Martyrdom does not seem to be envisioned here.
The context in 1 John 3:17–18 goes on to speak of not shutting

oneself off from the fellow Christian who is in need, when one has enough to be able to share.

In v 17 the plural (*tauta*) is used. However it clearly refers to the commandment of mutual love. The use of the plural does not seem to be significant; it is undoubtedly plural by assimilation to v 11. Such plurals occur repeatedly in the last discourses (e.g. 14:25; 15: 11,17; 16:1,4b,12,25; 17:1; 18:1).

E. CONCLUSIONS: THE COMMANDMENTS GIVEN TO THE DISCIPLES

With this first review of the commandment passages as a basis, we are now in a position to deal more directly with the three major problems confronting the person who would understand in detail these commandments given to the disciples. The solution of each of these problems is disputed.

First, there is strange alternation between the singular and plural of commandment. For example, in 13:34, when introducing the love command, the singular appears: "A new commandment (*entolēn*) I give you, that you love one another." In 14:15, the plural occurs: "If you love me, you will keep my commands (*entolas*)." In 15:10, the plural occurs again: "If you keep my commands (*entolas*), you will remain in my love." In 15:12, it is the singular: "And this is my command (*entolē*), that you love one another." In all, the singular occurs three times in the gospel in regard to the disciples (13:34; 14: 31; 15:12) and the plural occurs three times (14:15,21; 15:10). The same alternation occurs with regard to the commandments given to Jesus: the singular in 10:18 and 12:49; the plural in 15:10. The same alternation occurs in the epistles: the singular occurs ten times—in 1 John 2:7 (three times),8; 3:23 (two times); 4:21; 2 John 4,5,6; the plural occurs eight times: 1 John 2:3,4; 3:22,24; 5:2,3 (two times); 2 John 6.

Repeated attempts to explain this alternation have been found wanting, and scholars have been forced to assume that the use of the singular and plural is random and without significance, a solution which is of course less than perfect.[24]

Second, there is the question about the number of specific commandments spoken about in the gospel. There is of course no doubt about the presence of the commandment to love one another. This is one of the most famous features of the Johannine literature. And this love commandment is directed only at love of one another, the love of one member of the community for another. In the gospel such love is always termed "love for one another" (*agapan allēlous*), but in the epistle the commandment is also phrased as "loving one's brother" (*agapan ton adelphon autou*) (4:21).

As was mentioned at the outset, many scholars would see this as the only commandment. They would argue that "to keep the word" is simply synonymous with "keeping the commandments" and so is another form of general exhortation. Others would see an additional commandment: to "keep the word" of Jesus. These scholars argue that this is a second commandment which is literally "to keep the word of Jesus." That is, the disciples are to remain faithful to the word of Jesus, to keep his message in its integrity.

The third, and related, problem is the dispute concerning the meaning of the phrase *tērein ton logon* ("keep the word") in relation to commandment. Does the term *logos* ("word") function as a synonym for the term *entolē* as the Old Testament background of the phrase could indicate, or does it mean literally "to keep/hold fast to the word/message" of Jesus? Each of these three issues is a problem not only for reading the gospel but for the epistles as well.

1. The Structure of the Passages

The key to the solution of these problems lies in the way the two major sections dealing with the disciples' commandments are structured.

First: General Exhortation

First there is the general exhortation to keep the commandments. In chapter 14 this occurs in two similar statements:

14:15a: "If you love me, you will keep my commandments."
(*Ean agapate me, tas entolas tas emas tērēsete.*)

14:21: "The one who has and keeps my commandments is the one who loves me." (*Ho echōn tas entolas mou kai tērōn autas ekeinos estin ho agapōn me.*)

Each of these speaks only of the commandments in general, and exhorts to their observance. There is no mention of love (or any other) command in particular. In chapter 15 the general exhortation occurs in:

15:9b–10a: "Remain in my love. If you keep my commandments you will remain in my love." (*Meinate en tē agapē tē emē. Ean tas entolas mou tērēsete, meneite en tē agapē mou . . .*).

Here again a general keeping of the commandments (plural) is spoken of without mention of any specific command.

2. The Singular and Plural of Commandment

Brown and others have stated that there is no apparent distinction in meaning between the use of the singular and plural of commands.[25] However in the light of the parallel arrangement just described, this seems incorrect. Once it is noticed that the plural of commandment is restricted to these two sections of the gospel (14:15–24; 15:9–17) and in both cases refers to general exhortation (14:15,21; 15:10), then it becomes apparent that the author has used the plural deliberately, precisely here in his general exhortation.[26] The singular is used consistently and exclusively in those passages where a specific commandment is spoken of. This is true in the two passages currently under discussion but also in the other passages in the gospel where the singular occurs (10:18; 12:49–50; 13:34–35). As we shall see later, this explanation also accounts for every instance of usage in the epistles.

Second: Keeping the Commandments and Loving God/Jesus

The second structural similarity in the two sections is that in each of these general exhortations it is said that the keeping of the commandments is a necessity for continued love by Jesus and/or the Father.[27] So in 14:21: "The one who keeps the commandments is the one who loves me and the one who loves me will be loved by my Father and I will love him." In chapter 15, Jesus gives the somewhat strange exhortation; "Remain in my love" (i.e. "continue to be loved by me") (v 9b). The command to "remain in my love" is awkward. However, there is precedent in the Old Testament in the command to love God in Deuteronomy 10:12:[28]

> And now, Israel, what does the Lord, your God, ask of you
> but to fear the Lord, your God, and follow his ways exactly,
> to love and serve the Lord, your God with all your heart
> and all your soul . . . (NAB)

The only difference between the presentation in the two Johannine passages is that in 15:9b commandment is linked to continued love *by* Jesus; in chapter 14 it had been first linked to love *of* Jesus in v 15. Then in v 21 it is linked to love *by* Jesus. This statement of "conditional" love by Jesus is parallel to the love of Jesus by the Father which was conditional to his fulfilling the commandment given him by the Father.

Third Structural Feature: The Specific Commandments

The third feature of the two sections is that each moves on from general exhortation expressed in the plural to a specific exhortation expressed in the singular. In the first section, the commandment is defined in terms of "keeping the word" of Jesus: "If someone loves me, that person will keep my word" (*Ean tis agapa me, ton logon mou tērēsei*) (14:23). In the second instance (chapter 15), the commandment is specified as "loving one another": "This is my commandment, that you love one another as I loved you" (*Hautē estin hē entolē hē emē, hina agapate allēlous kathōs ēgapēsa hymas*).

The meaning of the commandment is clearest in chapter 15, and it is there that I will start. In 15:12 it is said that the command Jesus gives is that the disciples love one another. In the same verse the love of Jesus for the disciples is given as the model for their love. This is further developed in v 13 where it is said that greater love no one has than a person lay down his/her life for his/her friends. This command is repeated in summary fashion in 15:17: "I command you this[29]: that you love one another."

In chapter 14, it is said twice (14:15,21) that if one loves Jesus, that person will keep his commandments. However, in chapter 14 there is no reference to love of one another, but rather to "keeping the word" of Jesus. In 14:23 Jesus says that "if someone loves me, he will keep my word" (sing.) (*ton logon mou tērēsei*). Then in v 24 he again says: "The one who does not love me does not keep my words (pl.)" (*tous logous mou ou tērei*). "Keeping of the word" is given as evidence that one loves Jesus.

But the words which are to be kept are then defined as not being Jesus' own but those of the Father who sent him. The use of the singular of *entolē*, the specific mention of keeping the word, and the absence of a reference to the love commandment indicate clearly that the development of chapter 14 like that of chapter 15 is an explanation of a specific commandment: "keeping the words of Jesus." This is therefore a separate commandment from that of chapter 15.

3. The Meaning of Tērein Ton Logon

There is much disagreement about the meaning of the key phrase in chapter 14, "keep the word." Because the meaning of the phrase *tērein ton logon* is so important for understanding the Johannine commandments, it is important that we spend some time looking at the parallels which could clarify the meaning of the term.

(a) *The Usage in the Hebrew Bible*

Some scholars suggest that the phrase is to be understood against an Old Testament background as synonymous with "keeping the commandments." In their view, it is not a separate commandment but simply another form of the general exhortation. Perhaps the most respected expression of the view that "to keep the word" is to be taken against an Old Testament background is that of R. Brown who has taken this position in his commentary on the gospel and then again in his commentary on the epistles.[30] Brown is certainly on solid ground postulating an Old Testament background for the equation of "word" with "commandment." As Brown points out "the Ten Commandments are referred to as the 'words' of God (Ex 20:1; Dt 5:5,22–indeed 'word,' Heb. *dabar*, may be a technical term for covenant stipulation)." He also points to the interchangeability of "commandments," "word," and "words" in the Greek of Psalm 129: 4,25,28.[31] In addition, *tērein* is used elsewhere with the ten commandments in the New Testament (Mt 19:17; 1 Cor 7:19).

There are others, however, who see the phrase as referring, again within an Old Testament context, to a specific commandment apart from the love commandment. These scholars take the phrase to mean "keep/remain faithful to the word," i.e. the whole complex of revelation given by God through Jesus. A good example of scholarly opinion in this regard comes from a survey of opinion on 14:23–24. Bultmann[32] describes *logos* as the entire message of Jesus which in its entirety is described in the singular but which is always expressed in individual *logoi*. On the verse, Barrett[33] says, "The word (singular) of Jesus is the whole saving message he brought." Schnackenburg[34] says: ". . . the idea that Jesus' word is not his own, but the Father's who sent him is repeated here in an almost stereotyped manner . . ." Pancaro[35] says: "In our view it [*tērein ton logon/tous logous*] does not mean to keep the commandment(s) of Jesus. 'To keep the word' is not unrelated to 'keeping the commandments' of Jesus, but the two formulas express two distinct, although complementary, realities."[36] This too is a position based on solid Old Testament evidence.

There is some precedent for the use of "word" to refer to the entirety of the revelation of God from Qumran. 1QS says (5:14—DSSE 79): "All who transgress his word are unclean." 1QS also warns against of "despising" the word of God (1QS 5:19—DSSE 80). Here the "word" refers to the entirety of the message of God as it does in John. In addition there is the expression "holding fast to" (CD 3: 12—DSSE 100; CD 3:20—DSSE 100; CD 8:1—DSSE 105). This is very similar to the Johannine "*tērein*". But it is never associated specifically with "word." Instead we find it referring to holding fast to "his commandments" (CD 3:12), "unto it (the house built by the Lord)" (CD 3:20), "to these things" (his commandments)" (CD 8: 1—DSSE 105).

The major problem in the assessment of the Old Testament evidence as well as that from Qumran and the pseudepigrapha is that it is ambiguous. As scholars indicate in the earliest traditions, there is close to being an equivalence of *dabar/logos* with commandment. It is commonly used to refer to the decalogue. However later in the tradition there is evident a shift in the usage toward identifying it with all of the law, and eventually with all of the scriptures. Yet at any period there are instances where the meaning is ambiguous and where both uses of the word could be attested.

The review of the Old Testament evidence is further complicated by the fact that the verb *tērein* is not a common verb in the LXX. It occurs only thirty-eight times. The exact phrase *tērein ton logon/tous logous* occurs only once: 1 Kings 15:11—and therein with the plural. Typically, exploration is done of the term "word" (apart from the phrase) as evidenced in the studies of Grether[37] and Mackenzie.[38]

Therefore all it is possible to conclude from a study of this prior evidence is that either meaning would be possible and would be intelligible.

(b) *The Johannine Usage*

In the light of this ambiguity, the most reliable basis for understanding the term is its use elsewhere in the Johannine corpus. "Word" is a term used frequently within the gospel and epistles, and the exact phrase occurs in a number of contexts. A close examination of this material establishes beyond reasonable doubt that the phrase is not simply a synonym for commandment but does in fact refer to a distinct, specific commandment.

In the gospel, *tērein ton logon (tous logous)*—"to keep the word (words)"—occurs eight times: 8:51,52,55; 14:23,24; 15:20 [twice]; 17:6. The synonymous phrase *phylassein ton logon* occurs once: 12:47. This second phrase occurs elsewhere in the New Testament only at Luke 11:28. In the epistles, although the verb *tērein* ("to keep") occurs with *entolē* five times, it occurs only once with *logon:* 1 John 2:5. As was indicated above, the phrase occurs only in the Johannine literature in the New Testament.

(1) *The Usage in Chapters Eight, Fifteen and Seventeen*

In chapter eight the entire discourse is concerned essentially with the word/message of Jesus as it witnesses to Jesus. This is evident in the thematic statement in 8:14–16 that Jesus witnesses to himself, but it is also evident from the frequent use of the various forms of *logos* ("word") and *lalia* ("word/utterance") throughout the discourse.[39] V 26 says that Jesus speaks what he has heard with the Father; v 28 says: "What the Father has taught me, these things I speak"; v 31: "If you remain in my word, you are truly my disciples";

v 37: "You seek to kill me because my word does not abide in you"; v 40: "Now you seek to kill me, a man who has spoken the truth to you, which I heard from the Father"; v 43: "You, do you not know what I speak? because you are not able to hear my word."

Then in v 51, Jesus says: "Amen, Amen, I say to you, if someone keeps my word, he will not see death forever." This follows up on all of the previous references to his word and is a negative formulation of the common designation of the word of Jesus as the word "of life" and of "eternal life." In v 53, it is said that if one keeps his word, that person will not "taste" death. In 8:55, Jesus says that his opponents do not know God, but that he (Jesus) does and he keeps his word. Thus he has exhorted his listeners to remain in and to keep his word, just as he keeps the word of the Father. Clearly the reference here is to the word as message which Jesus received from the Father and which he has been bidden to speak in the world. There is never any suggestion in the commentaries that this means anything other than keeping the word/message which Jesus speaks.

In 15:20, Jesus asks his disciples to remember the "word" he spoke to them, that the slave is not greater than the master. "If they kept my word, they will keep yours" (*ei ton logon mou etērēsan, kai ton hymeteron tērēsousin*). Here again there can be no doubt that what is being referred to is the message of Jesus which others have kept or not, and the message of the disciples which others will keep or not.

The single instance of the phrase in chapter 17 (17:6) speaks of the disciples keeping the word of the Father. This is the only instance in the gospel of the disciples keeping the Father's word (elsewhere in the gospel it is Jesus' word). However this fits well with the concept that the word of Jesus is in fact not his but the Father's, especially since the prayer itself is addressed to the Father and puts the disciples into the presence of the Father.[40] Here *ton logos sou tetērēkan* ("they have kept your word") in v 6 is paralleled by *ta rēmata ha edōkas moi dedōka autois, kai autoi elabon . . .* ("the words which you gave me, I have given to them, and they accepted"). Again there can be no doubt that the meaning intended is the message of Jesus.[41]

All of these features of the material point in the same direction: that in the gospel *tērein ton logon* refers to keeping/guarding the message of Jesus rather than to keeping (in a general sense) a commandment, even though it is, of course, the keeping of the word that is commanded.

(2) *The Usage in Chapter Fourteen*

Having finished our examination of the phrase "to keep the word" elsewhere in the gospel, let us look at its use in the immediate vicinity to see how the usage in chapter 14 compares with the use elsewhere in the gospel.

First, it should be noted that in vv 15 and 21 it was said that the one who kept the commandment was the one who loved Jesus. Then in v 23 it is said that if one loves him, he will keep his word. The verse goes on to say that in this case the Father will also love that person and Jesus and the Father will come and abide in the person. V 24 states this in the reverse and Jesus' word is defined as the word of the Father who sent him.

Here we have an instance of the keeping of the word of Jesus fulfilling what is expected in terms of keeping the commandments, and being evidence that one loves Jesus. Clearly this is a commandment that is spoken of. In chapter 14 there is the general exhortation (vv 15,21) in preparation for a specific command, but there is no mention of loving one another, only of "keeping the word/words of Jesus." Thus, it would seem that what is intended by the words *tērein ton logon* is a specific command: to "hold fast to the words of Jesus."

Second, it will be remembered that there are two commands given to Jesus by the Father in the gospel: what to "do" (i.e. lay down his life for his friends, 10:18; 14:31) and what to "say" (i.e. his message, 12:49–50). These two commands then parallel the commands that Jesus gives to the disciples. Jesus had loved in response to commandment. The disciples are then to imitate Jesus' love by loving one another *as Jesus has loved them* (13:34–35; 15:12–13). What then of the command that Jesus speak the words of the Father? It is most likely that it is precisely this command that finds its counterpart in the command to the disciples to "keep" the words of Jesus.

Third, it should be noted that in 14:24b it is said that the word "which you have heard" is "not mine but his who sent me." Both of these expressions are used elsewhere in the gospel of the "word" of Jesus which he is bidden to speak, e.g. 5:24; 12:49–50.

Fourth, although this will not be apparent until later,[42] the commands to the disciples in the epistles are also twofold: to believe/to keep the word and to love one another. This is unequivocal in the instance of 3:23: "And this is his command, that we believe in the name of his Son Jesus Christ, and that we love one another, as he gave us a command." The arrangement of this verse is chiastic and this structure even more clearly reinforces the fact that there are two commandments spoken of. The presence of a second command is also unequivocal in 2 John 4: "I rejoiced greatly that I have found some of your children walking in truth, as we received a command from the Father." Thus there is clear evidence of two commandments in the epistles.[43] The fact that such a dual commandment occurs in the epistles, and the fact that faith, correct belief, is looked upon as a commandment in 2 John, prove conclusively at least that there was a tradition within the Johannine community of such a second commandment, of treating faith as a second commandment. If this is so, then surely this, together with the dual commandment given to Jesus by the Father (in the gospel) and the presence of the consistent parallel structure in the commands of 14:15,21–24 and 15:9–17, is sufficient evidence that 14:15,21–24 speaks of a command to keep (or remain faithful to) the message of Jesus.

However the Old Testament background as explained by Brown and others does still have a role to play since it was undoubtedly the intention of the author for *logos* in the gospel to echo the usage of such terms in the Old Testament while transforming them in their application to Christ. That is, the word of revelation of the Old Testament (the later meaning) becomes paralleled with the word of revelation of God through Jesus.

I have dedicated considerable attention here to the discussion of the phrase "to keep the word" because it is important that the plain meaning of the phrase be understood in order to understand why it is proposed that the phrase is a definition of a separate commandment and not simply a synonym for general exhortation to keep the commandments.[44]

Fourth Structural Feature: Correlation of the Disciples'
Commandment with That Given to Jesus

Finally, the fourth feature is that in each case the commandment given to the disciples is related explicitly or implicitly to the similar commandment given to Jesus by the Father. Thus in chapter 14, when the disciples keep the word of Jesus, it is identified as the word of the Father which they are keeping, the word given to Jesus to speak. This is evident particularly in 14:24b: *kai ho logos hon akouete ouk estin emos alla tou pempsantos me patros* ("And the word which you hear is not mine but that of him who sent me, the Father").

In chapter 15, the love of one another that is commanded of the disciples is related to the laying down of one's life for one's friends, as Jesus is said to do (10:15b,17) in fulfillment of the commandment of the Father (10:18). Thus what Jesus does in fulfillment of the commandment given him by the Father becomes the model for the disciples' own obedience both in their faithfulness to his word and in their living out the command of community love.

F. CONCLUSIONS TO THE CHAPTER

We have seen that there are two commandments given to Jesus by the Father. We have seen that these commandments are intended to encompass the entirety of his ministry: what he was bidden to say and what he was to do. It is also said that Jesus had to fulfill these commandments in order to remain in the love of the Father. The "conditional" phrasing of these statements is particularly striking when applied to Jesus. It would seem to imply that Jesus could conceivably not have wanted to fulfill these commandments or that conceivably he would not have and thus not have remained within the love of the Father! The language is certainly evocative of the phrasing of the conditional form of covenant in the Old Testament. If the continued love of Jesus by the Father was dependent upon his fulfillment of the commandments given to him, it is also true that the Johannine Jesus does fulfill the commandments and he does so precisely as an expression of his love for the Father.

Jesus in turn gives two commandments to the disciples. These are correlated with those given to Jesus by the Father. First the disciples are to cling to everything that he says, and, second, they are to imitate what he did by loving one another.

The most serious question faced by the first part of the investigation had to do with the number of commandments given to the disciples. We have seen extensive evidence that there are two commandments in the Johannine tradition, not one. In addition, we have seen that these two commandments are closely correlated with the two commandments given to Jesus. Just as Jesus is bidden to speak the word of the Father, the disciples are bidden to keep the word which Jesus gives them. Likewise, as Jesus was bidden to give his life for those he loved, so the disciples are bidden to love one another in imitation of Jesus.

In addition we have found that the puzzling alternation between the singular and plural of commandment can be explained if one recognizes that the plural occurs only in general exhortation and the singular is used to refer to a specific commandment. We saw that this proposal is confirmed consistently throughout the gospel and the epistles.

We have also seen the same conditional elements attached to the keeping of the commandments by the disciples as was evident in the case of Jesus. If they are to remain in the love of Jesus, the disciples must keep the commandments. And if they do keep the commandments, they will continue to be loved not only by Jesus but also by the Father. And just as Jesus' obedience to the commandments was evidence of his love for the Father, so the one who keeps the commandments of Jesus shows his/her love for Jesus.

One other point presents itself at this juncture, a point of no little significance. Alongside of the conception of the ministry of Jesus as "commandment" in the gospel, there is another theological conception of the ministry: the ministry as a "work" given to Jesus by the Father to complete. This second conception of the ministry is widespread in the gospel—much more widespread than the conception of the ministry as a "commandment." Consequently, before we begin the exploration of commandment in the epistles, we must pause to examine the relationship between "commandment" and "work" as theological conceptualizations of Jesus' ministry.

NOTES

1. The most primitive terminology for the decalogue does not use the term *mishpat* ("commandment"; Gk: *entolē*) but rather *dabar* ("word"; Gk: *logos*). For example see Exodus 20:1 (LXX) where the decalogue is introduced as "all these words" (*pantas tous logous*).

However various other terms were used interchangeably. For example in the same passage (Ex 20:6 LXX) those keeping my commandments are described as "*tois phylassousin ta prostagmata mou*" (literally, "those keeping my orders"). Later other terms are also associated with this concept: *dikaōma* ("decree"), *krimata* ("judgments"), and of course *entolē* ("commandment"). All of these terms refer to the individual prescriptions which make up the law. However in the New Testament, the variety of terms all but disappears and *entolē* becomes the common, and almost exclusive, term used to refer to the prescriptions of the law. The "law" is the whole of which the "commandments" are the individual elements. For a complete list of citations and fuller discussion see G. Schrenk, "*entolē,*" *TDNT* 4, 544–556. In Paul *entolē* becomes at times a synonym for the whole of the law when used in the singular (e.g. Rom 7:8,9,11) although even there the law and the commandments are distinguished presumably as the whole and the part (Rom 7:12).

2. Gender-neutral language will be used throughout this book. Its applicability will be guided by the following principles. In all references within and to the cultural world of the Bible, the references will be in the gender in use at that time. This use is intended to reflect the historical particularity of texts. This would include references to Yahweh as "he" when referring to the texts. It also includes the use of "he" to refer to the author of the gospel and epistles of John although the author(s) of the gospel/epistles is (are) anonymous. However when discussing the texts or making references from the point of view of our current understanding of them, gender-neutral language will be employed where appropriate.

3. P. Perkins, *Love Commands in the New Testament* (New York: Paulist, 1982) 109.

4. R. E. Brown, *The Johannine Epistles* (AB30; New York: Doubleday, 1982) 470.

5. M. J. O'Connell, "The Concept of Commandment in the Old Testament," *TS* 21 (1960) 351–403; S. Pancaro, *The Law in the Fourth Gospel* (NovT Supp 42; Leiden: E. J. Brill, 1975) 431–51. O'Connell mentions in his study that the article is intended as a preliminary to a full study of "commandment" in Johannine theology, but that study was never completed.

6. This is hardly the only position however. For example, among

commentaries published in the last five years, that of Kenneth Grayston, *The Johannine Epistles* (NCB; Grand Rapids: Eerdmans, 1984),
argues that the first epistle exhibits several more primitive traits than
the gospel and that these can be accounted for by dating the epistle
before the gospel (pp 10–14). However as will be seen in what follows
throughout this book, various features of both the gospel and the first
epistle make more sense if the gospel is dated earlier.

7. It also occurs in 8:5 in the pericope of the woman taken in
adultery, a passage that is not part of the original text of the gospel.
That instance is not considered here.

8. The translation of the commandment texts is my own. Other
translations throughout the book are from the NAB (1st ed.).

9. The phrase is found in classical and Hellenistic Greek. For a
discussion see H. Conzelmann, *1 Corinthians* (Hermeneia; Philadelphia: Fortress, 1975) 255, n.59. I will discuss the conception in
greater detail later. See below, especially chapter six.

10. The complex of love relationships in the Johannine literature
has been studied recently by F. Segovia, *Love Relationships in the
Johannine Tradition* (SBLDS 58; Chico: Scholars, 1982). Segovia's
study is of some interest because of his attempt to use the relationships
to determine authorship of various sections of the last discourses.

11. The noun *philia* ("friendship") does not appear, although *philos*
("friend") occurs six times in the gospel.

12. C. Spicq, *Agape in the New Testament* (3 vols.; St. Louis: Herder, 1966), has proposed the thesis that *philein* connotes a more deeply
affective love than *agapan.* This is accepted by R. Schnackenburg,
The Gospel According to John (3 vol; New York: Seabury, 1980)
2,462 and others. The synonymity of the two terms is defended by
Brown, *The Gospel According to John* (AB 29,29a; New York: Doubleday, 1966,70) 497–99, R. Bultmann, *The Gospel of John. A Commentary* (Philadelphia: Westminster, 1970) 253, n.2, and recently by
R. Joly, *Le vocabulaire chrétien de l'amour est-il originel?* (Brussels:
Université/Libre, 1968). The terms are interchanged: 11:3,5,36,
14:21; 15:9,13, 13:23; 19:26; 21:15–17, and it is difficult to find a
consistent distinction. See in addition to the above, the famous treatment of love in A. Nygren, *Agape and Eros* (2 vols; London: SPCK,
1932–37). For further bibliography on *agapē,* see F. Segovia, *Love
Relationships* 24–29.

13. For example, *agapan* is used of the Father's love for the Son in 3:35, but *philein* is used in 5:20. *Agapan* is used for the Father's love of the disciples twice in 14:23, but *philein* is used twice in 16:27. Examples could be multiplied. The major defender of the thesis that there is a distinction is C. Spicq, *Agape.*

14. The consideration of the literary features of the text will be postponed to chapter five.

15. *Logos* in this sense occurs in 2:22; 4:41,50; 5:24,38; 6:60; 7:36,40; 8:31,37,43,51,52,55; 12:48; 14:23,24 (twice); 15:3,20 (twice); 17:6,14,17; 18:9,32; 19:8,13.

16. As we shall see in the following chapter, the same is true of the "works" (*erga*) of Jesus which are the individual "components" of the overall "work" (*ergon*) given to him by the Father.

17. This passage is similar in several respects to 3:16–21: (1) The Son is sent to save the world (3:17; 12:47); (2) Jesus is described as "light" coming into the world, an image that occurs only in isolated passages in the gospel outside of the prologue (prologue: 1:4,5,7,8,9; other occurrences: 3:19,20,21; 8:12; 9:5; 11:9,10; 12:35,36 and 12:48); (3) Jesus does not judge (3:17; 12:47). However the judging which is brought about by unbelief is located in the present in 3:18, while it is located on the last day in 12:48.

18. Schnackenburg (*Gospel* 2,391) gives numerous parallels for the use of the term from Qumràn. But Schnackenburg (*Gospel* 3,87) does not think that "world" (in v 31) is the same dualistic use that is found in vv 17,19,22. I would disagree. On the expression "he has no power over me" (*en emoi ouk echei ouden*), see BAG 334, I,7.

19. For example, J. Becker, "Die Abschiedsreden Jesu im Johannesevangelium," *ZNW* 61 (1970) 220; G. Richter, "Die Deutung des Kreuzestodes Jesu in der Leidensgeschichte des Johannesevangeliums," *Bibel und Leben* 9 (1968) 30ff; R. Schnackenburg, *Gospel* 3,53; F. Segovia, *Love Relationships* 121–22.

20. Brown, *Epistles* 267.

21. See further on 2:7–8 below.

22. There is some textual uncertainty about the verb in 14:15. Codex Sinaiticus and P[66] read the verb in the subjunctive (*tērēsete*). The verb is in the imperative (*tērēsate*) in Codex Alexandrinus and Codex Bezae. Codex Vaticanus has the future (*tērēsete*). However the subjunctive is most likely to be the original. For a full discussion,

see Brown, *Gospel* 638; Schnackenburg, *Gospel* 3, 413, n.86; B. Metzger, et al., *A Textual Commentary on the Greek New Testament* (London: United Bible Societies, 1971) *ad locum.*

23. Brown, *Gospel* 663.

24. See for example Brown, *Gospel* 638, 641; *Epistles* 251; F.-M. Braun, "La Réduction du Pluriel au Singulier dan l'Évangile et la Première Lettre de Jean," *NTS* 24 (1977) 47–51.

25. Brown, *Gospel* 641; *Epistles* 250–51, 280. See also Bultmann, *Gospel* 541, n.4. F.-M. Braun ("La réduction," 47–48) suggests that the plural is equivalent to the singular and that it is similar to other plurals in the gospel which are used interchangeably with the singular (e.g. *ta haimata,* 1:13; *ta hydata,* 3:23, etc.). In addition Braun speaks of the excellence of the love commandment making it superior to all the other commandments. Schrenk ("*entellomai, entolē,*" 544–556) claimed that in 1 John the singular was never discussed without reference to the plural but does not seem to indicate that it was a characteristic for the plural to occur first, even though as he points out the only case where the plural does not occur first is in 4:31 (sic!). J. L. Houlden, *The Johannine Epistles* (HNTC; New York: Harper and Row, 1973) 102, calls the use of the plural unusual in the Johannine literature and states that "there is no sign that these writers thought in terms of any other commands besides that of mutual love."

26. In 15:17, although the word *entolē* does not occur, it seems that the commandment to love is equated with the plural (i.e. *tauta entellomai hymin, hina agapate allēlous.* The meaning of *hina* is generally taken to be epexegetical, i.e. "These things/this I command you, that you love one another." It is also possible, however, that the *tauta* refers to what has been said above, but this seems less plausible. The most likely explanation of this occurrence is that *tauta* is plural by assimilation to *tauta lelalēka hymin hina* ... of 15:11. Such expressions occur regularly throughout this section, to the point that Schnackenburg (*Gospel* 3,92) uses them in determining the structure of the discourse. John 15:17 is a summary statement, ending the treatment of the commandments, and such assimilation to v 11 would not be surprising in such a context. Thus I would not see this as an exception to the consistent use of the singular and plural of *entolē* by the author.

27. It is not my purpose here to present a full description of the love relationships within the gospel but only to outline the relationships of importance for the present discussion. For a discussion of this see Segovia, *Love Relationships*. For an examination of the background of the relation between love and keeping the commandments, see W. L. Moran, "The Ancient Near Eastern Background of the Love of God in Deuteronomy," *CBQ* 25 (1963) 77–87. For a study of love as it relates to commandment in the Old Testament see M. J. O'Connell, "Commandment," esp. 374–79, and other more general treatments of love such as C. Spicq, *Agape.*

28. On the passage in Deuteronomy, see M. J. O'Connell, "Commandment," 361–62, 375–77.

29. Literally, "these things." See the discussion of the plural above.

30. Brown, *Gospel* 641; *Epistles* 250–253, esp. 252.

31. Brown, *Gospel* 641. Pancaro (*Law* 403–411) provides an even more detailed treatment of this expression throughout the Old Testament (LXX and MT), rabbinic, Qumran, and pseudepigraphal tradition. Pancaro in turn refers to the work of O. Grether, *Name und Wort Gottes in Alten Testament* (Giessen, 1934).

32. Bultmann, *Gospel* 625, n.1.

33. Barrett, *The Gospel According to John* (2nd ed.; Philadelphia: Westminster, 1978) 466; see also 467.

34. Schnackenburg, *Gospel* 3,82.

35. Pancaro, *Law* 427.

36. See also F. Segovia, *Love Relationships* 148–51.

37. Grether, *Name und Wort Gottes.*

38. J. L. Mackenzie, "The Word of God in the Old Testament," *TS* (1960) 183–206.

39. For a full discussion, see U. C. von Wahlde, "The Witnesses to Jesus in John 5:31–40 and Belief in the Fourth Gospel," *CBQ* 43 (1981) 385–404, esp. 395–97.

40. In that sense, the prayer of chapter 17 seems to prepare for the more direct relationship between the disciples and the Father that is found in the epistles. It will be recalled that in the epistles, the images of light and love are applied to the Father whereas in the gospel they were applied to Jesus. The same is true of the commandments in the epistles which are said to be "of God" rather than "of Jesus."

41. *Tērein* (without *logos*) is also used several times in the discourse.

It is possible to get the sense of *tērein* from its use throughout. The first time it occurs (v 6) it is in the phrase *tērein ton logon.* However the other times it is used by Jesus in his prayer for believers. In v 11 it has the force of "keep/guard/preserve" when he prays to the Father to guard believers (*tērēson autous en to onomati sou*). In v 12 he recalls that he himself has preserved them in the Father's name. In v 15 he prays to the Father to preserve them from evil (*hina tērēsēs autous ek tou ponērou*). Given this context, there can be little doubt that the fact that the disciples have "guarded/held to" the word of the Father should be a reason for his "guarding" in his name and for his "guarding" them from evil.

42. See the discussion of *entolē* in the epistles in chapter three.

43. One must of course use such parallels cautiously, since it is precisely in crossing such borders that one runs the risk of seeing only the similarities without seeing the differences. In this case there are differences: namely that the commandments in the epistles are referred to as commandment of God rather than of Jesus. However this difference does not affect the fact of the parallelism with the general Johannine tradition.

44. The plain meaning of the second commandment "to love one another" is much more apparent. Consequently, the discussion of the background and of the particular formulation of the commandment will be postponed until chapter eight.

Chapter Two

"COMMANDMENT" AND "WORK": TWO JOHANNINE THEOLOGIES OF THE MINISTRY OF JESUS

As we saw at the end of the previous chapter, alongside "commandment" as a conceptualization of the ministry of Jesus, we also find the notion of the ministry as "work."[1] The relationship between these two concepts demands a closer look for the information that it could shed on the Johannine tradition of the commandments.

In various places in the gospel Jesus refers to his ministry as a "work" (*ergon*) given him by the Father to complete; he himself is said to "work" (*ergazesthai*). He in turn refers to his miracles as "works" (*erga*). This conception of the ministry occurs as early as chapter 4 and as late as chapter 17. Certainly it is a major theological conception and framework within which the ministry of Jesus is cast.

However, as we have seen, this conception exists alongside another: that of the ministry as a "commandment" (*entolē*) given to Jesus by the Father. It is generally presumed that these are simply alternate literary expressions of the same idea. E. Lohmeyer states this position clearly:

> The word "work" carries the same meaning as commandment or norm and is distinguished from these only in that the idea of commandment is marked with the notion of independent value or of its origin but the idea of work is stamped with the notion of a long-standing duty. Because of this, it is understandable that work is able to be a synonym for "Law" or "commandment."[2]

39

Another problem concerns the understanding of work itself as applied to Jesus in the gospel. S. Pancaro in his study of the law in the gospel treats at some length the conception of the "works of God" (*erga theou*) and attempts to show that the phrase is used in a way that would recall "nomistic terminology" (i.e. terminology dealing with the law). Thus he sees Jesus as fulfilling the law in his ministry as an obedient Son of the Father. Yet this conflicts with the view expressed in 5:19, that the use of *ergazomai* ("to work") reflects not obedience to the law but cooperation in the creative act of God. If this is true, then neither Pancaro's assessment of the background is correct, nor is Lohmeyer's assessment of the interchangeability of "work" and "commandment."

In addition, there are several features of the usage of these conceptions within the gospel itself which are puzzling and call for attention: Why does "work" occur much more frequently for the ministry of Jesus than "commandment"? Is it significant that the death of Jesus is twice referred to as a "commandment" but not as a work? "Work" is used more frequently to describe the obligations of Jesus. On the other hand, commandment seems to be used more for the obligations of the disciples. These features of the two terms then urge us on to look more carefully at these two terms in the hope not only of solving these problems but ultimately of understanding a little better the notion of commandment itself.

We must then begin by attempting (1) to describe the usage of work in the Johannine writings and (2) to determine whether it can be said to be integrated theologically with the concept of commandment.

A. *ERGON* IN THE GOSPEL

Ergon occurs twenty-seven times in the gospel.[3] The verb occurs seven times.[4] The usage is complex, however, and does not represent only one sphere of meaning. In fact, the word *ergon* is used in a variety of ways in the gospel, and only some of these can be said to be related to the conceptualization of the ministry of Jesus. It is partly this complexity that has made it so difficult in the past to fully appreciate its distinctive use as a theological conception of Jesus' ministry.

First, work is used to refer to the overall mission of Jesus. This is directly related to the usage described above. The ministry of Jesus is an *ergon* given to him by the Father: 4:34; 5:17; 17:4. The clearest example of this is the one just mentioned (5:17) where Jesus explains his working on the sabbath: *ho pater mou heōs arti ergazetai, kagō ergazomai* ("My Father works until now, and I work"). Another example of this conception is 4:34 which was discussed before. In each case there is a clear correlation between the work of the Father and the work of the Son. This "working" is seen as a cooperation of Jesus with the Father in the bringing of his work to perfection and completion. Although there is general agreement about the background of the instance in 5:17, there are those who would see the application of this term to Jesus as an example of applying the legal use of *ergon* ("doing the works of the law") to Jesus. This will be discussed further below.

Second, work is used in the gospel to refer to the "work" done by the Father: 4:34; 5:17 (and implicitly in 17:4). These uses although not directly referring to the ministry of Jesus are referred to by Jesus as the model of his own activity. Thus they are important for understanding the characteristic usage and can indeed be said to be a part of it.

In 4:34, Jesus says that his food is to do the will of the Father (*to thelēma tou pempsantos me*) and to bring to completion and perfection his work (*teleiōsō autou to ergon*).[5]

In 5:17, the working of the Father on the sabbath is used as a model of and justification for the work of Jesus. Here the "work" of the Father is commonly identified as his activity in creation (cf Gen 2:2ff). The common Jewish belief that if Yahweh ceased activity creation would dissolve, together with the extreme reverence for the sabbath, gave rise to the dispute evident among the rabbis whether God was allowed to work on the sabbath.[6] We will discuss the background of this conception more below, but what is important for the present is that Jesus is identified with this exalted activity of God and claims to be an extension of that very activity within the world. This Johannine conception is unique in the New Testament.

Third, work is used to refer to the miracles of Jesus. This is directly related to the usage of work discussed above. The *erga* (plural) are performed as part of his larger work which Jesus performs in accord with the Father:[7] 5:20,36 (twice); 7:3[8],21; 9:3[9]; 10:25,32 (twice),33,37,38; 14:10,11; 15:24.

Fourth, there is one instance in which the term refers to "works" (and from the context it is clear that this refers to miraculous works) which the disciple of Jesus will do: 14:12. In this sense the disciples are to exercise the same power as Jesus in performing works during their ministry. It is perhaps striking that this usage occurs only once in the gospel, especially when it is compared with the frequent statements in Mark that the power of Jesus was to be theirs (e.g. 3:14–15; 6:7; 9:38–41).

Fifth, work is used in the gospel to denote human actions. These actions have an ethical dimension which can be punished or rewarded and which exhibit their openness (or lack of openness) to Jesus. For example, 3:21 says: "But he who acts in truth comes into the light, to make clear that his deeds (lit. 'works') are done in God." This use also occurs in 3:19,20,21; 7:7.[10]

Sixth, work occurs in the idiomatic expression *ergazesthai ta erga* or the alternate *poiein ta erga* which would be literally translated "to work/do the works" of someone. It is clear from the context in these instances that these "works" do not refer to miracles, but simply to human acts/deeds. In this sense it is synonymous with "doing the will" of someone. In this usage we find a close linkage with the first of the uses above, but here the term takes on a broader meaning of identifying those actions which are done in accord with the will of someone else—thus its idiomatic meaning.

In 6:28–29 we find the crowd asking Jesus the question "What do we do in order to do the works of God?" (*Ti poiōmen hina ergazōmetha ta erga tou theou*). Jesus responds: "This is the work of God, that you believe in the one whom he sent" (*Touto estin to ergon tou theou, hina pisteuēte eis hon apesteilen ekeinos*). This is not a discussion of faith as opposed to good works as is often suggested, but rather the simple idiomatic expression of a question ("What is the will of God in our regard?") followed by the answer of Jesus that they should believe in the one God has sent.[11]

The case in 8:39,41 is even clearer. Here Jesus is disputing with his listeners about whom they really are followers of. The imagery is cast in terms of being "sons of" someone and having someone as their "father," an imagery that is common in Qumran and the pseudepigrapha. Jesus says (v 39) that he speaks what he has seen in the presence of his Father and that his listeners do what they have heard from their Father. The listeners respond that their father is Abraham. Jesus responds that if they were children of Abraham they would do the "works" of Abraham. But as it is they seek to kill Jesus and Abraham would not have done this. Jesus then reasserts that they do the works of their father. The listeners then say that their Father is God. Jesus then says that, if their Father were God, they would love him (Jesus) and listen to his word. But instead they are (v 44) children of ("followers of") the devil and they do his will. The devil is in turn a liar and there is no truth in him, but no one could say this of Jesus. Throughout this exchange, the use of work is clearly different from the characteristic Johannine use above.

It is the first of these uses which constitutes the dominant gospel use. However this first use (work as the description of the overall ministry of Jesus, the second (the description of the activity of the Father as "work"), the third (the description of the miracles of Jesus as "works"), and the fourth (the description of the future activity/ miracles of the disciples as "works")—all of these uses can all be integrated with one another as aspects of a single conceptual framework. It is this use which provides a conceptualization of the ministry parallel to that of the ministry as "commandment."

The last two types of usage reflect a dualistic framework that is not able to be integrated with the other four. In order to understand this more fully, it will be helpful to examine the background of the two uses of the term.

B. THE BACKGROUND OF THE USE OF *ERGON*

Each of the two usages of *ergon* that we have seen in the Johannine writings stems from a distinct linguistic and theological background.

Although there are many examples of "work" in the extant gnostic writings, the usage there does not closely parallel the dominant gospel use closely, since in much of the gospel usage the work of Jesus is so closely associated with creation and with the activity of "the creator God," the Father.

Rather, work in the "characteristic" gospel usage finds its closest parallels in the canonical Hebrew scriptures. It is used repeatedly of the activity of God in creation and to refer to his miraculous deeds on behalf of Israel. For example, in Psalm 8:3 the physical universe is so described: "When I behold the heavens, the works of your hands, the moon and the stars which you set in place . . ." His actions on behalf of Israel at the exodus are called "works" (Ex 34:10). In addition it is used to describe the continuous activity of God who rewards and punishes without ceasing (cf Is 5:12–13). Thus in the gospel of John a parallel is drawn between this activity of the Father and the activity of Jesus. Jesus is said to share in this power to the extent of having the privilege of employing it on the sabbath (Jn 5:19). In addition the disciples will also share in this activity and so in a special way they too are presented as sharing in the creative, miraculous and judgmental powers of God!

However, the second of the two types of usage, as they were described above, exhibits a linguistic usage which does not occur in the canonical Hebrew scriptures. The description of persons as "doing the works of someone" in the sense of "doing what is characteristic of someone" or "doing the will of someone" finds close parallels within many of the sectarian documents from Qumran and within the pseudepigraphical literature, especially within the T12P. In all of these instances, it is closely tied to and reflects the view of reality of modified dualism which pervades those documents. In this worldview, persons are described as being dominated by the spirit of God or of Beliar (Satan). In each of these cases, their actions then are said to reflect this influence; they are then said "to do the law of God or the works of Beliar" (*ē nomon kyriou ē erga Beliar*) (TLev 19:1).

At Qumran we find a similar use:

> And now, Children, harken unto me, and I shall uncover your eyes to see and consider the works of God; to choose that in which he delights and to reject that which he hates, to walk uprightly in all his ways and not to wander according to the designs of a guilty inclination and the allurement of lust (CD 2:14–16 DSSE 98).

Notice here that even though the phrase "works of God" is used, it clearly refers to works which are pleasing to God, which would be characteristic of God, or which could be said to be his will. In this dualistic use "works" always has an ethical dimension. This use is not an extension of the biblical use in which the term refers to miraculous activity in which there is a sharing in the creative power of God. This is substantially different from the use in the canonical scriptures and reflects a different worldview.[12]

C. *ERGON* IN THE EPISTLES

Turning to the use of work in the epistles we find a considerably different picture. First, the word occurs much less frequently. The verb occurs twice;[13] the noun occurs five times.[14]

The two times the verb is used, it is used in a sense similar to the fifth usage identified in the gospel: the "ethical," a use typical of the dualistic view of reality. In 2 John 8 it occurs in the context of an exhortation to the readers to remain faithful to the teaching of Jesus. The author urges his correspondent not to lose what he has achieved (*mē apolesēte ha eirgasametha*) but to gain the full reward. In 3 John 5 it is used in a very general sense which has its closest similarity in the first category above. Speaking to Gaius, the author says: "Beloved, you show fidelity in whatever you do for the brothers (*ho ean ergasē eis tous adelphous*), even though they be strangers."

In 1 John 3:8 the noun is used in the same way of the "works" of the devil which Jesus has come to destroy. The context is identical with that of the dualism of apocalyptic and inter-testamental in that it speaks of allegiance to one or other of the spirits when the author speaks of the one who sins being "of the devil." The term is used to refer to the "works" of Cain and the works of his brother Abel in 3: 12. Again there is evidence of the dualistic worldview when the author describes Cain as being "of evil."

In 3:18 work occurs in an exhortation to love not just in words but in "action" (*ergō*). This is a very general sense related to the first (ethical) sense but meant to contrast action with words.

The usage in 2 John 11 again fits the first category of the gospel very well. The author of the epistle exhorts his readers not to receive anyone who comes to them not bringing the correct teaching: "For the one who greets such a person takes a part in his evil deeds." The same is true of the use in 3 John 10 where the author criticizes Diotrephes for not receiving his letters. But the author says that when he comes to the community, he will recall himself the evil deeds which Diotrephes commits.

On the basis of this analysis, it becomes apparent that the overall usage of work in the epistles corresponds to the dualistic use in the gospel but shows no similarity to the more dominant use there. In the epistles the term is not used to refer to the "creative" activity of God nor of Jesus. Neither is it used to refer to the works which Jesus had promised the disciples would perform. In short, the usage dominant in the gospel does not appear in the epistles.

D. The Theological Conception in the Gospel

What have we learned about the characteristic use of work as used in the gospel of John? First, we learn that the activity of the Father is characterized as work and that this concept is derived from the view of God in the Old Testament who continues his creative activity always and who also performs his activity of rewarding and punishing without ceasing. Second, Jesus describes his activity as work also and puts it in parallel with the activity of the Father (5:17). It is this of course which gives rise to the first accusation of blasphemy on the part of the Jews, since they recognize in this claim to the reciprocal work of the Father and of Jesus a claim on the part of Jesus to equality with God (5:18). Third, we learn that Jesus says his purpose is to bring to completion the work of the Father (4:34; 17:4). In that sense, the individual miracles of Jesus are called works (see the list above under the fourth use of *ergon*). The concept provides the basis for the development of the discourse in the remainder of chapter 5. In addition, the works are one of the three essential witnesses to Jesus as listed in 5:31–40. They also provide the topic for the dialogue with the Jews in 10:22–39. As such the concept of work provides a major framework for the understanding of the activity of Jesus and of his relationship with God.

E. Final Conclusions

From our study so far we have seen that in the gospel and the epistles work is used with two distinct spheres of meaning. We have also seen that the backgrounds against which these two conceptions are to be seen are distinct. The second usage which is found in both the gospel and the epistles finds its closest parallels in the dualism of Qumran and the intertestamental literature. It is not found in the Hebrew Bible. On the other hand the background of the dominant gospel use is clearly found in the Old Testament itself. Although the Old Testament usage can refer both to the creative works of God as well as to his activity within history, it is the creative aspect of work which provides the closest parallels to the Johannine use.

What are we to make of this? Although it is striking that the characteristic use of work does not appear in the epistles, the significance of this cannot be fully appreciated until we look at the usage of commandment in the epistles. Consequently we will now turn to an analysis of commandment in the epistles.

NOTES

1. There are of course other expressions which mean very much the same: for example, "to do the will of God" (*to thelēma tou theou poiein*—4:34; 6:38) or "to do what is pleasing to God" (*ta aresta autō poiein*—8:29). However these are not major in that they are not as frequent nor do they function to structure the presentation of the ministry as do work and commandment; consequently these terms will not be studied here.

2. E. Lohmeyer, "Probleme paulinischer Theologie, II, 'Gesetzeswerke'," *ZNW* 28 (1928) 183.

3. 3:19,20,21; 4:34; 5:20,36 (twice); 6:28,29; 7:3,7,21; 8:39,41; 9:3,4; 10:25,32 (twice), 33,37,38; 14:10,11,12; 15:24; 17:4.

4. 3:21; 5:17; 6:27,28,30; 9:4 (twice).

5. The verb *teleioun* is of course difficult to translate exactly by a single English word since it has the connotation of both bringing to perfection and also of bringing to completion.

6. For a discussion and references, see Brown, *Gospel* 216–17; Schnackenburg, *Gospel* 2,100–01 and notes there.

7. This relationship is commonly recognized. See for example F.-M. Braun, "Réduction" 45–47; Schnackenburg, *Gospel* 518. Schnackenburg himself refers to H. van den Bussche, "La structures de Jean I–XII," *L'Évangile de Jean,* Recherches Bibliques 3 (1958) 61–109.

8. This is the only instance of the term in its use as "miracle" which is not on the lips of Jesus.

9. Here the usage is perhaps intended as a play on words, since in addition to its idiomatic meaning "to do the will of" it can also easily refer to the performance of a work in the sense of miracle, i.e. the healing of the blind man as is evident from the context.

10. This use is also implicit in 5:29, but the word does not occur there.

11. The usage in 6:28–29 is obscured somewhat by the fact that the phrase occurs in separate parts of a dialogue. This may account for the erroneous interpretation of these verses as dealing with the relation between "faith and works." For a full discussion, see my "Faith and Works in Jn vi 28–29," *NovT* 22 (1980) 385–404.

12. There are instances of "works" at Qumran which refer to the creative and/or historical acts of God (e.g. "the favors of God manifested in His mighty deeds"—1QS 1:21—DSSE 73), but this use is clearly distinct from the dualistic, and the two are only distantly related in thought.

13. 2 Jn 8 and 3 Jn 5.

14. 1 Jn 3:8,12,18; 2 Jn 11; 3 Jn 10.

Chapter Three

IN THE JOHANNINE EPISTLES: THE COMMANDMENTS OF GOD

What we have learned already about the Johannine command-ments in the gospel facilitates our study of the same term in the epistles. But we should be cautious not to think that we will simply find the same usage there as previously. In the epistles, there are significant differences. The most striking difference is that in the epis-tles the commandments given to the disciples are said to be com-mandments "of God" rather than "of Jesus." In addition, there is no mention of commandments given *to* Jesus as there was in the gospel, nor is there any mention of "work" as a parallel conceptu-alization of the ministry of Jesus or of the disciples.

Another significant change is the role of commandment within the documents as a whole. In the epistles, especially in 1 John, the theme of commandment becomes a major element in the shaping of both the theology and the literary structure of the document. Com-pared to the role of commandment in the gospel, the role in the epistles is much more dominant. All of this tells us to weigh the evidence carefully and not to attempt simply to harmonize the use in the epistles with that in the gospels. As was the case in the preceding chapters, we will begin with the "statistics."

A. THE STATISTICS

Commandment (*entolē*) occurs eighteen times in the epistles.[1] In the epistles, there is no mention of the commandment given by the Father to Jesus. The entire focus is on the commandment given to the disciples. The three problems that confronted the understanding of commandment in the gospel—consistent use of the singular and plural of the word commandment, the number of specific commandments referred to, and the meaning of the phrase "keep the word" (*tērein ton logon*)—occur again in the epistles but as we shall see the proposal we advanced above is confirmed by the way it continues to explain the usage in the epistles in a consistent manner.

B. THE COMMANDMENTS GIVEN TO THE DISCIPLES

In 1 John we again meet the issue of the number of commandments specifically referred to. However in at least some texts in 1 John there is clear evidence that there are two commandments intended.[2] We will begin by looking at the first epistle and specifically at the texts that give the clearest evidence of two commandments. As we did previously, we will begin with a thorough look at the details of each passage and then proceed to more general comments.

1. *1 Jn 3:21-24*

> (21) Loved ones, if our hearts do not accuse us, we have confidence before God, (22) and whatever we ask for, we receive from him, because we keep his commandments and we do what is proper in his sight. (23) And this is his commandment, that we believe the name of his Son Jesus Christ, and that we love one another as he has given us the commandment. (24) And the one who keeps his commandments abides in God and God in that person. And in this we know that he abides in us, from the Spirit which he has given us.

The context within which this passage occurs (vv 19–20) is commonly recognized as being one of the most complex in the Johannine literature. As Brown puts it, "the verses offer the prologue competition for the prize in grammatical obscurity."[4] Brown then goes on to list nine (!) problems involved in the interpretation of those verses. In spite of this complexity in the surrounding context, v 21 is clear in relation to its own following context: when the believer's heart does not hold anything incriminating,[5] the believer is able to be bold before God and (in v 22) the believer will receive whatever he asks for.

V 22 contains the first instance of the verb "to ask for" (*aitein*) in the first epistle (it will occur again in 5:14,15,16). The ability to ask and to know that one will receive is related to "boldness" (*parrēsia*) both here and in the instances later in the epistle. In the present, the asking is contingent upon obedience to the commandments and upon doing what is pleasing in "his" sight (v 22). In 5:14–16, a somewhat similar idea is expressed by saying that we should ask "according to 'his' will." In both cases the asking is not a simple prerogative of the believer but one conditioned by obedience and propriety.

In the gospel also, asking and receiving had been associated with obedience to the commandments in 14:13–14 and 15:7,16. Sometimes the verb *erōtan* is used, but there is no discernible difference in meaning.[6]

In v 22 the commandments are "his" (of God) (cf v 21) rather than of Jesus. The last clause of v 22 ("and do what is pleasing before him") is synonymous with keeping the commandments, although some would take the second clause as more inclusive.

"Belief" is not as common a term in the epistles as it is in the Johannine gospel. In addition to its use here, the verb occurs only seven times.[7] The only Johannine use of the noun form *pistis* occurs in 5:4. It occurs with the dative with "name" here and in 5:13. It occurs with the object ("spirit" in 4:1; "God" in 5:10) in the dative. It occurs followed by *hoti* ("that") twice in statements that define the object of belief (5:1,5), and once with the object (the Son of God) after the preposition *eis.*

The subjunctive of "believe" in v 23 is aorist, which usually indicates a single act of faith. Some manuscripts have changed the tense to a present subjunctive to stress the continuous aspect of belief.[8] Johannine forms of the verb believe (*pisteuein*) occur in a variety of configurations: with the accusative, with a following *hoti*-clause, with *eis* and, as here, with the dative. Although a variety of theories have been formulated to try to account for the usage, there are exceptions to all of them.[9] Consequently it seems useless to try to see a particular meaning intended here.

Of particular concern here is the use of "in the name of" (*en tō onomati*) in the definition of the "first" commandment. Grayston states that *onoma* commonly signifies a person's standing, authority, and power.[10] The two other instances of the phrase (2:12 and 5:13) corroborate this view. In 2:12 it is said that our sins are forgiven "*dia to onoma autou*" (literally, " 'through' the name of Christ"). Therefore the sins are forgiven through Jesus' standing before God. What is at issue in 2:13 is not the precise means by which the sins are forgiven in Christ, but the fact that the action which transpires between God and the believers occurs through some sort of mediation by Jesus.

In 5:13 the similar *eis to onoma* (with the accusative) (literally, " 'into' the name") occurs. Again the same process is evident: life is made available by God but only to those who believe *in the name of the Son of God.* Thus the position of Jesus as a necessary intermediary occurs again. This is affirmed by the previous statement in 5:11–12 that God has given life and this life is "in" his Son. The one who has the Son has life.

Consequently when we turn to 3:23, we find that the usage is consistent with these other texts and that in fact there are two important elements. First, this belief is belief in God, and, second, this belief is to be "in the name of his Son Jesus Christ." The essential element is therefore the place of Jesus in this belief, although belief *that* Jesus is the Christ (5:1) and *that* he is the Son of God (5:3) is also important.

Conclusions

As was mentioned above, this passage is the clearest example of the twofold commandment in 1 John. V 23 says explicitly: "And this is his commandment that we believe in the name of his Son Jesus Christ, and that we love one another as he has given us a commandment" (*Kai hautē estin hē entolē autou, hina pisteusōmen tō onomati tou huiou autou Iēsou Christou kai agapōmen allēlous, kathōs edōken entolēn hemin*). The arrangement of the verse and of the material immediately surrounding it is crucial to the understanding of the meaning of the verse. 3:23 is itself a chiasm and forms the central section of a larger chiasm extending from vv 22 to 24.[11]

V 22 begins the chiasm with a general exhortation (n.b. the plural form as in the gospel) to the keeping of the commandments.[12] This keeping of the commandments is complemented by a promise that one will then receive what one asks for. This first element of the passage is matched in v 24 by the concluding general exhortation to keep the commandments (again the plural). And again there is a complementary explanation of the benefits: that person will remain in God and God will remain in him, and that person will possess the Spirit.

V 23 then forms the center of the construction. It begins with the statement "and this is his commandment" which is then specified as to believe in Jesus Christ. Then in reverse order to this section, the second commandment, to love one another, is specified, and then the fact that this also is a commandment is stated, paralleling the statement in v 23a.

The structure can be diagrammed in paraphrase as follows:

A.   General statement: keep the commandments (and benefits).
   B.   "This is his commandment . . .
      C.   . . . that we believe in the name of his Son,
            Jesus Christ . . .
      C'. . . . and we should love one another . . .
   B'. as he gave us a commandment.
A'. General statement: keep the commandments (and benefits).

The fact that there is a double commandment referred to here is clear and needs no discussion. Brown lists it as the only example where a dual commandment occurs and one of two instances where belief is made the object of a command.[13]

This instance of the commandments is unique, however, in that the first commandment is described here as "believing in the name of Jesus." Elsewhere in the Johannine literature, the first commandment is identified as "keeping the word" ("of Jesus"—Jn 14:23–24; "of God"—1 Jn 2:5,7) or as "walking in truth" (2 Jn 4,6). This alternation in phrasing is not unique to the first commandment. There is also some alternation in the formulation of the second ("love") commandment. It is phrased variously as "to love one another" (*agapan allēlous*—Jn 13:34; 15:12,17; 2 Jn 5), "to have love for one another" (*agapēn echein en allēlois*—13:35), and "to love one's brother" (*agapan ton adelphon autou*—1 Jn 4:21).

Is there a difference intended in the various phrasings? It seems not. The difference is probably intended to emphasize the role of Jesus in salvation as the Johannine community conceives it. The word of God was described as the word of Jesus in the gospel, just as the commandments are. While he speaks of the roots of their obligations as founded in God, the precise dimension of belief that is in question is the role of Jesus (cf 5:1,5, etc.).

As we shall see below in chapter 6, one of the major problems facing the Johannine community at the time of the epistles was a dispute over the precise role and importance of Jesus within salvation. Thus to "believe in the name of Jesus" and to "keep the word of God" would be at least for the purposes of the author in his historical situation functionally synonymous since it was precisely that it was the word of God that they had heard from Jesus (cf 1:1–3, 2:7) that was the issue.[14] The common element clearly shared by all three formulations of the first commandment is that there is a correct belief to which the members of the community are called. Each formulation expresses this with varying degrees of specificity.

The use of the singular and plural of commandment throughout this section is of course consistent with the explanation proposed previously. The plural is used in general exhortation twice, in the first and last statements. In v 23a the singular is used because only the first commandment is spoken of. Then when the obligation of community love is specified in v 23b again the singular is used.

2. *1 Jn 2:3–11*

(3) And in this do we know that we have known him, if we keep his commandments. (4) The one who claims "I have known him" but who does not keep his commandments is a liar, and the truth is not present in that person. (5) The one who keeps his word—in this person truly has the love of God been brought to perfection. (6) The one who claims to abide in him ought to walk as he walked. (7) Loved ones, I do not write you a new commandment but an old one which you had from the beginning. The old commandment is the word which you heard. (8) Then again I do write a new commandment to you, one true in him and in you, in the sense that the darkness is passing away and the true light is already shining. (9) The one who claims to be in the light and who hates his brother is still in darkness even now.

(10) The one who loves his brother abides in the light and there is no stumbling block in him. (11) But the one who hates his brother is in the darkness and walks about in darkness and does not know where he goes because the darkness blinded his eyes.

Within this passage, the term commandment occurs six times. As was the case in 14:15,21–24 and 15:9–17 in the gospel and 3:22–24 in 1 John, the passage within which commandment occurs is carefully arranged, and understanding of that arrangement is important for understanding the use of commandment here.

Structure of 2:3–11

The section begins with a statement of the general theme in v 3. This is followed in vv 4–11 by three claims of the secessionists, each introduced by similar participial phrases. The topic of each of these false claims is linked verbally to the material which directly precedes it. The result is a "chaining" process which links the material together into a tightly knit whole. The first false claim (vv 4–5) picks up the theme of "knowing God" from v 3. The second false claim (vv 6–8) resumes the theme of being "in God" from v 5c. The third false claim (vv 9–11) resumes the theme of being "in the light" from v 8d. Each of the three claims is then countered by proposing a test for them given by the author. We will look at these in detail.

Introductory Statement (2:3)

The relationship of claim to test is laid out in the introductory statement (2:3): "We know that we know him by this, that we keep his commandments." This is the conclusion to the previous statement that, if we sin, we have a Paraclete before God, Jesus, who is a propitiation for our sins. V 3 then adds that we can be sure that we know Jesus if we keep "his" commandments. The author will insist throughout that there is a way to test any of the claims made with regard to Jesus.[15] Here the test is to determine whether that person keeps his commandments.[16]

The plural "commandments" is used here in general exhortation.

Identification of the giver of the commandment here requires some comment. Although "his" in v 3 could refer to Jesus as expressed in 2:1d, the parallelism in what follows strongly suggests that it refers to God as expressed in v 5b. The same is true of "his" throughout the section except where it clearly refers to the believer (vv 9–11).

First Claim (2:4–5)

In this first sub-section, the claims of the opponents (taken over from the previous verse) are spoken of under the image of "knowledge" and the test for this claim is whether one "keeps the commandments."

The author argues that if anyone says that he knows him (God) but does not keep his (God's) commandments, he is a liar and there is no truth in him. This general statement again uses (consistently) the plural of commandment. This is simply the reversal of what has just been said in v 3. "I have known him" (*Egnōka auton*) is a knowledge claim, a claim to a certain correct perception of who God is. It is the "belief" of the secessionists. But, as the author argues, anyone whose perception of God does not require the keeping of the commandments is a liar, and there is no truth in him.

Then the opposite is described: in the one who "keeps the word" of God, the love of God is brought to perfection. Thus "keeping the word of God" is now identified as a commandment, just as it was in the gospel. However we notice that here the word is identified as the word "of God" and not of Jesus. The same shift in attribution of the word (from Jesus to God) is evident in the attribution of the commandments.[17]

The exact nature of this commandment (defined as "keeping the word") is again disputed. Scholars tend to take the same positions as they did regarding the phrase in the gospel. Brown for example favors the equation of "word" with "commandment," making it simply a continuation of general exhortation.[18] Others would see it as a specific commandment referring to the need to be faithful to the entire message of Jesus.[19]

I would again propose that it refers to holding fast to the message of Jesus/God for the following reasons. First, we have seen in the gospel and in 1 John 3:23 that belief is a command in the Johannine tradition and so that possibility should be considered. Second, the fact that the singular of commandment is used indicates that a specific commandment (apart from the love command which is not mentioned) is intended. Third, it should be noted that the images most closely associated with "word" here are ones which would typically be associated with belief rather than the love command. The claim itself is "to know" Jesus; the claimant is said to be a "liar," and it is said that there is no "truth" in him. All of these terms have to do with the understanding of or belief in Jesus. If the claimant "knows" God really, then he will keep fast to his (Jesus'/God's) word.

It should be noted that in the first false claim, the necessity of understanding of Jesus is described in terms of moral action. But, as we have seen, for Johannine thought the commandment to "believe" is clearly a form of moral behavior in addition to being a "doctrinal" concern. Thus the fact that here it occurs as the evidence of "moral" action should not be surprising.

Given this cumulative evidence, "keeping the word of Jesus" is likely to be the intended meaning of *tērein ton logon* here: i.e. those who remain true to the understanding of God proposed by God himself can be said to truly know him.

This conception of the word of Jesus/God correlates well with the statement in John 12:49–50 where the word of Jesus is identified as ultimately the word of God. This identification of the word of Jesus as the word of God is also the ultimate grounding of the author's ability to refer to the commandments attributed to Jesus in the gospel as being "of God" in the epistles: since they are part of the word of Jesus, the commandments, like his word, are nothing other than the word of God.

Second Claim (2:6–8)

In the second false claim the relationship between belief and action is spoken of under the images of "remaining in him" and "walking as he walked." The image of "remaining in him" is of course taken over from the end of v 5 where it was said that they know that they are "in him." There is no evidence that a difference is intended between *menein* ("to remain/abide in") and *einai en* (literally "to be in") when they are used of the relationship between Jesus, God and the believer.[20]

The second claim is that the believer indwells with God. But the author argues that one cannot make such a claim if one does not walk as he (Jesus) walked.[21]

Implicit in the argument (between vv 6 and 7) is that "walking as he walked" involves the keeping of his commandments. V 7 begins by speaking of the commandments specifically. Here we find all singular uses of commandment: v 7 three times; v 8 once.

In v 7 the author says that the commandment is not a new one but one which they have heard from the beginning. What then is the commandment? It is nothing other than the "word (*logos*) which you have heard." Brown again argues that *logos* here is simply a synonym for "commandment."[22] It would then refer to the love commandment. This would of course provide a plausible reading since the love commandment is spoken of in v 9. But two elements of the context create problems for this interpretation. First, if we take Brown's interpretation, v 7b is meaningless. The last phrase of 7a ("an old commandment which you have had from the beginning") states that the commandment is "old" because it is the one which they have had since the beginning. Unless *logos* refers in some specific way to the message of Jesus, 7b (which in Brown's interpretation would state: "the old commandment is the commandment which you have heard") would add nothing to what had already been said.

The second problem is that, as we have seen in chapter one, throughout the Johannine writings "*hearing*" the word always refers to hearing the *message* of Jesus/God. This would suggest also that word means "message" rather than "commandment." On the other hand, the words make much more sense if, having provided the explanation of "old" in 7a (it is old because it is the one which you have heard from the beginning), he then goes on in 7b to say that the "old" commandment is the message which they have heard. This also fits well with the epistle's emphasis on what had been heard "from the beginning" (1:1).

Three times in the Johannine literature (13:34; 1 Jn 2:7–8; 2 Jn 5) commandments are referred to as "new." The Greek word used is *kainos* which has the connotation of "fresh" (as opposed to *neos* which also means "new" but with the connotation of "young"). This is the only instance of the commandment to believe being identified as a "new" commandment. In contrast to 13:34, in this verse the issue of "newness" versus "oldness" becomes explicit. The commandment is (in one sense) not new but old, because they have had it from the beginning. Here the author is explicitly contrasting the commandment with the ideas of the secessionists who bring in new things and go beyond what they have heard from the beginning (1:1; 2:13,14,24 (twice); 3:11; 2 Jn 5,6).[23] This is also the sense in which "new" is used in 2 Jn 5, as will be seen below.

But the author goes on to say that the commandment is "new" in the sense that it is true in him and in his readers, that is, inasmuch as the darkness has been taken away and the light is now shining. Thus it is the actuality of the commandment as it has been realized in Jesus and in the life of the Christian that makes the commandment a new one.

Then v 8 describes this message in the common symbols of darkness and light. Light is customarily used in the Johannine writings to symbolize the revelatory dimension of Jesus (Jesus as the light), just as love is used to symbolize the moral (Jesus as loving). Thus both the metaphor of light and the equation of the commandment with the *logos* suggests that the "test" of true indwelling here is correct faith.

What does this second section add to what had been said before? First, it addresses a different claim: the claim to remain in him. Second, this claim is also tested: by the evidence of whether one walks as Jesus did. This means to walk according to the commandment which the author writes to them. This commandment is the word which they have heard. Thus the message of Jesus provides an observable test by which the believer's claim can be verified. Third, the commandment to believe is qualified as being the one which they had heard from the beginning and which had come to reality in Jesus. Then not only are the images of belief changed, but the exhortation describes different aspects of belief than the previous claim.

Third Claim (2:9–11)

In the third false claim, the image of being in light is taken over from the previous section and binds this section to what preceded.

The one who claims to be in the light and hates his brother is in fact in darkness even now. Once again the basic topic is the relationship between a claim and a test of that claim. Here the claim is to be in the light, and the test is whether one lives out the love command. V 10 speaks of the one who loves; v 11 speaks of the one who hates. In both v 10 and v 11, the images of light and darkness reappear as the implied state determined by one's moral behavior.

Conclusions

Throughout the section the use of commandment is consistent in that the plural is used for general exhortation and the singular is used for specific commandment. We see both commandments referred to: the commandment to remain faithful to the word of Jesus in the first two, and the commandment to love in the last of the claims. Within this passage we see another feature of the commandments. They function as the means by which the claims of the opponents can be tested. They function as an integral part of the author's defense in the conflict raging within the community.

Finally we see that Jesus continues to be the model for the community in their obedience to the commandments. Twice he is held up as such a model. The believer is to walk "as he walked" (v 6) and the commandment which the believer is to obey has been realized in Jesus and so it should be realized also in the life of the Christian (v 8).

3. 1 Jn 4:21–5:5

(21) And we have this commandment from him, that the one who loves God should love his brother also. (5:1) Everyone who believes that Jesus is the Christ has been born of God, and everyone who loves the begettor loves the one begotten of him. (2) This is the way we know we love the children of God, that we love God and keep his commandments. (3) For this is love of God, that we keep his commandments. And his commandments are not burdensome, (4) because whatever is born of God conquers the world,

and this is the victory which has conquered the world, our faith. (5) Who is the one who conquers the world if not the one who believes that Jesus is the Son of God?

In this passage there are several references to the commandments as "his." The first instance is in 5:2. There it is a reference to God the Father, who is identified four words earlier. The two occurrences of "his" in 5:3 also refer to "God" earlier in the verse.

There is no dispute about the definition of commandment in 4:21. It is clearly the commandment to love: "And this is the commandment which we have from him, that the one who loves God also loves his *brother*" (*Kai tautēn tēn entolēn echomen ap' autou, hina ho agapōn ton theon agapa kai ton adelphon autou*).

V 21 is unique however in being the only instance in which the commandment of love is specifically identified as being love of one's brother. This confirms, as I have said above,[24] that the other references in the Johannine literature to love of one's brother are also intended to be references to the love commandment.

In addition the verse indicates that there can be no division of love of God from love of one's brother. Previously this had been true on the basis of what might be called an extrinsic relationship, i.e. it had been said that one could not love God without keeping his commandments, and one of the commandments was love of one another. Here however the basis of the relationship is different. This is what might be called the Johannine version of the great commandment, that one should love both God and neighbor. We will study the relationship between the synoptic great commandments and the Johannine tradition in chapter eight, but it becomes evident in passages such as this that although the Johannine tradition knows the content and theme of the great commandment tradition, the primary focus of the Johannine commandments themselves (keeping the word of Jesus/God and loving one another) is not the same as the focus of the great commandments in the synoptics.

As becomes evident from the argument in 5:1–2, the love of God and of one's brother are linked by reason of loving both the begettor and the begotten. Here, then, the basis for the love is cast in terms of an aphorism based on familial love: if one loves the parent, one ought to love the child. The application to the Christian is explained in 5:1. The one who believes that Jesus is the Christ is "born" of God.[25] This would apply both to the Christian and to one's fellow Christian: both are children of God. Therefore if one subscribes to the principle that one who loves the parent should love the child, then the one who loves God should love one's fellow Christian, since that fellow Christian is a child of God also.

In v 2, this argument takes a peculiar turn. Love for the fellow Christian is identified as *love for God and obedience to his commandments*. Thus the author turns the argument not to an exhortation to love of brothers in the sense of not "shutting off oneself from a brother in need" (1 Jn 3:17) but to a general exhortation to keep the commandments. By keeping the commandments, one exhibits love for the brothers. Thus here the author goes from the specific commandment to general exhortation.

Conclusions

Rhetorically this passage provides a reversal of the expected relation of commandments. It also provides another clear example of the author's "chaining" technique. In the first of the statements (4:21), the topic is initiated from the point of view of commandment. This is the commandment that the one who loves God should love one's brother. In 5:2 love of the brothers is the point of departure: we show true love for the brothers by keeping the commandments and loving God. And finally in 5:3, the argument begins with "love of God" which is defined and demonstrated in keeping the commandments.

From this point we learn (in v 3) that the commandments are not burdensome because the one born of God has conquered the world. The theme of "burden" (or the lack thereof) is also found in the synoptics at Matthew 11:30. Here though it has a special Johannine accent. According to v 4, presumably the commandments would be burdensome to the world, but because the Christian has been born of God and has faith in Jesus as the Son of God, the Christian has already conquered the world. This "conquering the world" is undoubtedly meant as an apocalyptic image. The believer has conquered the world through the atoning death of Jesus and through the life in Jesus and in the Spirit (cf the following 5:6–12).

Finally this passage is important because we find in it the main elements of the Johannine confession of Jesus: "that Jesus is the Christ" (5:1) and "that Jesus is the Son of God" (5:5). These were two disputed elements of the identity of Jesus within the Johannine community at the time of the first epistle, as we shall see in more detail in chapter six. These were also the two titles which made up the final statement of purpose within the gospel: "These things have been written that you might believe that Jesus is the Christ, the Son of God, and that, believing, you might have life in his name" (Jn 20:31).

4. 2 Jn 4–6

> (4) I rejoiced greatly that I have found some of your children walking in truth, just as we received the commandment from the Father. (5) And now I ask you, Lady, not as one writing you a new commandment but one which we had from the beginning, that we should love one another. (6) And this is the love, that we should walk according to his commandments. This is the commandment, as we heard from the beginning, that we should walk in it.

The meaning of commandment in 2 Jn 4–6 has been the cause of no little discussion and frustration. It is all the more frustrating because the verses make up the center of the author's theological argument in the letter.[26] Brown has called vv 5–6 a "syntactical quagmire." Houlden described the seeming randomness of the passage well when he said: "V 6 has one of our writer's familiar reversals of previous formulations. He loves to combine his favorite words in all possible directions."[27] However, careful attention to details of epistolary format, sentence structure and literary devices seems to clarify the passage and remove it from the realm of quagmire and uncover once again some elements of respectable rhetorical style. As I deal with each of the verses in turn, I will point out the various features alluded to above.

V 4

Because 2 John is a true letter, as opposed to 1 John which is most properly called a theological tract,[28] the understanding of the place of v 4 within the form of the letter will be helpful. The verse is neither part of the introduction (vv 1–3) nor fully part of the body of the letter (vv 5–12). Rather it is transitional in that it looks back to the introduction by including an expression of joy typical of that part of the letter format, but it also looks forward to the body of the letter by introducing what proves to be the topic of the letter.[29]

In v 4, the author describes the joy he experiences because of his knowledge that some of the members of the community are walking in truth, "as we received a commandment from the Father." The author is happy that some members have continued in their fidelity to the tradition. In this instance commandment clearly refers to belief. That this is the meaning of commandment here is generally recognized. Even Brown lists this as the second of the two passages where commandment refers to belief.[30] It is also to be noted that again the commandment is (consistently) referred to as "from the Father."

V 5

V 4 had been a report of obedience to a commandment and the "hinge" to the body of the letter. V 5 begins the body of the letter proper by introducing a new topic (cf *kai nyn*). This is an injunction to keep the other commandment of the tradition. This commandment is not new but one they have had from the beginning: "Let us love one another." Here the commandment referred to is clearly the love commandment and its meaning is not disputed. What is surprising is how this verse relates to the remainder of the letter where the chief concern is correct teaching/belief.

In v 4 the listeners are said to be walking in truth, and we have seen that the author has used images of truth when referring to his listeners as persons he had "loved in truth." In what follows the concern is those who have gone out from their midst, those who do not confess Jesus as the Christ coming in the flesh. In the remainder of the letter "remaining in the teaching of Christ" will be the criterion for accepting visitors who come to the community (v 10) and for determining the sin of the opponents (v 9, twice). What does the love command of v 5 have to do with this?

V 6

In v 6 we find two parallel statements, each of which provides a definition.[31] Each begins the same way—"and this is the love" (*kai hautē estin hē agapē* . . .) and "this is the commandment" (*hautē hē entolē estin* . . .)—and each is then followed by the epexegetical *hina* which provides a definition for each. V 6a has: "Now this is love: that we walk according to his commandments." Then v 6b has: "This commandment is (as you have heard from the beginning): that you walk 'in it.' "[32] Furthermore, each of the definitions is linked with the other and with the statement of the love command in v 5.

The result at first glance seems to be simply a sentence which is a play on words and circular in argument. The verse is at any rate annoyingly vague not only because of the seeming play on words but also because the ambiguous meaning of *agapē* in v 6a—does this love refer to love of the brothers or love of God?—and the unclear referent for *en autē* in v 6c—does this feminine pronoun refer to *agapē* (love), *entolē* (commandment) or *alētheia* (truth) all of which are feminine and have occurred previously in the letter? Let us look at each of these problems.

The Meaning of Agapē in V 6

Does *agapē* in v 6 refer to love of neighbor or love of God? There are two possible solutions which fit the grammar well and which are paralleled elsewhere in Johannine thought about love and the commandments. The first of these is that love does not refer to brotherly love but to the love which each should have for God and which is evident from the keeping of the commandments. If this is the case, the verse would read: This is love (for God), that we keep the commandments (in general). This interpretation would be consistent with the remainder of Johannine thought (see the same idea in 1 Jn 5:3 and in the gospel in 14:21,23 and 15:9b,10). There can be little doubt that v 6a is in fact a general exhortation; the plural of commandments clearly indicates this.

The second possible explanation proposes that *agapē* of v 6a refers to the brotherly love of v 5. Then this part of the verse means that brotherly love is shown in the keeping of the commandments. Although a somewhat unusual statement, this also has a precedent in Johannine thought. 1 John 5:2 states: "In this do we know that we love the children of God, that we love God and we execute his commandments" (*En toutō gignōskomen hoti agapōmen ta tekna tou theou, hotan ton theon agapōmen kai tas entolas autou poiōmen*). Here we have the reverse of what is normally said: one can tell love for the brothers by the way one obeys the commands of God.

Of these two the second best fits the context. First, it is the most natural explanation since love of the brothers has been spoken of immediately preceding in v 5. Second, the love of the brothers here forms a clear contrast with the warning given in v 11 that to greet the opponents is to take part in their evil deeds (and so, implicitly, not to show love for the brothers). Third, as we shall see, it fits more appropriately with the phrase "walking in it" as well as with the structure of the entire set of verses.

The Meaning of En Autē in V 6

The second problem associated with the verse is the obscurity of the phrase *en autē* ("in it") in v 6c. As we saw above, there are three possible referents for the pronoun. Each of these possibilities has its proponents, and the discussion of past proposals is summarized thoroughly in Brown's commentary.[33]

Although absolute certainty cannot be had, it seems most likely that the phrase is intended to refer to truth.[34] First, there is the fact that the verb "walk" (*peripateō*) has been used in the context only with the phrase "in truth" (*en alētheia;* cf v 4). In v 6, *peripateō* occurs with *entolas* (commandment) but the preposition *kata* (according to) is used instead of *en* (in). This is consistent with the usage in the remainder of the Johannine writings where, after *peripateō, en* occurs three times with *alētheia* in addition to 2 Jn 6, 2 Jn 4, and

3 Jn 3,4. Yet *peripateō en* never occurs with *entolē*. Thus there is considerable precedent for its use with *alētheia* but none for any other use.

Second, "walking in truth" is the content of a command in v 4; "walking in it" in v 6c is also the content of a command.[35] However when the command of fraternal love is spoken of in v 5 it is expressed in a *hina* clause. It would indeed be awkward then to see fraternal love as a referent of *autē* in v 6c.

Third, there is the awkwardness which results from taking *entolē* as the antecedent: "This is the command which we have heard from the beginning, that we walk in the command." This awkwardness argues against accepting the position of Brown,[36] Houlden[37] and others. Brown who sees the introduction of the love command as intended for its own sake nevertheless seems to be aware of the awkwardness of this interpretation: "By using the idiom of walking 'according to His commandments' and walking 'in it,' the author thinks of the commanded love as expressing itself in a way of life. Presumably the Presbyter feels there is some challenge to the necessity of such 'walking,' but he does not explain what this will be. Since in the next verse (7) he mentions secessionists . . . who are guilty of a christological error. . . ."[38]

Brown then goes on to argue from the similarity of language with 1 John that the author of 2 John is thinking of the same combination of ethical and christological errors discussed in 1 John. Undoubtedly the author of 2 John was aware of both kinds of errors, but it seems that in this letter he is concerned with the christological rather than the ethical, and so introduces the language of the ethical only as a way of exhorting to correct christology, which was of course "ethical" in the sense that holding fast to the message was in the Johannine tradition the object of a command just as was fraternal love. Keeping faithful to the words of Jesus then would fulfill both of the major commandments of the community: it fulfills the injunction to keep the words themselves, and it also fulfills the message to love the brothers inasmuch as keeping the commandments in general is a manifestation of love of the brothers.

The fourth reason for seeing truth as the antecedent of "it" is that this is the only possibility which fully respects the definitional character of the two clauses in v 6. If truth is the antecedent we have a clear and orderly progression from what seems to be the awkward intrusion of the love command though two subordinate definitions which then conclude by showing that the love command itself exhorts to keeping true to the message of Jesus and so walking in truth.

The fifth reason for seeing "truth" as the antecedent is that the concern of the entire epistle is with truth as we have seen. Consequently, that the commandment here would be addressed to this concern is very likely.

Conclusions

I would see the entire context proceeding as follows. After expressing joy that some of the members of the community are walking in truth (as they had received a commandment), the author turns in v 5 to an exhortation to the second of the commandments, that they love one another. What this has to do with walking in truth he then proposes to show. First the author defines the fraternal love, as he sees it in this application ("and this is the love . . ."), as keeping the commandments in general (v 6a). That is, the general obedience to the commandments is one manifestation of love of the brothers. But the author has one particular commandment in mind and he proceeds to define that: "And this is the commandment one heard from the beginning, that they walk 'in it.' " Here "it" refers to the truth. The author, returning to the expression he had first used in v 4, again exhorts them to remain in the truth of the teaching that they had received. Thus, the single reference to the love command (v 5) is introduced somewhat awkwardly as a means of strengthening the command to believe what they have received from the beginning. This becomes another example of the way in which the author of 1 and 2 John combines the commandments in such a way as to show that each is in fact a support of the other. If we love the brethren, then part of this commitment will be continued faithfulness to the true teaching of Jesus. Likewise, if they remain faithful to the true teaching of Jesus, they will see that this true teaching involves a demonstration of love for the others.

C. Conclusions to the Discussion
of Commandment in the Epistles

From our review of the commandment texts in the epistles we notice the following. We have seen that the use of the singular and plural of the term is consistent. This conclusion is of course closely tied into another more significant conclusion: that here also there clearly is evidence of two commandments in the Johannine tradition, not just one.

We have seen that in the epistles the author attributes the commandments to God (their ultimate source) rather than to Jesus because the opponents are calling into question the role of Jesus.

In the second Epistle, commandment also occurs in the same pattern as above, and both commandments are again mentioned, but the stress is on the "first."

Our exegesis to this point has been quite detailed. It was so necessarily. This detailed exegesis was necessary in order to establish several basic features of the Johannine commandment tradition. As we have seen, the Johannine commandments have suffered from a combination of misunderstanding and lack of attention. In this chapter we have come to see a commandment tradition within the Johannine community which focuses on only two requirements: that the members of the community "keep the word of Jesus" and that they "love one another." Presumably these two commandments were of considerable importance within the life of the community if they were in fact termed "commandments."

Yet why would the community speak of only two commandments? What was there in the community life that brought forth such a focus on these two elements as objects of "commanding"? The injunction to remain faithful to the word of Jesus, while noble, may well seem self-evident to the Christian of today. If there were something so important in this concern that it was seen as one of the two basic commandments given by God through Jesus, we are led to ask whether this commandment had some special meaning within the community of the time that is perhaps not so evident to us.

When we turn to the second of the commandments, the commandment of "brotherly love," our immediate reaction might well be different. Certainly this commandment has struck a sympathetic chord within the hearts of Christians throughout Christian history. But when looked at from a critical point of view, even this commandment raises questions for the Christian of today. When compared with the Matthean injunction of love even for one's enemies, the Johannine commandment has a double effect upon the reader. While this understanding of Christian love presents a particularly strong and compelling view of the possibilities of Christian love within the community, it is a Christian love which is much less broad by neglecting, if not excluding, the breadth of Christian love which should, as other parts of the New Testament tell us, extend to everyone. What is the intention of the commandment? Are we correct in maintaining that what is traditionally termed one of the most beautiful and intense injunctions to Christian love really is such?

The Johannine commandments, although they may seem at first sight to be almost self-evident, do not in fact easily yield to full understanding. If we are to fully understand them, we must come to grips both with the way in which they relate to the rest of Johannine theology within the gospel and epistles and how they relate to the history of the Johannine community itself.

NOTES

1. 1 Jn 2:3,4,7 (three times), 8; 3:22,23 (twice), 24; 4:21; 5:2,3 (twice); 2 Jn 4,5,6 (twice). The verb does not occur in the epistles.

2. In the past scholars who were compelled to recognize the presence of two commandments in at least one, possibly two, passages in the epistles continued to argue against there being actually two commandments in the tradition and tended to treat these instances as a kind of anomaly.

3. In the translation above, I have substituted "God" for the pronoun "him" (*autos*) in the first part of v 24 for the sake of clarity.

4. Brown, *Epistles* 453.

5. The verb *katagignōskein* is a forensic verb used infrequently in the Old Testament and New Testament. It refers to the knowledge which would be detrimental to a person in a legal trial.

6. P. Trudinger, "Concerning Sins, Mortal and Otherwise. A Note on 1 John 5, 16–17," *Biblica* 52 (1971) 541–42, argues that *erōtaō*

means to ask questions regarding rather than to petition. However this is not consistent in the Johannine usage (cf Jn 14:16; 16:26; 17: 9,15,20).

7. 4:1,16; 5:1,5,10,13.

8. Codex Sinaiticus, Alexandrinus and the Byzantine tradition. See Metzger, *A Textual Commentary, ad locum.*

9. Brown (*Epistles* 462–63; *Gospel* 512–15) discusses the various positions. Among the studies of belief in Johannine theology are those of A. Vanhoye, "Notre Foi, oeuvre divine, d'après le quatrième évangile," *NRT* 86 (1964) 337–54 and I. de la Potterie, *La vérité dans Saint Jean* (2 Vols; AnBib 73–74; Rome: Biblical Institute, 1977) esp. 1, 296–97; 2, 553–558.

10. Grayston, *Epistles* 117.

11. Also noted by S. Smalley, *1, 2, 3 John* (WBC; Waco: Word, 1984) 206. I. H. Marshall, *The Epistles of John* (NICNT; Grand Rapids: Eerdmans, 1978) 200–201, says that the passage "sums up the commands as one command which is then expressed as having two parts; in this way the fundamental unity of the two parts is made quite clear." This misreads the chiastic arrangement.

12. The second part of the verse, *kai ta aresta enōpion autou poioumen,* really is an example of hendiadys, paraphrasing the previous section of the verse regarding the commandments: to do what is pleasing before him is to keep the commandments.

13. For the other, see the section on 2 John 4 below. See Brown, *Epistles* 461–64, 706–07.

14. Of course what is at stake for the author of 1 John is that this word is what they have had from the beginning. The opponents, however, are not content to rest with that; they are going beyond the teaching which they had heard (2 Jn 9).

15. This testing of claims is a major technique of the author in his rebuttal of the opponents. It will be discussed fully in chapter six.

16. Brown (*Epistles* 278–79) observes correctly that there is more to this than simply the claim that one can deduce human behavior from one's knowledge of God. The opposite is also true: one can gain some knowledge of God through behavior when that behavior is governed by God's commandments.

17. This shift in attribution of "word" from Jesus to God is consistent throughout the first epistle. See 1:10 where *autou* refers to

God, and see 2:14 where the identification of the word as the word of God is explicit.

18. Brown, *Epistles* 254. Also R. Bultmann, *The Johannine Epistles* (Hermeneia; Philadelphia: Fortress, 1973) 25; Houlden, *Epistles* 68. Segovia (*Love Relationships* 42) treats the phrase here as a synonym of "keeping the commandments" even though in 14:15–24 he sees the same phrase as referring to belief, as "focusing on the person of Jesus, his origin and destiny" (pp 148–51).

19. Marshall, *Epistles* 124; Grayston, *Epistles* 64; Smalley, *1, 2, 3 John.*

20. The Johannine usage is distinctive and makes up a majority of the New Testament usage. Important studies include J. Heise, *Bleiben. Menein in den johanneischen Schriften* (Tübingen: Mohr, 1967); E. Malatesta, *Interiority and Covenant: A Study of einai en and menein en in the First Letter of Saint John* (AnBib 69; Rome: Biblical Institute, 1978).

21. For the discussion of the theological use of *peripatein* see especially de la Potterie, *Vérité* 646–657.

22. Brown, *Epistles* 253–54.

23. There is also the possibility that the reference to the "beginning" referred to the beginning of the individual Christian's existence, i.e. his initiation. I find this less likely.

24. See above the discussion of John 15:12.

25. This statement does not mean that the act of believing is what makes one "born of God" but simply that this belief (which is possible only through the presence of the Spirit within) is evidence that one is born of God. The actual birth results from the coming of the Spirit.

26. For a more detailed discussion of these verses see my article "The Theological Foundation of the Presbyter's Argument in 2 Jn (vv 4–6)," *ZNW* 76 (1985) 209–224.

27. Houlden, *Epistles,* 145.

28. See the full discussion in Brown, *Epistles* 86–92.

29. Thus I am in agreement with Brown (*Epistles* 682, 790–92) who discusses the problem and concludes by defining it as "transitional to the body of the letter" (p 682). So also J. L. White, "New Testament Epistolary Literature in the Framework of Ancient Epistolography," *ANRW* II. 25.2 (Berlin: de Gruyter, 1984) 1741.

30. Brown, *Epistles* 663. Brown does however argue that the verse

refs to both correction confession of Jesus and love of the brothers, a position I find unconvincing since love of the brothers is explicitly introduced later (v 5).

31. There are three textual variants of some concern here. Several mss have *houtos* for *hautē* before both statements and also have another *hina* before *kathōs*. These are admittedly more difficult readings but they are not sufficiently attested. The text followed here is that of the UBS version.

32. This parallel use of definitions has not been noticed previously and aids greatly in the solution of the problem. Brown (*Epistles* 192) provides a very helpful study of the definitional use of *kai hautē estin* . . . but fails to include *hautē . . . estin* which is functionally identical to the other phrase. Brown points out that the referent of the "Now this is . . ." statement is generally introduced in the verses that precede and then discussed or defined more fully in what follows. This is clearly the case in 1 John 3:23; 5:4,11,14.

33. Brown, *Epistles* 667–68. Brown himself does not claim a certain position but admits an inclination toward seeing command as the antecedent.

34. De la Potterie (*Vérité*) also defends the position that *alētheia* is the proper reference for the pronoun; see esp 651–55; also von Wahlde, "Foundation" 219–223.

35. Brown's concern (*Epistles* 667) that the antecedent of *autē* is too far removed seems irrelevant in the light of the contorted nature of the grammar throughout the verses.

36. Brown, *Epistles* 174.

37. Houlden, *Epistles* 145.

38. Brown, *Epistles* 684.

Chapter Four

THE JOHANNINE
COMMANDMENTS
IN THEIR GOSPEL SETTING:
A SOURCE-CRITICAL
EXPLORATION

In chapter two we saw that a comparison of the "commandment" passages with the "work" passages in the Johannine gospel indicates that each group of passages expresses a specific theological conception of Jesus' ministry. We also saw that on the whole the dominant conception of the ministry within the gospel is that of work rather than that of commandment. This, coupled with the fact that these two theologies of the ministry give no indication of being correlated or integrated with one another, leads us to question whether the commandment passages are in fact a later editorial addition to the gospel.[1] This chapter seeks to explore that question in more detail.

There is considerable discussion today about the literary makeup of the Johannine gospel. Although I have elsewhere presented some views regarding the earlier stages of the gospel's literary history,[2] it is not my intention to present a complete view of this history here. My intention is simply to review the commandment passages within their literary contexts to determine as far as possible whether the passages are original to the gospel or are additions by the redactor.

A. 10:7–18

The first of the commandment texts occurs within the passage containing the explanation of the parable of the shepherd (10:7–18). The explanation of the parable is bounded both by the parable itself which appears in 10:1–6[3] and by vv 19–21 which form the concluding reaction of the listeners. The section which contains the explanation of the parable is unfortunately quite complicated, and a thorough understanding of the commandment text must involve an analysis of 10:7–18.

1. Literary Characteristics of the Material

A critical reading of vv 7–18 reveals numerous literary inconsistencies which suggest that the passage is not the work of a single author. These inconsistencies may be summarized as follows:

V 7 begins with the statement by Jesus that he is the *gate* for the sheep. Yet in vv 11,14 Jesus is identified as the shepherd! The identification of Jesus as the gate is striking since the dominant figure of the parable is that of Jesus as the *shepherd* rather than the gate.

The second verse (v 8) speaks of "those who came before me" as being thieves and robbers and of the sheep not listening to them. Clearly this verse is not part of the development of Jesus as the gate since gates cannot be thieves and robbers nor do they "come before me." These verses (vv 7–8) obviously are not the work of the same author as the prior verse. V 9 returns to the statement of Jesus as the gate, but this time the statement is accompanied by a development which is consistent with the image of the gate: "Whoever enters by me will be saved and will go in and go out and will find pasture." Therefore we must posit another literary seam between vv 8 and 9.

V 10 returns to the context of v 8 by speaking of thieves and robbers, describing them as coming to steal, kill and destroy. Jesus on the other hand is described in this verse as having come so that they might have life and have it abundantly. This verse is consistent with the statement of v 8 but not with v 9.

V 11 speaks of the figure of the shepherd explicitly for the first time by identifying Jesus as the "good" shepherd. One would have expected this part of the verse to be the beginning of the explanation since it is a more logical development of the parable itself than was the image of Jesus as the gate. However the verse goes on to speak of the shepherd as laying down his life for the sheep. Although this image is not so striking in itself as to demand editing to account for it, when it is linked with the following verses (vv 12–13), it immediately becomes clear that even these verses are not compatible with the original parable since they introduce for the first time the figures of the hireling and the wolf (neither of which was part of the original parable) as well as the topic of dying for the sheep which also was not part of the original parable. All of this indicates that vv 11–13 also (except perhaps for the first part of v 11) are not an original part of the passage either.

V 14 repeats the statement of v 11, that Jesus is the good shepherd. This figure is then developed consistently with both the parable and with the image of the shepherd up through v 15a: "I know mine and mine know me, just the Father knows me and I know the Father." In these verses (vv 14–15a) we are evidently in contact with at least part of the original explanation of the parable. This is confirmed by the fact that the verses are also consistent with the understanding of the parable presumed in the discourse which follows (10:22–39).

But in v 15b the image of dying for the sheep returns and is evidently another brief editorial addition consistent with the material of vv 11b–13.

V 16 speaks of the sheep which do not belong to this sheepfold: "They too will hear my voice, and there will be one sheepfold and one shepherd." This topic like that of the hireling and wolf has no basis in the parable itself and is a secondary development.

V 17 returns to the image of the shepherd dying for the sheep. Jesus says that the Father loves him because he lays down his life, in order that he might pick it up again. V 18 continues this: "No one takes it away from me, but I lay it down of my own accord. I have power to lay it down and to take it up. This is the commandment given to me by the Father." Thus ends the explanation of the parable. In all we have identified what may be four layers of tradition: (1) the material associated with Jesus as the gate; (2) the material associated with Jesus as the shepherd; (3) the material referring to the hireling and to Jesus as dying for the sheep; (4) the material which makes reference to the sheep of other folds.

This complicated and involved passage with its various levels of interpretation are illustrated on the accompanying page. This chart demonstrates that there are three or possibly four separate levels of interpretation within the passage.

THE LITERARY STRATA IN THE EXPLANATION
OF THE PARABLE OF THE SHEEP

10:7–18

(7) Amen, Amen, I say to you,
"I am the gate for the sheep.
(8) All who came before me were thieves and robbers, but the sheep did not listen to them.

> **(9) I am the gate.** If someone enters through me, that person will be saved and will go in and out and will find pasture.

(10) The thief comes only to steal, to put to death and to destroy.
(11) I am the good shepherd.

> The good shepherd lays down his life for the sheep. (12) The hireling, not being the shepherd and not owning the sheep, sees the wolf coming and leaves behind the sheep and flees—and the wolf grabs and scatters the sheep—(13) because he is a hireling and the sheep are of no real concern to him.

(14) I am the good shepherd. I know my sheep and mine know me, (15) just as the Father knows me and I know the Father.
And I lay down my life for the sheep.

> > (16) I have other sheep which are not from this fold and I have to shepherd them also. They will hear my voice and there will be one flock, one shepherd.
> >
> > (17) My Father loves me because **I lay down my life** in order that I may take it up again. (18) No one takes it from me, but I lay it down of my own will. I have the power to lay it down, and I have the power to take it up again; this is the commandment I received from my Father."

2. The Repetitive Resumptive as an Indicator of Editing

In addition to the fact that a more consistent and coherent reading is achieved by distinguishing and isolating the various levels of meaning here, we also find considerable evidence within the passage of a common editorial technique in the gospel: the use of the "repetitive resumptive," i.e. the repetition of material as a way of bracketing inserted material.

Consistently in the gospel, certain types of repetition of material is an indication of editing. Typically the repetitive resumptive functions to bracket and so identify an addition by repeating a brief section of the original sequence from immediately before the insertion.[4] In the text above there are three indications of the repetitive resumptive (printed in boldface).

Each of these repetitions brackets material. The introduction of "I am the sheepgate" at the beginning of the explanation seems intended to introduce this secondary image of Jesus right at the beginning. Then allowing[5] for v 8, the beginning of the original explanation, the image of the gate is reintroduced in v 9 by means of the repetition and is given its only development. Here Jesus is presented as the only means for the sheep of gaining pasture and of being saved.

The second repetition ("I am the good shepherd") clearly brackets vv 11b–13. The third repetition ("I lay down my life") clearly brackets the next addition (v 16).

Thus we may be almost certain that we have identified and isolated each of the editorial expansions of the parable. When these are removed, there results what would seem to be a clear and coherent "original" explanation, consistent both with the parable which precedes and the discourse which follows.

However the problem is not completely solved since the editorial expansions (the figure of the sheepgate, the shepherd who dies for his sheep and the other sheep from other sheepfolds) are not consistent with one another. The solution of this part of the problem is beyond the bounds of the present occasion. We are able to indicate with some degree of certainty that the passage containing the commandment text (vv 17–18) is an addition to the original. This explanation is consistent with the fact that in the discourse which follows (vv 22–39), the so-called "original" discourse), the term "works" appears consistently. Thus we see that much as the two terms for God (Yahweh and Elohim) in Genesis are an indication of different strata in the creation story, so the two terms which conceptualize the ministry of Jesus—"commandment" and "work"—serve to indicate different strata in the material of chapter 10 of John.[6]

The literary indications of this division of material are sufficient to achieve a reasonable certainty about the division of the material in the explanation. Several features of this material call for comment.

First, there is the commandment itself. We have seen before that the commandment given to Jesus here is what to "do": to lay down his life for the sheep. Jesus does this in response to a commandment, and because of this he is loved by the Father. In addition it is said that Jesus does this of his own free will. It is not a matter of being taken by force; rather Jesus' obedience to the Father and his giving of his life is a matter of his own free choice. This view of the death of Jesus is what is properly called "expiatory," that is, his death brings about some good for the sheep. As has been demonstrated in the present literary analysis, there are serious reasons for suggesting that this entire complex of ideas is distinct and separate from the other complex of ideas dealing with the good shepherd. In addition, this "dying shepherd" complex can be shown to be secondary to the other in that the other complex is the only one which is consistent with both the parable itself and the continuation of the parabolic material in the discourse which follows.

What is most important for our purposes here however is the fact that there is such significant evidence that the material containing the commandment material is secondary and that, at the same time, the theology of the addition has clear theological parallels in 1 John.

3. Theological Parallels with 1 John[7]

(a) Association of "Expiatory Death" with "Commandment"

Commentators are in agreement that this is a description of the death of Jesus as expiatory. It is also noticed frequently that in the gospel there are clearly two strains of thought theologically about the death of Jesus. In the first, which is the dominant strain in the gospel, the death of Jesus is spoken of primarily in terms of "departure." His death represents the end of his revelatory ministry and the point at which he returns to the Father, but in these texts there is no clear indication that the death has an intrinsic value to it.

On the other hand, in a minority of texts within the gospel, the death of Jesus is spoken of in terms of being an "expiatory death"— a death "for" his own. What is important for our purposes is that the conception of the expiatory death of Jesus is found together with the conception of the ministry of Jesus as commandment in the explanation of the parable. Are there other texts in the gospel that associate these two? Are there texts in which the concept of death as departure is clearly associated with commandment? Let us answer each of these in turn.

Given the fact that commandment occurs only in four passages of any size in the gospel, it is significant that in the other commandment passage parallel to this, the passage which describes what the disciples are "to do" in imitation of Jesus (15:9–17), we again find a reference to the expiatory death of Jesus. When he gives his commandment to the disciples to love one another, he gives a model for this love, the love that he has shown to them. Then he goes on to qualify this by saying that greater love no one has than that he lay down his life for his own. This is significant in that there is this consistent association of the two distinctive concepts.[8] The second question raised above concerned the possibility of the occurrence of commandment with conceptions of the death of Jesus as departure. There is no reference to death simply as departure in 12:44–50, nor in 14:15,21–24.

It is also significant that in 1 John there is no mention of the death of Jesus as departure, but only of the expiatory nature of his death.

(b) Association of "Love" with Commandment

Yet another striking feature of the passages is that the relationship created and preserved by keeping the commandments is one of love. This feature is evident in all of the commandment passages except 12:44–50 and 14:31. Is this also a feature typical of 1 John as redactional in the gospel? Although the passages dealing with love are concentrated in the last discourses, there are occurrences of the theme elsewhere in the gospel. This makes it difficult if not impossible to reach definitive conclusions regarding the occurrence of this concept within the original gospel or the redaction. We will say more about this below. For now we are able to see that there is considerable evidence that the commandment passage is not an original element of the parable explanation.

B. 12:49–50

The second of the commandment texts in the gospel occurs as part of 12:44–50. In this passage Jesus speaks of the judgment which comes as a result of rejecting his word, the word which he was commanded by the Father to speak.

1. Literary Characteristics of the Material

It is commonly pointed out in gospel commentaries that this passage seems to have no relation to its surrounding context. In 12:36b it had been said that Jesus departed from the people and hid himself. Following on this, vv 37–44 provide in the words of the narrator a summary of the public ministry, a theological reflection on the ministry, and then a final statement about the failure of religious authorities to confess belief in Jesus. Suddenly in 12:44, with no mention of time, location, or purpose, Jesus begins speaking again. His words, which continue to 12:50, are also unrelated to the context which follows in 13:1ff (which begins the narrative of the last supper). This awkward placement of the material is generally taken to indicate that the passage is a secondary addition to the gospel.

The analysis I have just presented is agreed to by most scholars. However there is some disagreement about the authorship of the verses. Some claim that they are the work of the evangelist but added to the gospel here by an editor; others claim that they are the actual composition of an editor who is also responsible for their placement here.

For example, Schnackenburg lists it as one of the gospel's "situationless" passages (*situationsgeloste*) and regards it as an addition by editors from material composed by the evangelist (although it may have some revision by editors).[9] Yet he notes with some approval the many similarities to 1 John discovered by Boismard.[10]

As Brown says: "The discourse that Jesus gives in these verses is clearly not in its original context; for, since Jesus has gone into hiding (xii 36), this discourse has no audience or setting."[11] Brown suggests that "xii 44–50 is a variant of material found elsewhere in John but preserved by a different disciple. In the final redaction of the gospel this independent discourse was probably added where it would cause the least disarrangement. . . ."[12]

2. Theological Parallels with 1 John

It is commonly pointed out that these verses are very similar in thought and in language to 1 John. This line of thought is most fruitful. From an examination of the passage, one can see that many of these features are rightly considered major features of 1 John but appear in the gospel only in passages where there are indications of editing.[13] Let us look at some of these features.

(a) The Typical Use of "Light" and "Darkness"

While the terms "light" and "darkness" occur several times in the gospel,[14] they are not distributed evenly but typically occur in passages where there are significant literary features to indicate that these passages have been added to the gospel.[15] For example, the terms light/darkness also occur in the prologue, in 3:16–21, in 8:12, in 9:4–5; and in 11:9. All of these passages are frequently thought to be secondary.[16] In addition, as will be pointed out below, the theme of light is one of the two structuring elements of the first epistle. The appearance of the term "light" here is significant here in the last passage in the "Book of Signs" (chapters 1–12) since it suggests that the reader's opportunity to walk in the light is almost ended, a statement which confirms the picture of the first part of the gospel ending with chapter 12.

(b) Final Eschatology

Second there is the presence of statements of future eschatology in the passage. As was mentioned above, it is commonly recognized that the gospel is dominated by realized eschatology while in the first epistle a future eschatology predominates.[17] We will discuss this in detail later.

(c) Dualistic Use of Work

Next there is the dualistic use of "work" noted above, a use not characteristic of the gospel but found repeatedly in 1 John. This of course forms a unity with the dualism of light/darkness which helps structure the first part of the epistle.

(d) The Presence of Commandment

The final factor is the presence of the term "commandment" itself. The fact that the term occurs in this "situationless" passage, and that this is the only other passage in the gospel (in addition to 10:17–18) which speaks of the ministry of Jesus in terms of commandment, gives a very strong indication that the material is to be associated with the theological context of 1 John.

Thus if the passage's awkward relation to its surrounding material suggests that it is an editorial addition, this combination of theological and linguistic features typical of 1 John suggests a connection between the passage and the theological orientation characteristic of 1 John.[18] Admittedly such indications are not proof, but these conclusions clearly point in the same direction as those obtained in the analysis of the previous commandment passage.

C. 13:34–35

The third commandment passage occurs soon after the beginning of the last discourses, the complex of dialogue and discourse material which runs from 13:31 to 17:26. As was the case with 12:44–50, it is commonly thought that 13:34–35 interrupt the surrounding sequence of material and are a secondary addition.[19] Also, as was the case in 10:17–18 and 12:50, while literary analysis indicates that the verses have been added to the context, once again theological similarities with 1 John enable us to suggest their affinity. Let us look briefly at the reasons for suggesting that the verses are additions to their present context.

1. Literary Characteristics of the Material

The verses themselves follow the first words of Jesus about his departure. He has informed his disciples (vv 31–33) that the Son of Man has been glorified and that God has been glorified in him. Then in v 33 he has told them that he is going away and that they will not be able to follow him. Then in vv 34–35 he gives them the "new" commandment that they should love one another as Jesus has loved them. In v 35 it is said that it will be by this love for one another that they will be recognizable as his disciples. However the material of v 36 takes up the context prior to vv 34–35. Simon Peter without any reference to the new commandment asks Jesus where he is going, and Jesus responds that Peter will not be able to follow at the present time, but that he will follow later.

Peter's question in v 36 deals directly with Jesus' statement in v 33 without reference to what has intervened. Nor is there any further reference to the love commandment in what follows. The next mention of the love command will be in chapter 15.

In addition to the contextual problems created by the verses, other scholars add various other considerations. Some mention features of style.[20] Schnackenburg also includes other theological differences. For example he points out that the "new commandment" is nowhere developed thematically in the gospel. It is however treated in 1 John 2:7–8. There the author describes the commandment that he is writing to the community as "not new" but "old." But then again it is described as "new" in the sense that it has just come to be in the reality of Jesus.[21] Finally Schnackenburg points out that the theme of brotherly love so dominates the first epistle that it can be called a fundamental theme, yet it is not so within the gospel. I would add that the theme of *knowing* whether one is a brother by love for one another is another issue which is not significant within the gospel but which is clearly a polemical issue in 1 John 9 (cf 3:16–18; 4:7–11,20–21).

Segovia, following Becker, likewise points to the contextual problems. He then goes on to show that the verses are similar in many ways to 15:1–17, a section of the gospel that he would see (as would I) as also being a redactional addition.[22]

Together these various features indicate strongly that 13:34–35 have been added to the gospel and that they find their closest parallels in 1 John.

These two verses form a fragmentary addition to the gospel, but it is very possible that this brevity can be accounted for. Boismard has suggested that the verses have been put here at the beginning as a means of introducing the love commandment along with other themes considered important by the author and which will be developed in what follows.[23] I would suggest that this is correct and that the redactor who added the verses felt them sufficiently important to interject them at the beginning of the last discourses even though this meant interrupting the sequence of the departure dialogue.

2. Theological Parallels with 1 John

(a) The "New" Commandment

Once again we find that the theology of the verses has close affinities with 1 John. In what sense the commandment of love is "new" is not explained here—nor elsewhere in the gospel. However in 1 Jn 2:7–8, the newness of the commandment to believe is explained.[24] It is new in the sense that it has been realized in Jesus; it is not new in the sense that it was not part of the Johannine tradition from the beginning.[25]

(b) Love for One Another

Love for one another occurs two places in the Johannine gospel: here and in 15:12,17. It can hardly be called a dominant theme, yet in the first epistle "loving the brothers" occurs in 2:10; 3:10,14; 4:20,21 and "loving one another" occurs in 3:11,23; 4:7,11; 2 Jn 5. In each case it can be said to be a major topic and developed accordingly. While this cannot be said to be proof that passages containing this theme are redactional additions to the gospel, it is a consistent usage which when combined with other features confirms the conclusions reached independently.

D. 14:15,21–24

These verses occur, as did 13:34–35, within the first of the farewell discourses following the last supper. That discourse begins in 13:31 and ends in 14:31. This commandment section is unusual in that it begins with a verse (v 15) which is detached from the remainder of the commandment material (vv 21–24) but which seems connected in terms of thought. Although there is little or no prior scholarly discussion of these verses which suggests that the verses are a secondary addition, comments are frequently made about tensions and other difficulties within the material. A careful reading of the material, with the theology of commandment in mind, gives new insight into the passage and provides a helpful perspective for understanding the thought of the section in general and for discovering the evidence for editing.

1. Literary Characteristics of the Material

(a) The Overall Structure of the Section

The structure of the first farewell discourse (13:31–14:31) is determined by two elements of the material. First, I would agree with Becker[26] who suggests that the major division of the material is determined by the dual themes of the departure and the return of Jesus.[27] 13:31–14:17 concerns the departure of Jesus and 14:18–31 concerns his return.

Within this overall arrangement, the four questions/statements by the disciples are important for determining the subordinate themes and structure. The first question (13:36) asks where Jesus is going. The second asks the way to the Father (14:4). The third asks how one is to see the Father (14:8). The fourth does not occur until 14: 22 where Judas asks why it is that Jesus will reveal himself to them but not the world.

(b) The Context: Vv 8–14

Our concern for the context of the commandment passage begins with the third question (14:8) in which Philip asks Jesus to show them the Father. Jesus replies in surprise that he has been with them so long and they have not recognized him since the one who sees Jesus has seen the Father: "Do you not believe that I am in the Father and the Father in me?" Then Jesus gives two types of evidence for showing that Jesus and the Father indwell mutually. First, the words which Jesus speaks are not spoken by Jesus on his own but rather the Father present in Jesus speaks them.[28] Second, the Father present in Jesus is the one who performs his works. In v 11, Jesus asks the disciples whether they believe that he and the Father indwell. He then says that, if not, they should believe because of the works Jesus performs.

In v 12, there is a shift from a focus on the departure of Jesus to the plight of the disciples, but the over-riding theme remains the ways the relationship between the Son and the Father is revealed. Here Jesus says that the one who believes in Jesus will perform the same works that Jesus performs and even greater ones—because Jesus is returning to the Father. Thus the request of Philip to "show us the Father" is answered three ways: by saying that the words of Jesus are those of the Father; the works of Jesus are done in the Father; finally, even the works which the disciples will do are evidence for this relationship because the disciples are to ask the Father in Jesus' name and their request will be granted "so that the Father may be glorified in the Son." V 14 generalizes this even further by saying that *whatever* they ask in Jesus' name, he will do, so that the Father can be glorified in the son.

(c) The First Editorial Addition: Vv 15–17

14:15, the first of the commandment verses, is not an integral part of this sequence. In v 14 the topic had been the granting of whatever the disciples asked for in the name of Jesus. Without explanation, v 15 introduces a general exhortation to keep the commandments ("If you love me, you will keep my commandments"). V 16 introduces another shift by promising the sending of the Paraclete. This sending of the Paraclete is evidently made contingent upon the keeping of the commandments (cf. the sequence established by *kagō* at the beginning of v 16).

Prior to v 15 the requests of the disciples will be granted so that the Father may be glorified in the Son, i.e. so that the relationship of the Son to the Father may be made manifest. However in v 15 (and following) the asking is reinterpreted not in terms of "greater works" or of "granting whatever one asks" but in terms of sending the Paraclete. In addition, the sending is done not to glorify the relationship of the Son and Father but is made contingent upon obedience to the commandments of Jesus.

In vv 16–17, the "other" Paraclete is promised, and it is to be a gift of Jesus which will be with the disciples forever. In these verses we find another element of the redactor's reinterpretation of the original get-what-you-ask-for language. Here what we are told is that the disciples are to ask for the Paraclete rather than the performance of "works."

V 17 continues this new theme but also resumes partially the theme of "indwelling" found in the earlier verses. The disciples are told that the world cannot know the Spirit of truth because the world neither sees the Spirit nor knows it. But the disciples will know the

Spirit because it remains with them and is in them. Here it is relationship between the Paraclete and the disciples that is spoken of, not that between Jesus and the Father.

It is regularly suggested that the Paraclete passages are a secondary addition to the gospel.[29] Even Schnackenburg, who does not consider the passages to be secondary, comments on the "tension" that results from the mention of the Paraclete here: "What is the relationship between the Paraclete who is promised and Jesus, who is to come himself to the disciples after Easter?"[30] Our analysis here would confirm that opinion. We have seen how awkward the introduction of the commandment text and of the reference to the Paraclete is here in relation to what precedes. The resumption of the context in vv 18–19 is equally awkward.

(d) The Original Sequence Resumes

Vv 18–19 then speak of the return of Jesus. Jesus will return soon, and the disciples will see him because he is living and they will live. If Jesus is to return, as we read in v 18, then why is there mention of the Paraclete here and why does that mention not clarify the relationship between the coming of Jesus and the coming of the Paraclete? The first part of v 20 continues the theme of vv 18–19 well by saying that on that day they will see the relationship of the Father and Jesus. Without vv 15–17, we find in v 18 a logical continuation of the theme (resumed from v 14) of how Jesus shows the disciples the Father. He will not leave the disciples orphans but will come to them. They will see him but the world will not. On that day they will know that he is in the Father and that Jesus is in the disciples and the disciples in him.

When we examine v 20, we find that the first part of the verse contains the statement that "on that day you will know that I am in my Father" but then it adds that Jesus will be in the disciples and the disciples will be in Jesus. This extension of the relationships is awkward and not prepared for by the context. It is likely an addition to what was previously simply a further indication of the relationship of the Father and the Son—just as the original meaning of the working of the works had been.

(e) The Addition of V 21

Following this (in v 21) there is the reintroduction of the material concerning commandment. As was the case in the previous commandment text (vv 15–17) what had previously been an absolute promise is now conditional to the keeping of the commandments. In v 21 we hear first that the one who keeps the commandments is the one who loves Jesus. This is almost a repetition of v 15. Second, it is said that the one who loves Jesus will be loved by the Father and by Jesus—and Jesus will manifest himself to him.

(f) The Resumption of the Original Sequence in V 22

V 22 then returns directly to the theme of the manifestation of Jesus to the disciples (resuming the original context of v 19). It asks (in the person of Judas) why it is that Jesus will manifest himself to the disciples and not to the world. The fact that Judas' question is separated from the previous three questions by so many verses (i.e. the previous question had been in v 8) is in itself curious and raises the suspicion of editorial additions.[31] This is confirmed by the development of the thought.

If we look back at the last clause of v 21, we see that the mention of manifestation there seems "tacked on" and has not appeared in any of the commandment sections prior to this. Yet by being "tacked on" to the end of the statement on commandments, the manifestation of Jesus to the disciples is now presented as contingent upon the disciples' keeping the commandments and upon their loving (and being loved by) Jesus.

But the theme of manifestation, which is introduced so awkwardly at the end of the statement on commandments follows well from v 20a, since there Jesus had been speaking of his return and of the fact that they would know him on that day—and even better from v 19 where Jesus had said that he would return and the disciples *would see him.* In the first statement the ability of the disciples to see Jesus is unconditioned: they will see him (although the world will not) because he will be living and they will be also. However, the introduction of the material on commandments makes the manifestation of Jesus to his disciples dependent on the keeping of the commandments—just as the previous mention in v 15 had made the granting of requests from Jesus dependent upon obedience to the commandments.

(g) The Addition of Vv 23–24

But still the editing is not finished. The answer given to Judas' question by Jesus in v 23 is also awkward. As Schnackenburg points out, Jesus' reply to this question does not seem to deal directly with it.[32] In response to Judas' question, Jesus says that if anyone loves Jesus, that person will keep his (Jesus') word, and the Father will love him, and Jesus and the Father will come to him and make their dwelling with him. A final time the prerogative of the disciples is made contingent upon their obedience to the commandment, here the commandment to keep the word of Jesus. The sequence then continues well with v 24 stating that the one who does not love Jesus will not keep his words, and that the word which the disciples hear is not Jesus' but that of the one who sent him, the Father.

It is noteworthy that in the present text (vv 23ff) the question of Judas is never clearly and directly answered. It could be said that the verses explain why Jesus is going to reveal himself and the Father to the disciples and not to the world by saying that Jesus and the Father will come and make their abode only with the one who loves Jesus and keeps his word. But there is in fact nothing about "revelation" or "manifestation" in vv 23–24. In addition *monē* had been used previously only in v 2, but in the sense of a dwelling place. In v 2, there were many *monai* and they were in heaven. Here the term does not refer to a "place" or a thing but to the fact of the indwelling of the Father and Jesus in the believer. Consequently I would argue that vv 23–24 have also been added to an earlier version of the discourse.

This analysis arrives at the following form of the text. The indented sections are those that have been added.

14:8–24

> (8) Philip then said to him, "Lord, show us the Father and it is sufficient for us." (9) Jesus said to him, "I have been with you so long and you have not known me, Philip? The one who has seen me has seen the Father. Why do you say 'Show us the Father'? (10) Do you not believe that I am in the Father and the Father in me? The words which I speak to you I do not say on my own authority. The Father abiding in me performs his own works. (11) Believe me when I say that I abide in the Father and the Father in me. If not, believe because of the works themselves. (12) Amen, amen,

I say to you, the one believing in me will do the works which I do, and that person will do even greater ones than these because I am going to the Father. (13) I will do whatever you ask for in my name so that the Father might be glorified in the Son. (14) If you ask me for something in my name, I will do it.

(15) If you love me, you will keep my commandments. (16) And I will ask the Father and he will give you another Paraclete—so that he might be with you forever, (17) the Spirit of truth, which the world is not able to receive, since it neither sees nor knows it. You know it because it abides with you and will be in you.

(18) I do not leave you orphans. I will come to you. (19) Yet a short time and the world will no longer see me, but you will see me because I live and you will live. (20) On that day you will know that I am in my Father

and you in me, and I in you. (21) The one who has my commandments and keeps them is the one who loves me. And the one who loves me will be loved by my Father, and I will love and will manifest myself to that person."

(22) Judas, not the Iscariot, said to him, "Lord, what has happened that you will manifest yourself to us and not to the world?" (23) Jesus responded and said to him,

"If anyone loves me, that person will keep my word, and my Father will love him, and we will come to that person and will make an abode with him. (24) The one not loving me does not keep my words. And the word which you hear is not mine but of the one sending me, the Father."

2. Theological Parallels With 1 John

Because the farewell discourses are the major body of instruction given to the disciples in the Johannine gospel, it is the natural place for the editor, at the time of the community crisis of 1 John, to make explicit his understanding of what the tradition requires of the disciples. He will of course do this in a way that will effectively refute the understanding proposed by his opponents.

In the prior version of the gospel, a distinction had been made between the disciples and the world.[33] That distinction reflected the community's historical experience at the time when the disciples (who believed in Jesus) confronted an unbelieving world. In his farewell discourse to his disciples, Jesus made certain promises to them which would be their prerogatives over against the unbelieving world. These promises were that they would get what they asked for in his name, that he would manifest himself to them—and possibly the sending of the Spirit.

However, by the time of the first epistle, the conflict had altered. Now the conflict is between two groups of "disciples." The issue is not of belief versus unbelief but of correct versus incorrect belief. The editor (for reasons we shall see later) chooses to articulate correct belief in terms of keeping the commandments. It is a matter of the disciple who keeps the commandments and the one who does not, of the disciple who loves Jesus and the one who does not. What had earlier been put forward as an absolute promise (that the disciple will get what he/she asks for, that Jesus will manifest himself to the disciple) is now reinterpreted in terms of a promise conditioned by obedience to the commandments.

This is the approach of 1 John. Within 1 John, receiving what one asks for is contingent upon keeping the commandments. In 3:21–22 "asking language" is clearly related to the keeping of the commandments: "Loved ones, if our hearts do not impeach us, we have confidence before God, and whatever we ask for we (will) receive from his *because we keep his commandments and do what is pleasing before him.*" According to 1 John one cannot simply ask and hope to receive. One must keep the commandments and do what is pleasing to God; then one will receive what one asks for. Thus we see that once again the commandment tradition speaks directly to the historical circumstances of and reflects the theology of 1 John rather than that of the (prior edition of the) gospel.

E. 14:31

This brief mention of commandment occurs in the concluding verse of the first farewell discourse. V 30 states that Jesus does not have much more to say to the disciples and that the "ruler of this world" is coming. He then adds that the ruler of this world does not have anything with which to convict Jesus, but in order that the world may know that Jesus loves the Father, Jesus will do what the Father has commanded.

1. Literary Characteristics of the Material

Alone among the commandment passages, this verse shows no significant literary evidence of being added to the gospel. Nevertheless, because of the theological parallels with the rest of the commandment passages and because of the evidence of the apocalyptic language typical of 1 John, it is likely that the verse is also an editorial addition belonging to the same stratum as the other commandment passages.

2. Theological Parallels to 1 John

First, there is an emphasis on love in relation to the commandments. This love has a witness value similar to the witness value of the love for one another as commanded in 13:35. It speaks of Jesus obeying the commandment out of love, and it clearly refers to the second of the commandments given to Jesus. In addition, the description of Satan as "ruler of this world" echoes the dualistic view typical of apocalyptic. Elsewhere we have seen this apocalyptic view to be typical of 1 John and of additions to the gospel. On the basis of these factors I would argue that this brief passage (which is obviously "of a piece" with the other commandment passages) is also an editorial addition.

F. 15:9–17

1. Literary Features of the Material

These verses occur in what might be termed the "second half" of the parable of the vine. It is generally agreed among scholars today that 15:1ff was not the original sequel to 14:31. 14:31 speaks of a departure, thus suggesting a termination of the discourse. In addition, there is nothing in the discourse of chapter 15 which can be said to be prepared for in, or a sequel to, 13:31–14:31. The image of the vine and the branches is new and registers a complete break with what goes before.

There is some dispute about just where the passage ends, however. Some would say that a break occurs between vv 17 and 18;[34] others would say that no break occurs until 16:4a.[35] As Becker points out, the exhortation concerning the love commandment is not continued beyond v 17, and the theme of the hatred of the world for the disciples begins in v 18 and is not anticipated in what precedes.[36] In addition, the focus in 15:1–17 can be said to be within the community, while in 15:18–16:4 the focus is on problems the community will face from the outside.

The question of the subdivision of vv 1–17 is also disputed. Schnackenburg would argue for a break after v 11 on the basis of the *tauta lelalēka hymin* ("these things I have said to you") at the beginning of v 11 and because the discussion of commandment begins in v 12. Becker would argue that the break occurs after v 8 because that is the last reference to the image of the vine and because it is the last reference to belief and becoming disciples, while in v 9 the topic of love is introduced. He also points to the very similar commands: *meinate en emoi* (remain in me) in v 4 and *meinate en tē agapē tē emē* (remain in my love) in v 9. The peculiar formulation of the command in v 9 gives even more credence to the position that this was intended as the beginning of a new division of the discourse.

I would propose however that not only is there a break after v 8 but that there are a number of factors which suggest that vv 9–17 are in fact a secondary addition to the parable of the vine and so not originally part of it.

The major factor in reaching this conclusion about the verses is the presence of that editorial use of the repetitive resumptive. This has been discussed previously as an indication of editing in 10:7–18. Because of the nature of the editing here a more extensive discussion of the technique seems warranted.

Elsewhere I have suggested four criteria for determining whether repetition within a passage is in fact editorial repetition or simply stylistic.[37] First, there is the presence of the repetition itself. The more extensive and the more awkward this is, the more likely it is that the repetition is meant to be editorial. Second, there is the presence of various phrases such as *hote oun* or *hōs oun* (both translated "when therefore . . .") which are used in narrative materials to resume the sequence after the insertion. In discourse material, the simple repetition of the context before and after the insertion marks the material as secondary. Third, there is the presence of various literary anomalies (commonly called *aporiai*) within the addition. The presence of aporiai is generally considered to be the most significant and most objective of criteria used for determining breaks in sequence and the resulting redactional insertions. These aporiai can be either contradictions, inconsistencies or significant shifts in thought. Fourth, when the supposed insertion is removed from the context, the resulting sequence must be plausible as a hypothetical original. Ideally the reconstructed sequence would present a better sequence than the present state of the text. Of course in a given passage, these factors will be present in varying degrees and so the texts must be judged individually. However the greater the number of criteria present, the greater the likelihood of the repetition being a true marker of editing.

Applying these criteria to the present passage we find that all are applicable, some to a remarkable degree. First, there is the presence of repetition. In this passage the repetition includes parts of vv 7–8 which are then paralleled in v 16. This parallelism can be illustrated as follows:

1.　　v 7: *ean meinete en emoi . . .*
　　　　　　("if you remain in me . . .")
　　v 16d: *kai ho karpos hymōn menē,*
　　　　　　("and your fruit remains")
2.　　v 7b: *ho ean thelete aitēsasthe kai genēsetai hymin.*

("whatever you want, you will ask for and it will be granted to you.")

v 16e: *hina ho ti an aitēsēte ton patera en tō onomati mou dō hymin.*

("in order that whatever you ask for from the Father in my name, I will give to you.")

3. v 8b: ... *hina karpon pherēte* ...

(... "in order that you might bear fruit" ...)

v 16c: *hina hymeis hypagēte kai karpon pherēte* ...

("in order that you might go and bear fruit" ...)

A fourth parallel element (which cannot be diagrammed) is the fact that in the first two elements listed above, there is an expressed relationship between remaining in Jesus/their fruit remaining and their ability to ask for anything and to receive it.

Clearly this repetition is extensive. The fact that it is so extensive makes it unlikely that it is an accident or a stylistic trait. In addition the fact that in the intervening verses there has been no mention of any of these topics is also a significant consideration. After the mention of "fruit" in v 8, it is indeed remarkable that the word does not reappear until v 16 and then that it appears in such an "offhand" way. It is also true that the statement promising the listeners that if they ask they will receive what they ask for occurs infrequently in the gospel. The fact that it appears twice within these verses suggests that it is not simply a matter of stylistic repetition, but actually repetition in order to resume.

The second of the criteria is not fulfilled in this passage: there are no overt markers such as *hote oun* (when therefore) or *epeita meta touto* (thereupon, after that), etc. This is not surprising since the material being dealt with is discourse material rather than narrative. But the present instance parallels the presence of the technique in the addition to the discourse on the bread of life in 6:51–58 and in 10:7–18, where again there are no temporal markers because the technique appears in discourse material.[38]

The third criterion suggests that there must be literary features in the intervening material which are inconsistent with seeing the passage as a unified whole. Here there are several, although it must be admitted that they are subtle and only when viewed together do they argue for seeing the verses as inconsistent with the surrounding context. First there is the amount of repetition in vv 7–8 and v 16 which requires explanation. Second, there is the sudden introduction of the themes of love and of commandment in vv 9–15 which is not prepared for in the previous sequence. Third, there is the statement *meinate en tē agapē tē emē* (remain in my love) (v 9b) which is awkward in itself and within the context. There is a similarity between this statement and that of v 4 where Jesus exhorts his listeners: *Meinate en emoi* (Remain in me). In addition it echoes v 7, *ean meinēte en emoi* . . . (if you remain in me), in order to introduce the theme of remaining in the love of Jesus through obedience. The juxtaposition of these two statements raises the question of the relationship between the two. While it could be thought that the second is simply a variant of the first, this becomes more and more unlikely when it is realized that the second exhortation introduces a new vocabulary which leads into a new development, concerning commandment and concerning intra-community love.

Fourth, there is the fact that in the first part of the passage the topic is one of faith, while in the second part of the passage the theme has clearly shifted to one of love. While this again is not incompatible with authorship by a single individual, the presence of this tandem relationship within a context of the other literary features suggests that in fact the juxtaposition is a result of editing rather than single authorship. Finally another important argument for seeing the juxtaposition of these two concepts as a result of editing is the fact that these two concepts occur in precisely the same relationship within the scene of the footwashing in chapter 13, and there the presence of editing is widely recognized.[39]

Finally the fourth criterion for seeing the repetition here as a marker of redaction was that the resulting sequence should be intelligible and should perhaps provide a more satisfactory sequence than the present one. This is certainly true of 15:1–17. The presence of a secondary redaction in vv 9–16 explains all of the unusual literary features of the passage as well as the awkward repetition of the exhortation to "remain." Thus I would see vv 9–17 as an addition to the parable of the vine and would conclude that they do not reflect the same sitz im leben as that of the earlier stratum.

2. *Theological Parallels with 1 John*

In the secondary elaboration of the parable of the vine (15:9–17), we resume the description of the love commandment first introduced in 13:34–35. We see that keeping the commandments is necessary for remaining in the love of Jesus, just as Jesus kept the commandments of the Father and so remained in his love. In addition their love for one another is to be modeled on the love of Jesus for them. Jesus' love had been demonstrated by his death for his friends. But his listeners are his friends if they do what he has commanded. Finally v 17 repeats the instruction to love one another. Throughout, the element of the conditional is clear.

It was pointed out above that at least some of the Johannine commandment texts are associated with an expiatory view of the death of Jesus.[40] Brown and others have argued that this view of the death of Jesus can only be called minor in the gospel, while it is the predominant one in the epistles.[41] Again we find that this passage echoes clearly the thought of 1 John over against the dominant thought of the gospel.

In addition, in the gospel there is little reference to specific ethical directions. However in 1 John there is more of such ethical concern. In the gospel, the only texts dealing specifically with ethics are those associated with commandment passages: 13:34–35; 14:15,21–14; 15:9–17. The same is true in the epistles. This is yet another indication that commandment and its associated concepts are more at home in the epistles than in the gospels.

G. Conclusions from the Literary Analysis of the Commandment Passages

The literary analysis just conducted has yielded results which are on the whole quite illuminating. One one hand there are clear indications in a number of the passages that the material dealing with the commandments is secondary. This was especially true in the case of 10:17–19, 12:44–50, 13:34–35, and 15:9–17. The indications regarding 14:15,21–24 were somewhat more subtle due to the interspersing of the additions throughout a section rather than in a single block. Nevertheless the literary and theological inconsistencies in those verses were significant enough to reasonably suggest secondary authorship even there. Finally in the light of this consistency, it becomes all the more likely that 14:31 is also an addition.

If then, as the literary evidence suggests, the commandment tradition is not original to the gospel, why was it added? Repeatedly we have seen that the commandment passages show considerable affinities to the thought framework and the theology of 1 John. Undoubtedly the commandment passages were added to the gospel by someone with a point of view similar to that of the author of 1 John (not necessarily the same person as the author however) in order to provide a foundation, anchored within the community's narrative of the life of Jesus, for his view of two essentials of the community's obligations.

When we speak of these passages being added, it could well give the impression that they were the creation of a redactor. However I think this unlikely. Given the repeated emphasis within 1 John on "what was from the beginning," it seems unlikely that the author would have created the commandment tradition out of whole cloth. More likely is the suggestion that a redactor in touch with the tradition as it was understood by the author of 1 John incorporated at a later date the commandment material which had been part of the community tradition from the earlier period but which had not been part of the written gospel.

But as we indicated at the end of the previous chapter, there are still numerous questions about the meaning of the commandments: their content and their relation to the specific historical circumstances of the community. However, recovering the historical circumstances of the community struggle and the nature of the dispute which so painfully tore the community apart has been less than easy, as we shall see in the next chapter.

NOTES

1. Of course there is also the possibility that the work passages are secondary and the commandment theme original. However this is unlikely as the following analysis will show.

2. U. C. von Wahlde, *The Earliest Version of John's Gospel: Recovering the First Edition of John's Gospel* (Wilmington: Glazier,

1989). I have also given a brief overview of my view of the gospel's composition history in the introduction to this book. If the analysis presented here is correct, the commandment passages belong to the work of the redactor (i.e. the author of the third "edition" of the gospel).

3. Some have thought that vv 1–6 are a combination of two parables: one focusing on the image of shepherd and the other on the image of gate. There are, it must be admitted, no literary indications of editing in the parable, and the only way to judge on internal grounds is from the consistency of the parable. The argument for seeing vv 1–6 as a combination of two parables rests primarily on the fact of the introduction of the figure of the doorkeeper in v 3 and on the argument that in the second part of the parable the opponents are spoken of as strange shepherds rather than as thieves and bandits as they are in the first part of the parable; cf. Brown, *Gospel* 392–93. However in my opinion this is a too precise reading of the material. Among those who see only one parable are: E. Haenchen, *A Commentary on the Gospel of John* (Hermeneia; Philadelphia: Fortress, 1984) 2, 48; R. Schnackenburg, *Gospel* 2, 282–83. In the second part, the figure of the doorkeeper is not prominent in its own right but only as a necessary element of the larger parable. In the second part also the opponents are not clearly identified as distinct from the thieves and bandits of the first part. There are three prominent features to the portrayal of the shepherd: he goes through the gate, the gatekeeper opens for him, and he knows his sheep by name. This is contrasted with the thieves and robbers who go over the wall and who do not know the sheep by name. Admittedly there is some inconsistency in the parable in that the gatekeeper would obviously have some difficulty letting alleged shepherds out through the door if they had not entered through the door but come over the wall. But to argue this is to press the parable for too much consistency.

4. The most complete survey of this technique is found in the article by F. Neirynck, "L'Epanalepsis et la critique littéraire à propos de l'Évangile de Jean," *ETL* 56 (1980) 303–338. See also M.-E. Boismard, "Un procédé rédactionnel dans le quatrième évangile: *La Wiederaufnahme,*" in *L'Évangile de Jean: Sources, rédaction, théologie* (BETL; ed. M. de Jonge; Leuven: Gembloux, 1978) 235–41; U. C. von Wahlde, "A Redactional Technique in the Fourth Gospel,"

CBQ 39 (1976) 520–33; idem, "*Wiederaufnahme* as a Marker of Redaction in Jn 6, 51–58," *Biblica* 64 (1983) 542–49. The Old Testament use of the technique has also been studied; see the bibliography listed in von Wahlde, "*Wiederaufnahme*" 545, n. 17.

5. We must remember that the process of editing was not intended to achieve the smoothness or consistency that the modern reader would demand of a text.

6. One must be careful of course not to simply use *any* instance of "work" to judge such strata but only those which are part of the group so defined in chapter two.

7. Although the similarities between the commandment passages and 1 John are consistent and impressive, I am not of the opinion that the redactor responsible for the addition of the commandment passages to the gospel is the same person responsible for the writing of 1 John. I would argue only that it is a person who shared the theological convictions and historical circumstances of the author of 1 John.

8. It is not true that the expiatory passages are all associated with commandment. Certainly I do not intend to imply that the commandment passages constitute the only addition to the gospel or even that they constitute the entirety of a particular stratum. My object here is much more narrow: to indicate that the commandment passages are secondary within the gospel and that they find close parallels in 1 John.

9. Schnackenburg, *Gospel* 2, 411–12.

10. Schnackenburg, *Gospel* 2, 420. The reference is to a series of treatments by M.-E. Boismard, "Le caractère adventice de Jn 12, 45–50," *Sacra Pagina* (ed. J. Coppens; Miscellanea Biblica. Congressus Internationalis Catholicus de Re Biblica; Vol. 2; Gembloux: Duculot, 1959) 189–92; "Les citations targumiques du quatrième évangile," *RB* 66 (1959), 377–78; "L'évolution du thème eschatologique dan les traditions johanniques," *RB* 68 (1961), 507–14.

11. Brown, *Gospel* 490.

12. *Ibid.* Bernard considered it to be out of place and put it after 12:36a. See J. H. Bernard, *A Critical and Exegetical Commentary on the Gospel According to St. John* (Edinburg: Clark, 1928) xxv–xxvi. Bultmann called it a displaced fragment from a discourse on light (*Gospel* 313). The most extensive study of the section has been

done by M.-E. Boismard in a series of articles ("Le caractère," 189–92; "Les citations targumiques," 374–78). Boismard points out various differences in style, in eschatology and in christology and assigns it to an editor. Boismard's arguments from style are particularly difficult to assess. Frequently it could be said that what appears to be personal style could in fact be caused by dialectical rather than personal differences of language. Sometimes too the differences can be accounted for by differences in conceptual framework. Boismard's analysis of christology is also not convincing. He argues that it is a Moses typology focusing on being sent. But there is mention of the Father, and even though there is no mention of the Son, this is not really significant since it is clear that "the Father" refers to the Father of Jesus. However his arguments about differences in eschatology are more convincing since it is generally agreed that the future eschatology is foreign to the evangelist's theology, yet it dominates the first epistle.

13. Of course it would be necessary to do a literary analysis of the complete gospel in order to establish fully that these passages are indeed additions also. However for the present we must rely simply on the observations of those others who would have studied the passages in the past.

14. *Phōs* occurs in Jn 1:4,5,7,8,9; 3:19,20,21; 5:35 (not in the same sense); 8:12; 9:5; 11:9,10; 12:35,36,46. *Skotia* occurs in 1:5; 6:17 (not in the theological sense); 8:12; 12:35,46.

15. See the discussion in Schnackenburg, *Gospel* 1, 407–10.

16. On the prologue, see the various discussions of the possibility of a pre-gospel hymn—for example Haenchen, "Excursus: The Pre-Johannine Logos Hymn," in *Gospel* 1, 131–140 and the bibliography there. On 3:16–21, see Schnackenburg, *Gospel* 1, 361 ("Verses 13–21 do not form part of the Gospel narrative, but come from a kerygmatic exposition of the evangelist which was originally independent, very like the kerygmatic parts of 1 John"). On 9:4–5 see the authors and the discussion in R. Fortna, *The Gospel of Signs* (SNTSMS 11; Cambridge: The University Press, 1970) 72. On 11:7–10, see Fortna, *Signs* 78–79; Brown (*Gospel* 432) also seems to favor the view that the verses are added.

17. Realized eschatology refers in part to the belief that judgment (and the possession of eternal life) is a present event within the life of the believer, occurring within the encounter with Jesus. Future

eschatology however proposes that the true act of judgment of the believer is something that will occur in the future (at the end of the world) and that at that time the full possession of eternal life (or condemnation) will occur. Much more will be said on this topic in the following chapter. On the presence of the two forms of eschatology within the gospel see for example Schnackenburg, *Gospel* 3 420–421; Bultmann, *Gospel* 313; Brown (*Gospel* 490–491) considers the passage to contain both realized and final eschatology.

18. If these passages show significant signs of being added, and if they agree with the structure of the epistle, then we have at least preliminary evidence that the features of the gospel's structure which parallel the epistle have been added to the gospel at about the time of the composition of the epistle, precisely to provide a new theological assessment of the ministry of Jesus.

19. See, for example, Bultmann, *Gospel* 525 n. 1; Schnackenburg, *Gospel* 3, 53–55; J. Becker, "Abschiedsreden," 220; Segovia, *Love Relationships* 122; M.-E. Boismard, *L'Évangile de Jean,* Vol. 3 of *Synopse des quatres Évangiles en francais* (Paris: Cerf, 1977) 347.

20. Schnackenburg, *Gospel* 3, 53.

21. Schnackenburg, *Gospel* 3, 53–55.

22. Segovia, *Love Relationships* 121–25. More recently, Segovia, "The Structure, *Tendenz,* and *Sitz im Leben* of Joh 13:31–14:31," *JBL* 104, 3 (1985) 471–93, esp. 491–93. Becker "Abschiedsreden" 220.

23. Boismard, *Évangile* 345.

24. We have discussed this above in chapter three.

25. In this sense, the mention of "newness" is similar to the gospel's reference to the Spirit as "another" Paraclete. The material needed to fully explain this element is found only in 1 John.

26. Becker, "Abschiedsreden" 222–223.

27. This is also the position of Schnackenburg, *Gospel* 3, 73–74. Both Becker and Schnackenburg point out that in the introduction (14:3) there is a mention of the dual elements of departure and return; this is echoed in v 28 where the two elements are again mentioned together.

28. This will be repeated in 14:24b.

29. For a discussion of this issue see chapter 5 and note 54 there.

30. Schnackenburg, *Gospel* 3, 77.

31. In effect the material on commandments has already answered Judas' question: Jesus will not manifest himself to the world because the world does not keep the commandments and is not loved by Jesus or the Father.

32. Schnackenburg, *Gospel* 3, 81.

33. That distinction continues in the editorial additions (cf 14:17), but now the world is exemplified in the opponents, not in the Jews.

34. For example, J. Becker, "Abschiedsreden," 229.

35. For example, R. Schnackenburg, *Gospel* 3, 91–2. Schnackenburg, who favors seeing 15:1–16:4 as a unity, argues that both formal features of the text as well as similarities in content indicate that the discourse should extend to 16:4. However, it seems that the weightier factors point to a division of the discourse after v 17 rather than after 16:4a, and it is this position that I will adopt.

36. Becker, "Abschiedsreden" 230–31.

37. von Wahlde, "*Wiederaufnahme*" 544–46; see also my "Redactional Technique" 524–26.

38. *Wiederaufnahme* 546–49.

39. For a helpful survey of recent literature on the topic, see F. Segovia, "John 13 1–20, The Footwashing in the Johannine Tradition," *ZNW* 73 (1982) 31–51.

40. For a full discussion of the theology of Jesus' death as expiation for sin, see below, pp. 156–158.

41. Brown, *Epistles* 98–99.

Chapter Five

THE CRISIS OF 1 JOHN: A RADICAL VIEW OF THE SPIRIT

The first epistle of John was written at a time of great turmoil within the Johannine community. Just as the gospel had been composed to deal with the split between Johannine Christianity and its parent Judaism, so the first epistle was written to confront the problems caused by a rift within the Johannine community itself. The basis for the split within the community was the way in which both groups believed the Johannine tradition should be interpreted. That both groups were very close to one another in their understanding of Jesus is evidenced by the way the two groups agreed with regard to their status as Christians. For example, both claimed to know God, to possess the Spirit, to walk in light, to abide in him, and to be children of God. But the two groups differed in the way in which they understood these claims to be realized. Even here there is considerable similarity, but the differences are significant. 1 John attempts to explain the falsity of the opponents' claims and to confirm the correctness of his own followers' viewpoint. Our purpose here is to discuss the nature of this theological crisis within the community as it is manifest in 1 John.

1 John is one of the shorter books of the New Testament. But within its few short pages it contains a wealth of material. For 1 John is a handbook for the understanding of what may have been the Johannine community's greatest crisis, and, as the subtitle of this book indicates, the epistle encapsulates a struggle for the understanding of the entire Johannine tradition—a struggle in which the Johannine commandments played a major role.

Our treatment of the Johannine crisis will fall into two sections, divided among the next three chapters. In this and the following chapter, we will explore an historical question: What was the nature of the conflict which divided the Johannine community at the time of the first epistle? In chapter seven, we will attempt to answer a literary-theological question: What is the meaning of 1 John and how does it attempt to deal with the community's crisis? That is, how is 1 John organized, what approach does the author take in confronting his adversaries, and finally how does the Johannine commandment tradition fit into this historical and literary context? In chapters five and six, we will be using 1 John as a "sourcebook" for historical information; in chapter seven we will attempt to understand it as a literary and theological work in itself.[1]

A. SOME PAST APPROACHES TO 1 JOHN

Any attempt to discover the precise nature of the theological crisis within the Johannine community is made more difficult because of the fact that there is so much disagreement about the interpretation of the epistle. A glance at four recent commentaries on the Johannine epistles will illustrate just how divergent this interpretation is.

Pheme Perkins' commentary appeared in 1979.[2] In it she argues that the key to the epistle's thought is a sensitivity to the language of oral cultures.[3] Reading the gospel in this light leads her to conclude that there is essentially one group of dissidents and one problem confronting the Johannine community: an ethical one. The dissident members fail to acknowledge a role for brotherly love within the community. The christological arguments, she would claim, are in fact a rhetorical device to discredit the opponents by linking them with the "Jews" of the gospel. In other words the author pictures the opponents of 1 John in the same light as the Jewish opponents of the gospel.[4] Perkins' view of the structure of the epistle is that it contains four major divisions plus a prologue, a conclusion, and an appendix.[5]

Kenneth Grayston, whose commentary appeared in 1984, argues that the epistle was not written after the gospel as most commentators think, but before it.[6] The gospel reflects an attempt to solidify the position of the author against his opponents and it also betrays a more fully developed style and theology. He argues that there is one group of opponents but there are two basic problems: one is christology and the other is ethics. The author's view of the opponents' christology is that they have exaggerated the role of the Spirit to the point that it has made the role of Jesus superfluous. Since the opponents claim that they now have the same Spirit Jesus did, they have no need of him.[7] Grayston sees the structure of the epistle as falling into six major sections.[8]

Stephen Smalley's commentary also appeared in 1984. He posits a writing after the gospel,[9] but claims that there is not one but two groups of adversaries that the author is confronting. One group is Jewish-Christian and finds it difficult to accept the messiahship of Jesus. Their christology tends to be too "low" in the christology range (exaggerating the human element). Another group which is basically Gentile has come from a pagan religious background which emphasizes dualistic, gnostic categories. This group has an excessively "high" christology (over-emphasizing the divinity of Jesus).[10] Although, like Perkins, he argues that there is basically only one problem confronted by the author, in contrast to Perkins he argues that the main issue is christology and ethics only by extension.[11] His view of the structure is the most elaborate of those presented here. He argues for a division of the epistle into two major sections. Each of these sections contains four subdivisions. The subdivisions of each half parallel each other thematically.[12]

The most extensive of the four commentaries is that of Raymond Brown which appeared in 1982. Brown posits a division of the epistle into two major sections, each of which parallels thematically (by the use of the images of light and love) the major parts of the Johannine gospel.[13] He sees one group of opponents and two major problems: christology and ethics.[14] But Brown says that the opponents, rather than denying the role of Jesus in salvation, as Grayston proposes, *minimize* the importance of the earthly life of Jesus by taking the high christology of the tradition even higher. Thus they are led to claim that the life of Jesus could not be salvifically important since Jesus did nothing on this earth that had not been seen or heard with the Father. They err in the direction of too high a christology.[15] The opponents' ethical position is derived from the gospel also. They claim to be sinless because they do not commit the sin of unbelief, the dominant sin of the gospel. They err in failing to love the brothers, but Brown argues that they fail to love the brethren in that they do not love the brethren of the author's segment of the community and instead love only their fellow secessionists.

The most striking feature to emerge from a review of these recent commentaries is the great diversity in the interpretation of 1 John. Yet a correct understanding of the Johannine crisis is necessary for a proper understanding of the Johannine commandments both in the gospel and in the epistles. For the Johannine commandment tradition took shape within and was a direct response to that conflict, a conflict that eventually brought a permanent rupture to the Johannine community.

The central issue in the crisis is the nature of the opponents' understanding of the Johannine tradition. That is clear from a reading of 1 John. However our access to their position is only through the references made by the author of 1 John. This characteristic of our evidence has caused some to question whether we are therefore *a priori* unable to obtain an accurate picture of the opponents' position.[16] However as will become apparent, the author of 1 John is quite thorough in his description of the claims of his opponents although his references are scattered throughout the epistle. By studying the author's references to the opponents' positions we are able to piece together the outlines of their theology.

B. The Statements of 1 John About the Adversaries

In his refutation of the opponents' position, the author of 1 John presents statements which represent both his own position and that of his opponents.[17] These statements are of three basic types.

The first type is the "claims" that the two groups make regarding their status as Christians.[18] For example both groups claim "to be in communion with" God; they both claim "to know" him, "to be in the light." The second type of statement is those of the author (and those he attributes to his opponents) about Jesus. The author says that the true Christian confesses the Son, but that the opponents deny him. The author confesses Jesus Christ come in the flesh; the opponents do not. The third type of statement has to do with various ethical considerations. For example, the author charges that the opponents falsely claim never to sin. In addition, the opponents do not show love for the brethren, and they shut themselves off from those in need. Let us begin by looking at each of the three types of statements in detail.

1. The Claims of the Two Groups Regarding Their Special "Status" as Christians

The claims of the two Johannine groups regarding their status as Christians describe various aspects of the relationship between the believer and God (the Father), Jesus, and the Spirit. From the pages of the first epistle, we are able to cull a listing of claims of the two opposing Johannine groups. These are listed in Table One.

This long listing of the shared claims indicates the extent to which the language and the claims of the two Johannine groups are the same. The secessionist group did not attempt to simply deny the claims of the Johannine community; it was at odds about how those claims were to be realized.

The list has been arranged in two sections. The first section (numbers 1–10) has to do with claims which are shared but about which there are differences as to how they are realized. The second part (numbers 11–13) contains claims which the faithful make but to which there is no parallel claim on the part of the secessionists. This absence of parallel claims regarding the latter claims is puzzling. Given the consistency with which the other parallel claims are mentioned, it seems that this omission is not simply accidental but a genuine absence of such claims on the part of the secessionists. Strikingly, all of the "missing" claims involve "the Son," Jesus. Clearly the opponents claim to possess the Father and to possess the Spirit, but there are no competing claims regarding the Son. The opponents do not claim to have communion with the Son (but only with the Father); they make no claim to possess the Son; nor do they claim to abide in the Son but only in the Father. This is very significant because it calls into question those theories which see the role of Jesus being diminished rather than done away with.

Of course any theory which speaks of the role of Jesus "being done away with" must face the very difficult question of how a group which did not believe in Jesus could in any sense of the word be

1. Both the faithful (1:3) and the opponents (1:6) boast of having COMMUNION WITH THE FATHER.

2. Both Johannine groups claim to KNOW GOD. This is apparent in the case of the faithful in 2:3–4 (implicitly), 13–14; 4:6,7, and in the case of the opponents in 2:3–4; 4:8a.

3. The faithful claim to ABIDE IN GOD (2:5–6,24,28; 3:6,24; 4:12,13,15,16); so do the opponents (2:6, and implicitly in several of the above texts).

4. The faithful claim to be IN THE LIGHT (1:7; 2:9–10); so do the opponents (2:9–10).

5. The faithful claim an ANOINTING BY THE SPIRIT (2:20; 3:24; 4:13); the opponents claim an anointing also (implicit in 3:24, also evident throughout 4:1–6).

6. The faithful claim a SPIRIT THAT BELONGS TO GOD (4:1,13; 5:6); their spirit is called the Spirit of truth (4:6); the opponents also claim possession of the spirit (4:1). However, the opponents, in the opinion of the author, reflect a spirit which does not belong to God. Their spirit is also called "he who is in the world" (4:4); and "the spirit of deceit" (4:6). The opponents can be called "false prophets" (4:1).

7. The faithful are GOD'S CHILDREN (3:1,2,10; "begotten by God": 4:7; 5:1); the opponents are children of the devil (3:8,10).

8. The faithful have PASSED FROM DEATH TO LIFE (3:14); the faithful have life through Jesus (4:9) and God gave eternal life, and this life is in his own Son (5:11) and the one who possesses the Son possesses life (5:13); the opponents are still in the abode of death (3:14,15) and they do not possess the Son of God and so do not possess life (5:12).

9. The faithful BELONG TO THE TRUTH (3:19) and know the truth (2:21); but the opponents do not know the truth (2:22; implicit in 3:19).

10. The faithful LOVE GOD (4:20—implicit); the opponents claim this also (4:20).

11. The faithful claim to have COMMUNION WITH THE SON (1:3); there is no mention that the opponents claim this.

12. The faithful claim to POSSESS THE FATHER AND THE SON (2:23; 5:11–13); the opponents claim to possess the Father (2:23) and the Spirit (4:1–6) but there is no mention of any claim on their part regarding the Son.

13. The faithful claim to ABIDE IN THE SON AND FATHER (2:24) and abide IN CHRIST (2:28); the opponents claim only to abide in the Father.

considered Christian, an objection raised by Brown.[19] However, before dealing with this issue, we must look at the second group of statements: the positions of both groups regarding the identity and role of Jesus.

2. Orthodox and Secessionist Views Regarding Jesus

Once again, gathering into one place the various belief statements makes it easier to understand the claims of the two groups more precisely. The language of "belief" here refers primarily to the convictions of these two groups about the identity, meaning, and "purpose" of Jesus within the schema of salvation. Again the positions of the two groups and the textual references are listed in Table Two as they appear throughout the epistle.

It is easy to see from this second list that one of the major areas of dispute within the community was the place and the meaning of Jesus within salvation. The opponents deny that Jesus is the Son of God, that he has come in the flesh, that he is the Christ and that his death was an atonement for sins. This confirms the picture that we received from the first listing, where we observed that the status-claims of the two groups were much the same except where they involved "the Son." Here too it would seem that there are no claims at all put forward by the opponents regarding Jesus.

It is clear from Tables One and Two that the opponents do not deny a role for *the Father* or *the Spirit*. But the issues regarding Jesus, the Son, are of a different sort. The author of 1 John handles each of these issues differently. He simply denies that the opponents possess the Father unless they possess the Son. With regard to the Spirit, he counters by claiming that although the opponents do possess a spirit, it is not the Spirit of Truth. With regard to the Son however, the author affirms his own position in considerable detail, showing the place of Jesus in salvation.

The fact that the author of 1 John simply denies that the opponents actually possess the Father and the Spirit while he elaborates in detail on the role of Jesus makes it all the more likely that the author's statements about the opponents' denial of a role for Jesus are to be taken literally. In my opinion, prior theories of the origin

---

TABLE TWO:
THE DIFFERENCES BETWEEN THE TWO
JOHANNINE GROUPS REGARDING "BELIEF"

1. The faithful BELIEVE IN THE NAME OF JESUS (3:23); the opponents do not (implicit in 3:23).

2. The faithful believe that Jesus is the SON OF GOD (1:3,7; 2:23–24; 3:8,23; 4:9,10,14,15; 5:5,9–13,20; 2 Jn 3,9); the opponents do not (2:22–23; 5:10–12).

3. The faithful CONFESS THE SON (2:23; 4:15); the opponents DENY the Son (2:22,23; 4:1–3; 5:10–12).

4. The faithful confess JESUS CHRIST COME IN THE FLESH (4:2; 2 Jn 7); the opponents do not (2 Jn 7).

5. The faithful believe that Jesus is the CHRIST (especially 5:1; but also 1:3; 2:1; 3:23; 4:2,15; 5:6,20; 2 Jn 3,7,9); the opponents do not (especially 2:22; by implication 4:2; and elsewhere in the texts referred to for the faithful; 2 Jn 9).

6. The faithful think that Jesus is an ATONEMENT FOR SINS (1:7,9; 2:1–2,12; 3:5; 4:14); but the opponents do not (see the context of 1:10).

7. The faithful are ROOTED IN THE WORD/TEACHING OF JESUS which they have heard from the beginning (1:1–3; 2:7,24; 3:6,11; 2 Jn 8,9); the opponents are not (implicit in the above texts, explicitly in 2 Jn 9).

---

of the community's divisions do not fully and satisfactorily account for these aspects of the opponents' position.

The adversaries could not simply be the same as the Jews of the gospel since the author of 1 John clearly speaks of a group which has been "Christian."[20] It is of course certain that what would have bound the Johannine Christians together initially was their common conviction that God had brought about eschatological salvation through

Jesus. But we are told (2 Jn 9) that with the passage of time some of the group became "progressive," going beyond what had been "from the beginning." As seen from the lists of claims and from the pages of 1 John, these others have evidently begun to alter their conviction regarding the place of Jesus in this plan of salvation. I would propose that it is in some form of "going beyond" the original message of the community that the error of the opponents is to be located.

However before we can make a final judgment about the position of the opponents we must look at the statements of the epistle about their ethical beliefs.

3. Orthodox and Secessionist Views Regarding Ethics

In addition to differences regarding their status as Christians and their understanding of the role of Jesus, the two Johannine groups represented in 1 John disagreed about various aspects of ethics and its context. Once again we will begin by gathering together the various pertinent statements in the epistles. (See Table Three.)

As can be seen from the listing, aside from the general statements which assert that the author's followers keep the commandments and act justly, there are a variety of more specific issues involved in the community dispute. There is a dispute whether the believers can be said to be free from sin. If they are freed from sin, there is a dispute about the role of Jesus in that forgiveness. There is a dispute about the coming of the parousia, a dispute about the extent of the eternal life believers possess in the present, a dispute about the coming of a general judgment and finally a dispute about whether the opponents love the brothers.

It is also evident that at least some of these differences are related to one another. Thus the opponents' full and perfect possession of eternal life is the ground of their claim to sinlessness. Since they possess life in its fullness now there is no need to speak of a parousia or of a final judgment. And sinlessness is the opponents' ground for not keeping the commandments and the commandment that the author has in mind is the one about love of the brethren. What then are we to make of these various differences between the two Johannine groups?

TABLE THREE:
DIFFERENCES BETWEEN THE TWO GROUPS
REGARDING ETHICS

1. The opponents boast that they are FREE FROM SIN (1:8,10); the faithful admit that they have sinned (1:7,9; 2: 1–2,12; 3:5; 4:10; 5:16–17). The faithful claim to be free from sin also (3:6,7,9; 5:18) but not in the same sense as the opponents.

2. The faithful act JUSTLY (2:29; 3:7; by implication in 3:12); the opponents act sinfully (3:4,8,10).

3. The faithful KEEP THE COMMANDMENTS (2:3–8; 3: 22,24; 4:21; 5:2,3); the opponents do not (2:4; implicit in 3: 22,24; implicit in 4:20 and in 5:1–5).

4. The faithful LOVE THE BROTHERS (2:10; 3:14,16, 17,18,23; 4:7–12,19–21; 5:1); the opponents do not (especially 3:17–18; also 3:10,14–15; 4:19–21).

5. The faithful expect a FINAL COMING WHICH INVOLVES JUDGMENT (2:28 = final coming; 2:18–19; 4: 17). In addition, the author makes a distinction between the "now" and the "future" which the opponents do not.

6. The faithful claim that JESUS HAS FREED THEM FROM SIN (1:9; 2:2; 3:5,8; 4:9–10) especially by his death (1:7; 3:16).

C. The Theological Position of the Opponents:
A Radical Pneumatology

I would argue that the "opponents" of 1 John represented a completely spiritual understanding of the ministry of Jesus. Rather than focusing on the images of the glorious restoration of a Davidic king in the last days, they held to the wisdom-oriented conviction that, in accord with their Jewish traditions and in accord with at least one strand of scriptural expectations, in the last days Yahweh would send his Spirit upon the people in a new and complete way. These Johannine Christians then, true to their understanding of their scriptures, held to a somewhat prophetic view of the ministry of Jesus and argued that the true purpose of his ministry was the announcement of and the preparation for the eschatological outpouring of the Spirit.

Once Jesus had returned to heaven, God would send the Holy Spirit in its eschatological manifestation. It would be the possession of the Spirit which would be the principle of eternal life. Consequently, the believers now would see no distinctive identity for Jesus nor would they have any permanent need of Jesus within salvation or within the community tradition since ultimately it was the Spirit that mattered.

This eschatological outpouring of the Spirit would be enough for the community. It would teach them everything they needed to know and they would have no need to be rooted in a "tradition" since they now possessed the Spirit of Yahweh who had also guided Jesus. They would be convinced that their reception of the Spirit cleansed them from sin and made them sinless for the future. Therefore to speak of an atoning death by Jesus would make no sense and they would have no need of ethical direction or be bound to "love the brothers" since all guidance now came directly from the Spirit. They would have no future, final judgment to fear since they had been made sinless by their possession of the Spirit. And in fact there would be no second coming of Jesus, no parousia, because the Spirit had come in a definitive way already.[21]

Of course such a proposal, to be true, would have to be shown to be (1) a plausible reading of the Johannine tradition as evident in the gospel. It would also (2) have to be a plausible reading of at least one current of eschatological hopes within Judaism at the time of Jesus. Finally (3) it would have to be a plausible reading of the opponents' position and the author's refutation as contained in 1 John.

In what follows I will indicate how the theory finds corroboration in all three areas!

D. The Eschatological Outpouring of the Spirit
as the Principal Purpose
of the Ministry of Jesus

1. The Foundation in the Johannine Gospel

(a) The Spirit In John's Gospel[22]

From the gospel, it is clear that the efficacy of the ministry of Jesus himself is portrayed as directly related to his own possession of the Spirit. This is true of Jesus throughout the New Testament tradition, but the portrayal is given a particular nuance in the Johannine gospel. Jesus receives the Spirit in a special way at the beginning of his ministry ("I have seen the Spirit descending as a dove from heaven and it remained upon him" 1:32).[23] The efficacy of Jesus' baptism of others is described in terms of its being done in the Spirit. John the Baptist says of him: "The one upon whom you see the Spirit descending and remaining upon him, this is the one baptizing in the Holy Spirit" (1:33).[24] Jesus speaks the words of God because God has given him the Spirit (3:34; 6:63). In 3:34, it is explicitly stated that God has given Jesus the Spirit *without measure* (boundlessly).[25]

Second, the gospel portrays the ministry of Jesus as not being of itself effective of belief but attributes the full causality of belief to the Spirit. In spite of statements that indicate that the encounter with Jesus and belief in him is what gives life,[26] there are other statements which clearly associate eternal life with the possession of the Spirit. "The Spirit is that which gives life" (6:63). "Unless one is born of water and the Spirit, that person is not able to enter the kingdom of God. That which is born of the flesh is flesh and that which is born of the Spirit is spirit" (Jn 3:5–6). "God is Spirit and he seeks those who will worship him in spirit" (4:23–34). In reference to Jesus' statement at Tabernacles regarding living waters, the evangelist says that this referred "to the Spirit which those who believed in him were to receive" (7:39). Thus it seems that belief is presented as a pre-condition for the reception of the Spirit, and thus eternal life. But belief itself was not the principle of life.

Furthermore, it is repeatedly said that the belief even of the disciples was linked to the giving of the Spirit (as we saw above) and that this was linked to the period after the glorification of Jesus. It is when the disciples receive the Spirit that they are able to truly believe.[27] "The Spirit was not yet (given) because Jesus had not yet been glorified" (7:39). "His disciples did not understand these things at first, but when Jesus was glorified, then they remembered that these things were written about him and that they did these things to him" (12:16). "When therefore he was raised from the dead, his disciples remembered that he said this and they believed the scriptures and the word which Jesus had spoken" (2:22). The departure of Jesus is linked to the giving of the Spirit. "I will ask the Father and he will give you another Paraclete, to be with you forever" (14:17). "The Paraclete, the Holy Spirit, which the Father will send in my name . . ." (14:26). "When the Paraclete comes which I will send to you from the Father . . ." (15:26). "When the Spirit of truth comes, he will lead you in all truth" (16:13).[28] This giving of the Spirit is presented by John the Baptist as the sum and substance of the ministry of Jesus: ". . . this is the one baptizing in the Holy Spirit" (1:34).

Besides this emphasis on the Spirit in the gospel, there is relatively little emphasis on the role of Jesus' death as having a function in itself.[29] Rather the dominant picture of the death is as a departure.[30] The clearest expression of this is 16:28 ("I left the Father and came into the world; now I leave the world and return to the Father").

Given the importance of the Spirit for the disciples and for Jesus himself, it would be possible to read the Johannine gospel in such a way that the purpose and result of Jesus' ministry was primarily the giving of the Spirit. Although there are passages which speak of the atoning death of Jesus (e.g. 1:29; 10:15), it was the possession of the Spirit that was central.[31]

The author of 1 John describes this conviction of his opponents as the conviction that Jesus came in "water only" (1 Jn 5:6).[32] Throughout the gospel, the image of (living) water is associated with the Spirit. Coming in water, in the context of the gospel, then means that Jesus has come to give the Spirit. Jesus promises the Samaritan woman living water (4:10–15); from his side will flow living waters (7:37–39)—waters which are identified as the Spirit; at the scene of his death, there does in fact flow water (19:34). And of course the assertion that Jesus "baptizes" (an action usually associated with water) "with the Holy Spirit" (1:33) confirms this imagery. Thus the author of 1 John is able to describe the position of the opponents as claiming that Jesus came "in water only," that is, that he came only to give the Spirit.

Once the Spirit has been given, it could be argued, the believer had no more essential need of Jesus since possession of the Spirit united the believer directly with God.[33] Jesus was important insofar as he was the agent by which the eschatological outpouring of the Spirit was accomplished, but he himself would then hold no permanent or continuing role in salvation. Although Jesus had been important for a time, he was no longer so.[34] Even though it might be claimed that Jesus was pre-existent, the possession of the Spirit made the believer on a par with Jesus with regard to the possession of eternal life, justice, sinlessness, "Christ-ness" and sonship.

(b) Lack of Doctrinal and Ethical Material

In addition to the actual portrayal of the Spirit in the Johannine gospel, there are other elements of the gospel that would serve to enlarge the role of the Spirit within the tradition.

One such feature is the relative lack of doctrinal and ethical material within the gospel. It is a well-known comment of Bultmann that the Johannine Jesus is a "revealer without a revelation."[35] The comment has been a topic of much discussion, but the fact that it could be made at all points to an important facet of the gospel: apart from the christological teaching of the gospel, there is precious little of the didactic. The same is true of the kind of ethical material which abounds in the synoptics. One looks through the Johannine gospel in vain for ethical direction other than the love commandment. There are brief references to "one whose deeds are evil" but there is no explicitation of what it is that makes the deeds evil.[36] The same is true of other doctrinal matters.

Given the relative lack of didactic and ethical material, together with the emphasis on the role of the Spirit in teaching the community, one can see how a one-sided reading could easily move away from any association with the tradition of Jesus' teaching. Such a tradition would naturally tend to rely more heavily on the Spirit for guidance in specifics. A group which emphasized these elements of the tradition could easily move in the direction of currents which emphasized the immediate experience of God and which are frequently called "mystical" or "gnosticizing." The opponents could well say that the Spirit is enough; the teaching of Jesus is not of essential importance, since the Spirit which informs the Christian is the same Spirit which informed Jesus. The Christian might argue that there would be no danger of error since it was the same Spirit which informed both.

(c) Lack of an Authoritative Teacher

Still another factor which aids in putting the Spirit into a unique perspective within the Johannine tradition is the lack of a community structure which would contain an office of an authoritative teacher, as was found in other Christian communities at about this time. Although there is mention of a "we" in the first epistle which is distinguished from "you," nevertheless it is true that the basic role (and authority) of both groups within the Johannine tradition was that of *witness* to the tradition. The author reminds them of what they have heard from the beginning of the tradition, i.e. from Jesus; he asserts that they have no need for anyone to teach them. And so even the role of the author of 1 John would be most properly described as "witness" and exhorter rather than as teacher.[37] All of these features indicate how unique and how important the role of the Spirit was in the Johannine tradition.

(d) The Paraclete Passages in the Gospel

But what of the Paraclete passages? It would seem that they would be a significant obstacle to a theory such as I have presented here. Those passages which speak of the Spirit as the Paraclete clearly link the "teaching" of the Spirit with the historical ministry of Jesus in such a way that they make it difficult to see how Jesus could ever be "done away with." Would not the Paraclete passages have confirmed the position of the author and made it impossible for the opponents to substantiate their position from the gospel itself? There are two possible approaches to this problem.

Brown, in his attempt to derive the positions of the adversaries from the gospel in the form that we now have it, argued that the adversaries had their own interpretation of the various statements which would seem at first to contradict their views. This avoids the risk of a circular argument whereby what does not fit the position of the adversaries is attributed to a redactor. This is certainly a valid approach. Furthermore it has the merit of not being dependent upon any particular theory of the relationship between the epistle and the gospel. However, while this approach is a possibility, it can create another problem: the explanation of how the adversaries interpreted away "contradictory" passages can well seem forced and unconvincing.

Brown uses this principle himself in his discussion of the Paraclete passages.[38] He suggests that both the author and the secessionists paid homage to the Johannine tradition and to the role of the Spirit but combined them in a different balance. Three factors lead Brown to believe that the secessionists assign a "creative" role to the Spirit which the author of 1 John would not: they are designated by the author as "progressives," the intensity of the author's stress on what was from the beginning and the infrequency of explicit references to the Spirit in 1 John. Brown supposes, that the author, in the judgment of the secessionists, did not take seriously enough the promise of Jesus that he had much more to tell his disciples than he told them during the ministry and that the Paraclete would declare the things to come (16:13).[39]

This is possible. However, rather than attempt to explain away the passages as does Brown, I would suggest that there is another approach which ultimately may hold more hope of giving a satisfactory answer. This approach takes seriously the possibility that certain passages are the work of a later editor. While one must be cautious in attributing material to an editor, it seems overly cautious to deny the possibility of editing *a priori*. Although this is not the place for a complete literary analysis of the Paraclete passages, it should be pointed out that the secondary character of the Paraclete passages has been proposed by scholars with some regularity.[40] More to the point for our purposes is the demonstration of how the Paraclete passages conform to and support what we shall later see as the theology of 1 John rather than the theology of the "dominant" view of the Spirit in the gospel.

In the first Paraclete passage (14:16–17) little is said of the Paraclete except that he is identified as the "Spirit of truth." The passage however is significant for two reasons. First, it makes reference to the Spirit as "another" Paraclete. Nowhere else in the gospel is Jesus referred to as a Paraclete. This comes to expression only in 1 John. Thus it is clear that this Paraclete expression presumes a view in which Jesus is the *first* Paraclete, a position that the opponents of 1 John evidently would deny. Second, this first saying is important because it refers to the Spirit as the "Spirit of truth," a title which makes full sense only within an apocalyptic framework where it is compared with the "Spirit of deception" (e.g. 1 Jn 4:6).

Never in the gospel is a contrast with, or even the possible existence of, a spirit of deception made explicit. In the gospel, except for the implicit usage such as in the present text, the apocalyptic contrast of spirits is not an issue. However, in the much more apocalyptic first epistle, the issue is an explicit one: test the spirits. This is an important distinction between the two documents. In the gospel the issue is whether one is born again of the Spirit, whether one has received the Spirit, the importance of the Spirit over against the "flesh." However in 1 John the issue becomes not *whether* one has the Spirit, but *which sort* of Spirit one has! Thus the terminology found here and in the remainder of the Paraclete passages presupposes an apocalyptic worldview which is nowhere explicit in the Spirit passages of the gospel.

In the second Paraclete passage (14:26) we see the first of the functions of the Spirit. He will teach the disciples all things and remind them of all that Jesus has said. While the first part of the saying could be interpreted to agree with the opponents who claim to be taught by the Spirit, the second part clearly anchors this teaching in the words of Jesus. This anchoring in the words of Jesus is again one of the clear polemical points of the first epistle.

In the third of the Paraclete sayings (15:26–27), we have, in addition to theological considerations, strikingly clear evidence of editing. In 15:22–25, Jesus recounts the three essential witnesses to himself (his word, his works, and scripture). These of course are a repetition based on the paradigmatic listing in 5:31–40. What is striking is that here the list is extended to five by the addition of the witness of the Paraclete and of the disciples! Each of these latter two clearly confronts the position of the opponents in 1 John.

The mention of the Paraclete, again as the Spirit of truth, which proceeds from the Father, will witness about Jesus. The Paraclete is specifically connected to Jesus, rather than an independent witness. In addition, the statement that the disciples are said to be witnesses because they have been with Jesus "from the beginning" occurs only here in the gospel. But emphasis on what was from the beginning and on witness to what was from the beginning is a recurrent, polem-

ical theme within both the first epistle (1:1; 2:7,13,14,24 [twice]; 3:
11) and the second (vv 5,6).

The fourth of the sayings (16:7–11) speaks of the Paraclete as
convicting the world about sin, justice and judgment. It is significant
for the present that in the explanation it is said that the Paraclete
convicts the world about judgment because the "ruler of this world"
is already judged. Once again we see terminology characteristic of
the apocalyptic worldview which dominates 1 John but which is
largely absent from the gospel.[41]

The fifth saying (16:12–15) again speaks in terms which are
clearly supportive of the polemical views of the author of 1 John.
The Spirit of truth will lead the disciples to all truth. More importantly,
he will not speak on his own, but only say what he has heard. In
addition, the Paraclete will glorify Jesus! That is, he will take from
what belongs to Jesus and will announce it to them. Finally the entire
relationship is summarized: what Jesus has is from the Father, and
so the Spirit will take from what is Jesus' and will announce it to the
disciples. Nothing could more clearly or definitively link the Spirit
with the words of Jesus!

Thus given the similarities between the Paraclete sayings and 1
John in theology, polemic, and worldview, it seems much more likely
that the Paraclete passages are in fact part of the redaction of the
gospel and not, as some would argue, part of the original edition.
The Paraclete figure is anchored in the words of Jesus; it takes the
community back to what they have heard "from the beginning."
This is what the author of 1 John considers essential for a correct
interpretation of the tradition as we shall see below.[42]

2. Jewish Background for Such a Conception of the Eschatological Outpouring of the Spirit

The Jewish expectations regarding the eschatological era are well
known, and this is not the place to review them in all their variety.[43]
However in our study of them we must be constantly on our guard
not to read the viewpoints of later Christian theology back into Jewish
expectations. The primary thrust of Israel's hopes for the future was
a restoration—of the covenant, of the nation, and of the land.[44] The

expectations about the precise form which this renewal and establishment were to take were of course diverse.

A second element in these hopes has to do with speculation that
this renewal or coming about of the new age would entail the action
of a divine agent. The divine agent was not always a part of such
speculation. Where the agent does occur, his role in the establishment
of this new age is described in various ways, and it is clear that the
agent was always a secondary element. Of course the role of the divine
agent is of paramount importance in Christian interpretation of the
eschatological events, but this was hardly the only possible scenario.

A. E. Harvey makes the following observation regarding Hebrew
messianic expectations: "What is important [in Jewish thought] is
the character of that new age itself, the nature of God's ultimate
kingship. The identity and role of any human agent is a secondary
matter."[45] A similar point is made by G. Vermes with regard to interpretation of "messianic" texts at Qumran: ". . . the interest of the
Church in the messianic role of Jesus is apt to assign a greater importance to Messianism in Jewish religion than the historical evidence
justifies. . . ."[46] Mowinckel points out that in those forms of future
hope where the emphasis came to be put on the religious aspect of
the future age, on the kingly rule of Yahweh, there was less and less
room for the messianic king. It was for the presence of God himself
among his people that the nation longed.[47] Recently M. de Jonge has
affirmed this approach: "It is even less helpful to denote the expectation of God's final intervention in the future as 'messianic expectation.' The appearance of a mediating figure ('human', 'angelic',
'divine'), whatever name or title he may have, is not a regular or
indispensable element. . . . We shall do well to concentrate on the
actual terms used in our sources. . . ."[48]

Among the blessings of the messianic age, the preeminent was
to be Yahweh's gift of his Spirit to the nation and to all mankind. In
the past it was this Spirit which came upon the king and distinguished
him as the instrument of Yahweh. So also it was the Spirit which
empowered the prophet and at times the priest. However, with the
coming of the new age there was to be a new and definitive outpouring
of the Spirit upon all mankind.[49] It was this that would definitively
bring about the presence of God among his people. This outpouring
of the Spirit would bring about a change within the hearts of mankind

and cause a new faithfulness to the law. This dimension of eschato-logical expectation is clearly attested in the Hebrew scriptures and in the Qumran documents.[50]

Joel 3:1–2 says:

Then afterward I will pour out my Spirit upon all mankind. Your sons and daughters shall prophesy, your old men shall dream dreams, your young men shall see visions; Even upon the servants and the handmaids, in those days, I will pour out my Spirit. (NAB)[51]

Isaiah 32:19,15 speaks first of the purifying punishment and then of the new age:

Down it comes, as trees come down in the forest! The city will be utterly laid low. Hill and tower will become wasteland forever for wild asses to frolic in, and flocks to pasture, until the Spirit from on high is poured out on us. (NAB)

Ezekiel 11:17,19 says:

I will gather you from the nations and assemble you from the countries over which you have been scattered, and I will restore to you the land of Israel. I will give them a new heart and put a new Spirit within them. (NAB)

Ezekiel 36:26,27 says:

I will put my Spirit within you and make you live by my statutes, careful to observe my decrees. (NAB)

Also Ezekiel 39:29 says:

No longer will I hide my face from them, for I have poured out my Spirit upon the house of Israel, says the Lord God. (NAB)

From Isaiah we see that this figure who has the Spirit is also said to be "anointed" (i.e. *messiah, christos*) because of this giving of the

Spirit. In Isaiah 42:1, there is a figure spoken of who is said to have the Spirit:

> Here is my servant whom I uphold, my chosen one with whom I am pleased, upon whom I have put my spirit; he shall bring forth justice to the nations. (NAB)

This figure is said in 61:1 to be "anointed," again precisely because he has possession of the Spirit.

> The spirit of the Lord God is upon me, because the Lord has anointed me. (NAB)

We know that these passages were interpreted in a messianic sense by Christians from their application to Jesus in the New Testament (e.g. Isaiah 42:1 is used in Mark 1:11; Matthew 3:17; Luke 9:35; Isaiah 61:1 is used in Matthew 11:5; Luke 4:18; 7:22; Acts 4:27; 10:38).

This description of the eschatological outpouring of the Spirit accounts well for the claims made by the opponents of 1 John. They, in accord with their Jewish heritage, believe in the Father; they believe that the hoped-for age has come; they therefore claim to be recipients of the Spirit in its eschatological manifestation. Certainly, within both sectors of the Johannine community, there is evidence that this outpouring of the Spirit is all-important. The Jewish hopes for the future age which we have reviewed make it plausible that for one segment of the Johannine community, a community which exhibited a strong belief in one dimension of eschatological hope, the figure of Jesus could well be made, for the reasons explained here and below, eventually to recede into the background relative to the Spirit.

At Qumran the end times will also involve the giving of the Spirit although it is portrayed within an apocalyptic framework. The Community Rule (1QS) describes the present time as dominated by the two spirits and the future giving of the spirit.[52]

> The nature of the children of men is ruled by these two spirits and during their life all the hosts of men have a portion in their divisions and walk in both their ways. . . . For God has established the spirits in equal measure until the

final age. . . . But in the mysteries of His understanding, and in His glorious wisdom, God has ordained an end for falsehood and at the time of the visitation He will destroy it for ever. . . . [At the appointed time of judgment] God will then purify every deed of Man with his truth; He will refine for Himself the human frame by rooting out all spirit of falsehood from the bounds of his flesh. He will cleanse him of all wicked deeds with the spirit of holiness; like purifying waters He will shed upon him the spirit of truth (to cleanse him) of all abomination and falsehood. (1QS 4:15–21—DSSE 77–78)

3. The Spirit in 1 John: The Approach of the Author

When we look to the pages of 1 John we find a portrayal of the adversaries which is compatible with the interpretation of the Spirit in the gospel and with those strains of Jewish eschatological thought described above. The final question then is whether this theory is also compatible with the role of the Spirit as it is presented in the first epistle.

Although it is often claimed that the pneumatology of the first epistle is less developed than that of the gospel,[53] the pneumatology is just as developed but less explicit. Pneumatology plays an essential role theologically in the argument of the epistle. But any argument from the Spirit in 1 John is made more difficult by the fact that not only must the author establish clearly his own position (presumably on the basis of his own possession of the Spirit), but he must also refute the position of his opponents who would claim the same authority for their position. If the pneumatology of the epistle seems less developed, it is also because the epistle is concerned to both explain theology and at the same time to provide "external," observable tests by which the orthodoxy of the opponents can be determined.

When he speaks of the Spirit the author of 1 John must be careful, for he is not simply speaking of a group which does not have the Spirit (as was the case of the opponents in the gospel context) versus those who do (the Christians); rather at the time of 1 John the dispute was between two groups who claimed possession of the Spirit. Let us look briefly at the Spirit texts in the first epistle.

Reference to the Spirit in 1 John occurs first under the rubric of the "anointing" which the faithful member has (2:20). It is this anointing which enables the believer to identify the false members of the community who are departing from the community's midst. The anointing gives them knowledge (2:20). It enables them to know the truth (2:21). They have no need to be taught by anyone since they have this anointing (2:27) and already know the truth. And implicitly it is this anointing which enables them to confess Jesus as the Christ since the "liar" is the one who denies that Jesus is the Christ.

In 3:24 we find that it is the Spirit which enables the person to know that Jesus "remains" in them. But it is important to test the spirits because not every spirit is from God (4:1–6). The external test of a spirit is whether that spirit confesses Jesus as the Christ come in the flesh (4:2–3). The Spirit which remains in the believer is greater than that which is in the world. Finally another way in which the spirits can be distinguished is that the spirit which listens to us is of God (4:6). The fact that this is one of the passages in which differing claims are explicitly contrasted indicates the importance of the Spirit for both the believer and the adversaries.

Finally we are told that the Spirit witnesses to Jesus (5:6–9). There are three that witness to Jesus: the Spirit, the water and the blood. The "water and the blood" refer to the fact that Jesus is coming to give the Spirit and to die to take away sin. And the Spirit testifies to the reality of both.

From these passages, it is clear that the position of the author is very close to that of the opponents, in the sense that the eschatological outpouring of the Spirit is claimed as an inner possession which makes knowledge of the truth possible. The opponents claim that they have no need of Jesus to teach them, and the author of 1 John claims that the believers have no need of anyone to teach them. But the author and the opponents differ in that the author constantly anchors his conception of the Spirit in the ministry of Jesus. This anchoring in the ministry is something that has subtle but far-reaching implications, as we shall see in the next chapter.

NOTES

1. In this sense, the text is seen as a "window" onto the Johannine world. While it is also true that the text is a "mirror," the image proposed by Murray Krieger in *A Window to Criticism* (Princeton: Princeton University, 1964), 3–4, it is not *just* a mirror. Reader/response criticism has provided valuable insights into the Johannine literature. A. Culpepper's book, *The Anatomy of the Fourth Gospel* (Philadelphia: Fortress, 1983), is a good example of such an approach. Reader/response criticism poses another set of questions to the text. Culpepper's balance is evidence that the approaches should be complementary rather than mutually exclusive.

2. P. Perkins, *The Johannine Epistles* (NTM 21; Wilmington: Glazier, 1979).

3. *Ibid.* xvi–xxiii.

4. *Ibid.* 4–5.

5. *Ibid.* 5.

6. K. Grayston, *Epistles* 12–13.

7. *Ibid.* 14–22.

8. *Ibid.* 4–5.

9. S. Smalley, *1, 2, 3 John.*

10. *Ibid.* xxiii.

11. *Ibid.*

12. *Ibid.* xxiii–xxiv, 17, 139. Smalley actually posits five subdivisions in the second half, but he does not claim a parallel for 4:7–5:4.

13. R. E. Brown, *Epistles* 116–128.

14. *Ibid.* 47–68.

15. *Ibid.* 50–54, 73–78.

16. Perkins represents one extreme view. She claims that we can know almost nothing of the positions of the opponents in a rhetorical culture (*Epistles* xxi–xxiii).

17. There are various ways of approaching the statements regarding the opponents. Bogart, in *Orthodox and Heretical Perfectionism in the Johannine Community as Evident in the First Epistle of John* (SBLDS 33; Missoula: Scholars, 1977) 27–30, argues that it is unlikely that the epistle contains exact verbatim quotes of the opponents, but that there was a genuine difference of views rather than simply a misunderstanding of one another. Bogart argues that excessive dis-

tortion of the position of the opponents would do little to help in a situation such as is encountered in 1 John, because the issue is the precise nature of the understanding of the Johannine tradition. I would agree.

According to J. Painter, "The 'Opponents' in 1 John," *NTS* 32 (1986) 49–50, in 2 John the opponents are labeled progressives; in 2 John 10–11 the welcoming of teachers who may have views similar to those of the opponents becomes an issue. Therefore the establishment of a criterion for distinguishing positions would be important for the community. Careful inquiry about the correctness of one's theological views was a part of the Qumran community's process (1QS 5:1–7), and there is no reason to think that something similar did not occur elsewhere. I find this to be a very reasonable approach.

Brown (*Epistles* 47–48) is correct in seeing some of the statements to be possible errors on the part of the author's own followers. For example the warning about those who still fear instead of loving (1 Jn 4:18) may well be intended for the faithful members who have not fully appropriated the tradition. Such statements have been excluded from the listing here.

It was pointed out at the beginning of the chapter how diverse the approaches are to understanding the position of the opponents. As will be seen in what follows, I am of the opinion that 1 John reports reliably the position of the opponents. This is a decision that cannot be made *a priori* but only after a thorough examination of the document itself. The reader, by reviewing the three tables listing statements about the positions of the opponents, will be able to judge for himself/herself how detailed and accurate the report of the opponents is. If some of the comments of the author seem to be a rhetorical extreme (you have no need of a teacher; you will know God directly), it should be recalled that these are simply paraphrases of claims made within the prophetic literature for the eschatological period.

18. Brown (*Epistles* Appendix 1, Chart 4) gives a listing of "Epistolary Statements Pertinent to the Adversaries' Views." He divides into three categories: (1) "General description; attitude toward Jesus"; (2) "Moral behavior; attitude toward sin; failure to love the brothers"; (3) "How the readers should react toward the adversaries." However the "claims" that each group makes for itself is also important in defining the perimeters of their positions. I would judge this to be

more important than the ways the readers should react to the adversaries.

19. Brown, *Epistles* 73–74.

20. Perkins (*Epistles* 42,51) and Brown (*Epistles* 92) are among those who suggest that the epistle uses much of the type of rhetoric addressed to the Jews in the gospel but now aiming it at the opponents of 1 John. This is not to say, however, that the opponents are those Jews.

21. This position is not an entirely new one. A somewhat similar form has been put forward recently by K. Grayston, *Epistles* 19 and his commentary on 2:18–27; 4:1–6; 5:6–12.

Grayston proposes that the epistle was written before the gospel and that this accounts for the fact that several passages in the gospel would seem to refute the position of the adversaries.

Grayston's position expresses well one type of criticism directed at the approach taken by Brown: "It would be very difficult to argue that the dissidents had read the Gospel, seized on these passages [i.e. those which would contradict their position] and the Paraclete sayings, divested them of their association with Jesus, and constructed their own spirit theology; just as difficult as arguing that the writer of the Epistle had read the Gospel and almost entirely forgotten its teaching when he wrote of the Spirit" (p. 20). I would argue that the most likely explanation is that the epistle was written after the *second edition* of the gospel and that the gospel was redacted by someone (other than the author of 1 John) to clarify the gospel tradition on those aspects which were ambiguous enough to have been helpful to the position of the opponents.

J. Painter (" 'Opponents' " 51–53) has also suggested that the opponents emphasized the role of the Spirit to the exclusion of Jesus. However Painter argues that the opponents' perspective was a Gentile one rather than Jewish. He states: "There is nothing in 1 John to suggest a Jewish background *for the opponents* and there are hints of a Gentile background" (p. 65). In my opinion, there are so many parallels between the position of the opponents and Old Testament passages associated with Jewish eschatological hopes that I find it difficult to think of the opponents as coming from anything else than some form of Jewish background. Painter, correctly I think, argues that there is less emphasis on the Spirit in 1 John because both groups claim possession of the Spirit and therefore the topic was very ambiguous as a proof of the author's position. Yet he argues from the lack of dependence upon the Old Testament that the opponents were Gentiles. I would argue the reverse: just as references to the Spirit would be weakened since both sides claim the Spirit, so defense from the Old Testament would be ambiguous since both groups based themselves on Old Testament hopes.

D. B. Woll, in *Johannine Christianity in Conflict: Authority, Rank and Succession in the First Farewell Discourse* (SBLDS 60; Chico: Scholars Press, 1981), describes the situation as one "in which claims to direct, independent access to divine authority have, in the author's eyes, gotten out of control by becoming a threat to the primacy of the Son." Thus although the position I am posing is presented in more detail than previous proposals, it does stand within a clear line of understanding of the Johannine community and the problems which could possibly arise from its distinctive theology. I would see the current study to be a more thorough working out of the position, showing that the position finds parallels in the Old Testament and within the Johannine gospel as well as within various non-canonical materials. See the important book by G. Burge discussed in the following note.

Various other aspects of the "pneumatic" dimension of the Johannine tradition have been stressed in, for example, E. Kasemann, *The Testament of Jesus* (Philadelphia: Fortress, 1968) 36ff; D. M. Smith, "Johannine Christianity: Some Reflections on Its Character and Delineation" *NTS* 21 (1975) 222–248, esp. 232–33, 243–44; Marshall, *Epistles* 21; K. Weiss, "Die 'Gnosis' im Hintergrund und im Spiegel der Johannesbriefe," in K.-W. Troeger, *Gnosis und Neues Testament* (Berlin: Evangelische Verlagsanstalt, 1973.)

22. The Spirit in the gospel of John has been the object of relatively few book length treatments. Of the earlier ones, the most important is that of F. Porsch, *Pneuma und Wort* (Frankfurter Theologische Studien 16; Frankfurt: Knecht, 1974). The recent studies of G. Burge in *The Anointed Community* (Grand Rapids: Eerdmans, 1987) is also quite helpful. His book begins with a thorough survey of past studies. See also E. Frank (*Revelation Taught: The Paraclete in the Gospel of John* (ConNT 14; Gleerup: Liber, 1985).

Of these I have found Burge's book to be the most helpful. Although

Burge's book came to my attention after the present book was complete, I find considerable agreement between his thesis and the view presented here. To quote from Burge's epilogue: "In brief, the final crisis of the Johannine community was essentially pneumatic. The spiritual inspiration and experiential focus of the community were pressed into use without serious controls and, in the process, seriously strained. 1 John counters this situation with a new dialectic between tradition and experience. The former sayings of Jesus (in the Gospel) must serve as an anchor and limit to unbounded prophetic inspiration" (p. 224).

23. However high the christology of the community, there are numerous references to Jesus' reception of the Spirit in a special way and to the fact that this reception of the Spirit was directly related to the efficacy of his ministry.

24. The notion of "baptizing in the Holy Spirit" does not refer to something Jesus does during his ministry but to what he does at the end of it. Schnackenburg (*Gospel* 1, 305) relates the conferral of the Spirit to 3:5 where birth is from water and the Holy Spirit. But this does not occur within the ministry of Jesus. Such baptism in the Spirit then refers not to an activity during the ministry of Jesus but to the outpouring of the Spirit at the glorification of Jesus and presumably in the sending of the Paraclete. This would relate well to 19:39 where the witness of the beloved disciple confirms that from the pierced side of Jesus comes forth the living waters promised in 4:10–15 and 7:39. So also Brown, *Gospel* 946–51.

25. The messiah's possession of the Spirit was also a characteristic of Jewish thought. See in the Old Testament, Isaiah 42:1; 61:1; etc. For a discussion of Old Testament and Qumran texts, see the discussion in Harvey, *Jesus and the Constraints of History* (Philadelphia: Westminster, 1982) 136–153, esp. 152–53; in the New Testament, Acts 4:27; 10:38. For the conception in the pseudepigrapha, see S. Mowinckel, *He That Cometh* (ET; New York: Abingdon, 1954) 308–311. See also the full discussion in chapter six below.

26. For example, there are frequent statements that it is the encounter with Jesus which gives life: 3:36 ("The one who believes in the Son has eternal life"); 6:40 ("Everyone who sees the Son and believes in him has eternal life . . ."); 6:47–48 ("The one who believes has eternal life. I am the bread of life"); 6:63 ("My words are Spirit

and life"); also 5:24 (the one who believes in the Father has eternal life). There are other references which are ambiguous in that they associate the giving of life with Jesus, but it is not possible to tell precisely *how* Jesus gives life (e.g. 1:4; 4:14; 5:40; 6:27,33,35; 8:12; 10:10,28; 11:25; 14:6; 17:2; 20:31).

27. The determination of the exact time of the giving of the Spirit is disputed. The possibilities include the following: (1) Jesus baptizes in the Holy Spirit during his earthly ministry; his words are spirit and life; (2) the Spirit is given only after the glorification of Jesus; (3) Jesus gives the Spirit to the disciples gathered in the upper room after the resurrection; (4) the Spirit is sent only after Jesus has returned to the Father. It is certainly fair to say that the dominant impression of the gospel is that it is not immediately and simply imparted through the words of Jesus in spite of the statements that would seem indicate that. The Spirit is accessible only after the glorification of Jesus (7: 39), and according to the Paraclete passages the Spirit comes after the departure of Jesus to the Father.

28. Related to this are the statements of 2:17,22 and 12:16 where it is stated that the belief of the disciples did not occur until after Jesus' resurrection, thus indicating how "late" true belief was thought to occur.

29. This is true in spite of the texts such as 1:29; 3:15–16, 6:51b, 10:15; 15:13, etc. The relationship between the role of the Spirit and the death of Jesus in the forgiveness of sins is a topic that will occupy us further in chapter six.

30. T. Forestell, in *The Word of the Cross: Salvation as Revelation in the Fourth Gospel* (AnBib 57; Rome: Biblical Institute, 1974) 191, states: "The cross of Christ in Jn is evaluated precisely in terms of revelation in harmony with the theology of the entire gospel, rather than in terms of vicarious and expiatory sacrifice for sin." Grayston (*Epistles* 51), speaking of the various descriptions of the death of Jesus in the gospel, also recognizes the problem of the purpose of Jesus' death: "That Jesus' death is in some way related to the benefits he confers is presumed but not readily demonstrated."

31. The case is strengthened by the possibility that those passages were added by an editor. Such is the case in regard to 10:15 as we have seen.

32. The author of 1 John argues that Jesus did not come in water

only but in water and blood (1 Jn 5:6). We shall discuss this further below.

33. G. Bornkamm, in "Der Paraklet im Johannes-Evangelium," *Geschichte und Glaube,* Part I. *Gesammelte Aufsätse,* Vol. 3 (BEvT 48; Münich: Chr. Kaiser, 1968) 68–89, made use of the image of the "forerunner-fulfiller" motif to describe the relationship between Jesus and the Paraclete. Just as John the Baptist had been a forerunner to Jesus, so in some sense Jesus was a forerunner to the Paraclete ("Der Paraklet" 71). But Bornkamm goes on to argue that the author has made significant changes in the Paraclete tradition by making the Paraclete dependent upon Jesus and essentially one with him. However, it might well be argued that the Paraclete passages, as distinct from other Spirit passages, make the relationship to Jesus clear, while the Spirit passages themselves tend to reinforce the picture originally described by Bornkamm, i.e. of the Spirit as the fulfiller of what Jesus had been the forerunner.

34. "In their own estimation the spirit is from God, and possession by the spirit makes them those who belong to God. Since this spirit does not confess Jesus, they claim access to the Father without him. They are no longer interested in Jesus come in the flesh because they themselves possess the spirit . . ." (Grayston, *Epistles,* 79).

35. Bultmann, in *Theology of the New Testament* (Vols. 1–3; New York: Scribner's, 1955) 2, 66, states: ". . . Jesus as the Revealer of God *reveals nothing but that he is the Revealer.* . . . John, that is, in his Gospel presents only the fact (*das Dass*) of the Revelation without describing its content (*ihr Was*)." The statement has been discussed frequently. See for example R. E. Brown, "The Kerygma of the Gospel according to St. John," *Int* 21 (1967), 387–400.

36. Sin in the gospel is conceived primarily as unbelief, apart from the presentation of the love command. There are minor references to "evil deeds" and "good deeds" (3:19–21), but these speak of nothing specific. But if the love command has been added later (as I would suggest) precisely to deal with the ethical misunderstanding of the opponents, then we get a much clearer picture of the previous version of the gospel, a version which put relatively little weight on both the didactic and the ethical material from Jesus' ministry.

37. See Brown, *Epistles* 94–97.

38. *Ibid.* 372–74.

39. *Ibid.*

40. H. Windisch is perhaps the most famous proponent; see his *The Spirit-Paraclete in the Fourth Gospel* (tr. J. W. Cox; Facet Books, Biblical Series 20; Philadelphia: Fortress, 1968). However, it seems unlikely that the Paraclete passages were independent, fully-formed units when they were incorporated into the gospel, as Windisch suggests. Among other proponents are J. Wellhausen, *Erweiterungen und Änderungen im vierten Evangelium* (Berlin: Reimer, 1907); Bultmann, *Gospel* 566–72; G. Bornkamm, "Der Paraklet" 68–89. G. Johnston, in *The Spirit-Paraclete in the Fourth Gospel* (SNTSMS 12; Cambridge: The University Press, 1970), suggests that similarities with 1 John in the passages argue that the author of 1 John was the author of the gospel. Grayston (*Epistles* 92) also entertains this possibility. The curious designation of the Spirit as "another" Paraclete has long been pointed to as an indication that the author was writing with 1 John 2:1 in mind, for there Jesus is referred to simply as "a Paraclete." For literature and further discussion see especially O. Betz *Der Paraclet* (Leiden: Brill, 1963); J. Becker, "Abschiedsreden."

41. It should be noted that the worldview of the gospel is not apocalyptic except for a few isolated passages. More will be said of this below.

42. Woll (*Johannine Christianity*) argues within the context of the first farewell discourse of the gospel (13:31–14:31) that the Paraclete assures that the status of disciple is mediated and that access to the Father is not direct (pp. 92–96). The Paraclete recalls the words of Jesus (p. 95).

43. See, for example, P. Volz, *Die Eschatologie der jüdischen Gemeinde im neutestamentlichen Zeitalter* (Hildescheim: Georg Olms, 1966 [1934]; J. Klausner, *The Messianic Idea in Israel* (New York: Macmillan, 1955); D. Gowan, *Eschatology in the Old Testament* (Philadelphia: Fortress, 1986); also the works referred to below.

44. See, for example, S. Mowinckel, *He That Cometh* 143–49, 338, and texts cited there; J. Carmignac, "Les dangers de l'eschatologie," *NTS* 17 (1971–72) 365–390; D. Gowan, *Eschatology* 1–20. Israel's hopes concerning the future age changed and developed, but the elements discussed here are constant elements within that development.

45. A. E. Harvey, *Constraints* 145.

46. G. Vermes, *The Dead Sea Scrolls: Qumran in Perspective* (Philadelphia: Fortress, 1977) 163.

47. Mowinckel, *He That Cometh* 280.

48. M. de Jonge, "The Earliest Christian Use of *Christos:* Some Suggestions," *NTS* 32 (1986) 321–343, 329. We will return to de Jonge's study further below.

49. Gowan, *Eschatology* 69–78.

50. The lines of future expectation at Qumran are essentially the same although the mention of a special outpouring of the Spirit is less clear there. Nevertheless the function of the Spirit there takes on many of the forms associated with the eschatological outpouring. There is some evidence which seems to point to a special giving of the Spirit in the future age. 1QS 4:19–21 (DSSE, 77–78) states: "God will then purify every deed of Man with His truth; He will refine for Himself the human frame by rooting out all spirit of falsehood from the bounds of his flesh. He will cleanse him of all wicked deeds with the spirit of holiness; like purifying waters He will shed upon him the spirit of truth (to cleanse him) of all abomination and falsehood. And he shall be plunged into the spirit of purification that he may instruct the upright in the knowledge of the Most High and teach the wisdom of sons of heaven to the perfect of way." On the covenant and future hopes at Qumran, see Vermes, *Perspectives* 163–69.

51. This event was to be the fulfillment of the words of Moses (Num 11:29): "Would that all the people of the Lord were prophets! Would that the Lord might bestow his spirit on them all!"

52. This dualistic framework is an important way in which these materials differ from the canonical presentation of the eschatological outpouring of the Spirit. Such a combination of Old Testament theology with another framework is also a characteristic element of 1 John.

W. Nauck, in *Die Tradition und der Charackter des ersten Johannesbriefes* (WUNT 3; Tübingen: Mohr, 1957) 26–66, pointed out that the concept of covenant in 1 John combined Old Testament theology with modified dualism. As will be apparent later, this present study proposes that a similar process took place with regard to the concept of commandment.

53. It might well be said that the role of the Spirit is not very

developed in the gospel either, apart from the Paraclete passages. Yet within the Paraclete passages the variety of roles assumed by the Paraclete match to a surprising degree the roles assigned to the Spirit in 1 John. On this, see for example the comparison between the Paraclete passages and 1 John 2:20–27 by Schnackenburg, *Die Johannesbriefe* (HTKNT 13; 5th ed.; Freiburg: Herder, 1975) 152.

Chapter Six

THE IMPLICATIONS OF
A RADICAL VIEW
OF THE SPIRIT: A NEW VIEW
OF FAITH AND LIFE

At the heart of the crisis in the Johannine community was the way both groups understood the purpose and effect of Jesus' ministry. In the previous chapter we focused on the evidence within the gospel and within 1 John that there were in fact two differing views of the role of Jesus and the Spirit. Our focus in this chapter is on the opponents and on the various *implications* of their understanding of the Spirit, the effects (in their view) of the eschatological possession of the Spirit. These effects influenced their understanding of the identity of Jesus and his role within salvation as well as almost all aspects of their Christian life. And while there was no aspect of the Christian life untouched by this radical view of the Spirit, the opponents' view was particularly difficult to refute since in so many respects their view was so close to that of the author of 1 John and his followers.

Before beginning the analysis, I will provide an overview of all the claims of the opponents and how they are derivable from radical convictions about the roles of Jesus and the Spirit. This overview will hopefully guide us in the pages ahead.

As can be seen from the accompanying chart, the opponents' understanding of the outpouring of the Spirit and its implications forms a coherent viewpoint. Of course nowhere in the first epistle is the position of the opponents described so explicitly or systematically. Rather the discussion in 1 John takes place in a way which takes this "view" for granted. As is evident, the viewpoint is not a complex one

TABLE FOUR:
THE OPPONENTS' UNDERSTANDING OF THE SPIRIT
AND OF THE IMPLICATIONS
DERIVED FROM THAT UNDERSTANDING

A. THE ADVERSARIES' VIEW OF HOW ONE COMES TO KNOWLEDGE OF GOD

1. Possession of the Spirit makes direct knowledge of God possible.
   The implication therefore is that there is no need
   (a) for intermediaries such as Jesus who would bring the word of God nor
   (b) for any human teachers who might claim to do the same.

B. THE ADVERSARIES' VIEW OF JESUS AND THE CHRISTIAN: CHRISTOLOGY AND ANTHROPOLOGY

2. Possession of the Spirit gives one an anointing.
   The implication therefore is that there is no unique role for Jesus as "Christ" ("anointed")
   since all now have an anointing just as Jesus did.

3. Possession of the Spirit gives eternal life and so makes one a child of God.
   The implication therefore is that there is no unique status for Jesus as Son of God
   since all Christians now have divine life and by that fact are truly "sons (daughters) of God."

C. THE ADVERSARIES' VIEW OF CHRISTIAN LIFE: ETHICS, JUDGMENT, AND RESURRECTION

4. Possession of the Spirit frees the believer from sin.
   The implication therefore is that
   (a) the believer is perfect and will sin no more.
   (b) the believer has no need of ethical directives (or "love of the 'brothers' ") since perfect conduct is spontaneous.
   (c) the death of Jesus is not the means by which sin is done away with.

5. Possession of the Spirit gives eternal life.
   The implication therefore is that it is not correct to say that life comes by means of an atoning death of Jesus.

6. Possession of the Spirit gives eternal life
   (a) in its eschatological fullness
   (b) now.

TABLE FOUR:
THE OPPONENTS' UNDERSTANDING OF THE SPIRIT
AND OF THE IMPLICATIONS
DERIVED FROM THAT UNDERSTANDING (*Continued*)

The implication therefore is that
(a) there is no meaning to a "second" coming of Jesus because it is not necessary.
(b) there is no future judgment for the believer since there will be no need for it.
(c) there is no meaning to a future physical life beyond the grave, nor of a future resurrection of the body.

but simply one which attempts to spell out the various implications of the eschatological outpouring of the Spirit.

However to demonstrate that the viewpoint presented above is correct, it would have to be shown, in a manner similar to that employed in the previous chapter, that the opponents' position is a plausible and consistent reading of certain strands of Jewish hopes regarding the eschatological outpouring of Yahweh's Spirit. In addition it would have to be shown that the opponents' position represents a plausible and consistent interpretation of the major strand of the Johannine gospel tradition. Finally, their position also would have to be shown to be mirrored within the text of 1 John and to be refuted by the author of the epistle.

In what follows, we will see that this is indeed the case. The chapter will contain three major sections following each of the major divisions presented in the accompanying chart.

A. THE POSSESSION OF THE SPIRIT AND DIRECT KNOWLEDGE OF GOD

One of the characteristic claims of the Johannine community was that the Christian is able to "know" God. It is a claim which was made by both groups within the community. And while the author denies that the opponents have true knowledge of God, he does not deny that such knowledge is possible. In fact he claims it for his group. In every case this knowledge of God is a result of the possession of the Spirit.

There are three elements involved in this claim to know God. First, there is the claim itself, i.e. that knowledge is possible; second, that this knowledge of God will be direct; and third, that such knowledge will be brought about by the Spirit. Each of these elements is a possible derivative of the Jewish hopes regarding the eschatological outpouring of the Spirit.

1. The Spirit and Direct Knowledge of God in the Old Testament

Although the Johannine terminology of "knowing" God is frequently associated with gnostic thought, it is also an essential element of Jewish covenant theology. From the beginning of his relationship with Israel, God had made himself known through his actions on behalf of Israel. God made himself known through his actions in the exodus (Ex 7:5,17). His dwelling with the people in the tabernacle would be a means of knowing the Lord (Ex 29:45–46). The actions of Yahweh in history were a way of knowing him (Ex 25:55,7,11,17).

Repeatedly in its history, Israel had been warned that it did not know God because of its sin! Isaiah 1:2–4 expresses this well:

Sons have I raised and reared but they have disowned me! An ox knows its owner, and an ass, its master's manger; but Israel does not know, my people has not understood. Ah! sinful nation, people laden with wickedness, evil race, corrupt children! (NAB)

Jeremiah 9:2 says:

They ready their tongues like a drawn bow; with lying, and not with truth, they hold forth in the land. They go from evil to evil, but me they know not, says the Lord. (NAB)

However in the final age, this will change. Israel will be healed of its sins (which have caused them not to know God) and they will in fact know him and know him directly (and no longer indirectly through God's actions). Isaiah 54:13, which is quoted in John 6:45, says:

All your sons shall be taught by the Lord. . . .

As Jeremiah says of the time of the new covenant (Jer 31:34):

No longer will they have need to teach their friends and kinsmen how to know the Lord. All, from the least to the greatest, shall know me, says the Lord. . . . (NAB)

This statement is so close to the formulation of 1 John 2:27 that one must conclude that even the author and his community were so convinced that they lived in the period of the eschatological possession of the Spirit that they too could claim this privilege. With regard to the same eschatological event Jeremiah 24:7 says:

I shall give them a new heart to know that I am the Lord. (NAB)[1]

In Isaiah 59:21 we see that the Spirit places the words of God in their mouths, a concept closely related to having direct knowledge of God:

My Spirit which is upon you and my words that I have put into your mouth shall never leave your mouth, nor the mouths of your children, nor the mouths of your children's children from now on and forever, says the Lord. (NAB)

Because the words of the Lord are in their mouths through the action of the Spirit, one would conclude that they will be instructed directly and thus have no need of anyone to teach them.

2. Direct Knowledge of God and the Johannine Community

The claim to direct knowledge of God was the foundation for many of the other claims of the opponents regarding Jesus. For once there was a principle of direct access to God through the Spirit independent of any human intermediary, then this would have consequences for the understanding of Jesus' role as teacher. The opponents take just this approach and so deny any permanent validity for the words of Jesus. They are "progressives" who go beyond the teaching of Jesus (2 Jn 9).

In the gospel both "knowing" and "not knowing" were important facets of the presentation of the ministry of Jesus. The verb *ginosko* occurs forty-nine times in the gospel and twenty-four times in the epistles. Jesus is presented as constantly "knowing" what was to happen (2:24,25; 4:1; 5:6,42; 6:15; 10:14,27). He also knows the Father (10:15). On the other hand unbelievers are expected to "know" (7:17; 8:32; 10:38; 17:3,23) but "do not know" who Jesus is; they do not know the Father (3:10; 8:27,28,43; 10:6; 14:17; 16:19; 17:25) but believers do (6:69; 17:7,8), although even their knowledge is incomplete before the giving of the Spirit (12:16; 13:7,12; 14:7,9,17,20; 15:18).

In addition, it should be recalled what was said in the previous chapter about the absence of much of the specific didactic and ethical material in the gospel, the focus on the role of the Spirit rather than on the role of teacher. All of these are to be explained by the emphasis on the knowledge that comes from the Spirit.

3. The Correction by the Author of 1 John

From the pages of 1 John we see that the author himself considers the Christian's possession of the Spirit to give the believer direct access to God. As is the case in almost all aspects of the community dispute, there is only a fine line between the position of the opponents and of the author. Throughout 2:18–27, the author of 1 John affirms much of what the opponents say but balances it with other claims. The author recognizes and affirms the possibility of direct knowledge of God (2:13,14,20–21; 4:7; cf also 2:4). In 2:20 he tells his readers that they have an anointing (*chrisma*) from the holy one and this makes them able to know the truth (2:21).[2]

In addition he argues that it is the anointing which enables them to have knowledge (2:20). The clearest example is in 2:27 which says that this anointing gives them the ability to know without being taught by others. The opponents on the other hand also have a spirit (implicit in 2:27, also 4:1–6), and they claim to know God also (2:4). But the author of 1 John also insists that the Spirit leads them back to the words of Jesus (2:24: "Let what you have heard from the beginning remain in you"). The same Spirit infuses both Jesus and the believer, and therefore the Christian must remain rooted in the Jesus of the ministry. One cannot simply rest on the inspiration of the Spirit but must also remain faithful to the words of Jesus. "What you have heard from the beginning about the word of life . . . is what we proclaim to you (1:1,3; see also 1:5; 2:5,7,27; 3:11).

This is the first of several "both/and" positions that the author of 1 John takes and which will characterize his approach with regard to the opponents throughout 1 John. The true believer has "both" direct access to God through the Spirit "and" direct access to God through the words of Jesus. The author speaks against a *one-sided* interpretation of the tradition and for a *balance* between the roles of Jesus and of the Spirit.[3]

Not only does the author provide a balanced ("both/and") position regarding knowledge of God, he also gives *an external criterion* by which the position of the opponents can be tested: the remembered words of Jesus.[4] The remembered words of Jesus, what was heard and seen and touched (1 Jn 1:1) (in addition to the inspiration of the Spirit), found the true Christian's faith. This providing of an external criterion will also be a consistent feature of the author's refutation of his opponents.

B. The Possession of the Spirit and Christology/Anthropology

In addition to their claims to direct access to God, which would make unnecessary any intermediary (such as Jesus) as teacher, the opponents' claims to possession of the Spirit also make unnecessary the other claims made for Jesus by the tradition.

The adversaries' view of the Spirit has implications for the role of Jesus within salvation.[5] 1 John speaks of these implications in three categories: the failure of the opponents to confess that Jesus is "the Christ," their failure to confess that he is "Son of God," and their failure to confess that he has come "in the flesh." We will look at each of these briefly.

1. "Jesus Is Not the Christ"

If the opponents deny that Jesus is the Christ, they are in reality denying that he is *the* (unique) Christ since they too have the same anointing from the Spirit that empowered his ministry.[6] From the opponents' perspective, it could be argued that even if Jesus was anointed (i.e. *christos*) and did possess the Spirit, now that the community members themselves possessed the Spirit in its eschatological fullness, Jesus did not have any permanent role nor perform any unique function with regard to their salvation.

(a) Anointing and the Spirit in the Old Testament

There is clear evidence in the Old Testament, and elsewhere in the New Testament, that the designation of someone as *christos* was to be linked to that person's possession of the Spirit.[7] The anointing of David by Samuel provides the model for this: "Then Samuel, with the horn of oil in hand, anointed him in the midst of his brothers; and from that day on, the Spirit of the Lord rushed upon David" (1 Sam 16:13).[8] This is also the case in Isaiah 61:1: "The Spirit of the Lord is upon me, because the Lord has anointed me."[9] This very passage is put in the mouth of Jesus in Luke 4:18ff to describe Jesus' messianic empowerment.[10]

(b) Anointing in the Gospel

In the gospel the claim is repeatedly put forth that Jesus is the Christ. Although the gospel repeatedly says also that Jesus will give believers the Spirit, nowhere is the believer actually called "christos." The absence of the explicit designation may be accounted for by the fact that, just as the gospel focuses on the identity of Jesus (as anointed), so 1 John focuses on the Christian and the prerogatives of the Christian (as anointed). Yet if Jesus was legitimately called Christos because of his anointing with the Spirit, then it could also be concluded that the believer could be so designated at least in a derivative sense.

(c) Anointing of Jesus and the Christian in 1 John

Just as Jesus was *christos,* so the believer is also. And in 1 John, even at a time when the term was in danger of misinterpretation by the opponents we see that the believer is said to have a *chrisma* (2: 20,27). The important element was obviously how this possession of the Spirit was to be interpreted and the precise nature and extent of the benefits it entailed.[11]

How then are the Christian and Jesus different? Jesus is anointed in a unique way. He is the unique Son of God; his words have a unique value as revelation.[12] However all the claims made for the believer in 1 John have a dual aspect ("both/and"). We are both sinless and sinful; we both need no teacher and we need Jesus' words; we both have life and yet that life is not perfect.

The description of Jesus has none of this "both/and." His possession of the "eschatological gifts" is perfect. This is traceable to his possession of the Spirit—a possession which is perfect and unique. As the gospel had indicated (Jn 3:34–35): "For the one whom God sent speaks the words of God, for he does not give the Spirit in a limited way. The Father loves the Son and has given everything over into his hands." This passage, which is frequently thought to be a secondary addition to the gospel,[13] spells out the relation of the Spirit to Jesus in explicit terms. In this passage, it is said clearly that Jesus is the one who has the Spirit without measure.[14]

Previously (at the time of the previous edition of the gospel) the issue had been whether Jesus possessed the Spirit and whether he would be the divine agent by which the eschatological Spirit would be poured out. This had been cast in such a way as to respond to a Jewish community which did not accept that the eschatological "moment" had arrived nor that Jesus was such a divine agent. At that time the issue of the exact relation between Jesus and the believer would not have been spelled out in all its detail. It was only later, when the gospel was read in different historical circumstances, that misinterpretation occurred and clarification became necessary.

2. "Jesus Is Not the Son of God"

The opponents in 1 John also deny that Jesus is the Son of God (2:22–23; 5:10–12). As was the case with regard to the prior claim, this denial was evidently intended to mean that the opponents deny that Jesus' sonship is in any way unique. If the Christian by the eschatological possession of the Spirit is truly a son/daughter of God, then how is Jesus unique?

The claim to divine "sonship" is built on three related aspects of their possession of the Spirit. First, the reception of the Spirit in both the Old Testament and the Johannine tradition is described in terms of a possession of a new (eternal, divine) form of life. Second, the entry into this life is described in terms of a begetting which then (third) makes the Christian a child (son/daughter) of God. All of these dimensions of Johannine thought are clearly echoed in Old Testament thought.

(a) The Spirit as the Principle of Divine Life, Begetting and "Sonship" in the Old Testament

Just as natural life is created through God's gift of a natural spirit, so divine (eternal) life comes about through the infusion of the Holy Spirit. In the Old Testament the character of the natural spirit as the principle of natural life is evident in several texts. For example in Genesis 2:7 we read:

> The Lord God formed man out of the clay of the ground
> and blew into his nostrils the breath [spirit] of life. (NAB)

But the natural spirit as the principle of natural life is even more clearly present in Ezekiel 37:4–10. There the focus of attention is on the way Yahweh will revivify Israel, but this is done using the image of Yahweh giving life to "dry bones" through the infusion of his (natural) spirit.

> Then he said to me: Prophesy over these bones, and say to them: Dry bones, hear the word of the Lord! Thus says the Lord God to these bones: See! I will bring spirit into you, that you may come to life. I will put sinews upon you, make flesh grow over you, cover you with skin, and put spirit in you so that you may come to life and know that I am the Lord. I prophesied as I had been told, and even as I was prophesying, I heard a noise; it was a rattling as the bones came together, bone joining bone. I saw the sinews and the flesh come upon them, and the skin cover them, but there was no spirit in them. Then he said to me: Prophesy to the spirit, prophesy, Son of man, and say to the spirit: Thus says the Lord God: From the four winds come, O spirit, and breathe into these slain that they may come to life. I

prophesied as he told me, and the spirit came into them;
they came alive and stood upright, a vast army. (NAB)

I have quoted this passage in its entirety because it shows so
clearly how the giving of a (natural) spirit was seen as the principle
of life. In an analogous way, the receiving of the Holy Spirit gives
divine life. That this is so is evident from the way divine sonship is
described in the Old Testament.

The various Old Testament sources of evidence for a human as
"son of God" have been the object of repeated study.[15] The most
likely source of the imagery in Jewish sources is the application of
the term "son" to the Israelite king (cf 2 Sam 7:14; Pss 2:7; 89:26–
27)—an application which was a source for the use of "*christos*" also
(Ps 2:2; 89:21,39). When the king was anointed, he received the Spirit
of Yahweh and became a "son of God." The day of his coronation
was described as the day the king was "begotten" by Yahweh.

The king is said to be anointed, to be a son of God, and to be
begotten by God. The king's anointing was the occasion of his reception of the Spirit (1 Sam 16:13). The reception of the Spirit was
the basis for his divine begetting and his sonship.[16] The three elements
are combined, for example, in Psalm 2:2, 7: "The kings of the earth
rise up, and the princes conspire together against the Lord and against
his anointed. . . . I will proclaim the decree of the Lord. The Lord
said to me, "You are my son; this day I have begotten you."

The evidence from Qumran clearly indicates that these scriptural
texts which were originally applied to the king were applied by the
Qumran community to their kingly messiah. In a fragment from
Cave 4, the 2 Samuel text is joined with Psalm 2 and interpreted as
applying to the one to come.[17]

Thus there can be no doubt that in the Old Testament it was
the Spirit of Yahweh which was the ultimate principle of divine life
and which, through divine begetting, was the means by which the
king was raised to the level of divine sonship.

(b) Divine Life, Begetting Through the Spirit, and "Sonship"
in the Johannine Gospel

In the Johannine tradition the "gift" of the Spirit as it was understood in the Old Testament was taken quite seriously and becomes

the principal attribute of the believer: the principle of life whereby the person is said to be "begotten" of God, and to be a "son of God."

It is true that the Johannine community had perhaps the highest christology of any early Christian group as Brown states.[18] The opponents do not quarrel with this high christology but simply argue that they too possess the essential attributes of such life, begetting and sonship. The opponents do not seek to deliberately devalue the status of Jesus; rather they elevate themselves by claiming similar prerogatives for themselves.

There is ample evidence within the Johannine tradition for the description of the believer as a "child" (son/daughter) of God. In both the gospel and the epistles, believers are repeatedly said to be "children" (sons/daughters) of God (Jn 1:12; 11:52; 1 Jn 3:1,2,10; 5:2[19]), or to be "born of God" (Jn 1:13; 3:3–8: 1 Jn 2:29; 3:9 (twice); 4:7; 5:1 [thrice], 4,18 [twice]) by means of their possession of the Spirit (Jn 3:5,6,8).[20]

The gospel clearly states that one could become a child of God (1:13) and describes how that would come about (most specifically 3:5–8). Likewise in 1 John there are repeated references to being a child (*teknon,* 1 Jn 3:1,2,10; 5:2, or *teknion,* 4:4). The importance of this designation for the Johannine community and the seriousness with which it was taken by the community can be seen from the fact that although elsewhere in the New Testament Christians are called "children," the image of "being born of God" is never applied to the Christian. Only in the Johannine tradition is such an explicit image used of the status of the believer.

The Christian, according to the gospel, seeks to have life (3:15,16,36; 5:29; 6:40,47,63,68; 8:12). Jesus has come to give eternal life (10:10,28; 17:2,3; 20:31). This eternal life is the "living water" which Jesus will give (4:14); and the living water is a symbol of the Spirit (7:38–39). It comes about through the reception of the Spirit which those who believe in Jesus will receive (7:39).[21]

Given the importance of the claim to being sons and daughters of God coupled with the fact that the Christian is said to have "eternal life" (the very life of God) *in the present,* there arises again the possibility of distorting this prerogative to the point that the essential difference between Jesus and the believer is at first blurred and eventually done away with. For the opponents, this means that there is no longer any need to speak of Jesus as "Son of God" in any unique sense since all Christians may claim this prerogative. Brown for example recognizes this possible ambiguity: "*Teknon* is the technical Johannine term covering divine sonship/daughterhood, since *huios,* 'son,' is reserved for Jesus in relationship to God. . . . John's language of begetting by God makes more realistic the imagery of 'children of God' than if he spoke of adoption; it also brings the status of the Christian children close to that of Jesus, God's Son."[22] This is the closeness that the opponents blur and eventually eliminate, just as they had blurred and eventually eliminated the distinction between Jesus as Christ and the Christian as "christ-ed."

(c) The Position of 1 John

If both groups claim to have eternal life, to be begotten of God and to be "sons" of God, then what is the difference between the two groups? In response to the opponents, the author of 1 John seeks to make two points. First, his opponents have a wrong understanding of sonship. Second, they fail to pass the "tests" of living out true sonship.

First, one must test the spirits (4:1–6); not all spirits are the Holy Spirit. Therefore not all life is eternal life nor is all begetting of the Holy Spirit. The opponents claim to be children of God but are really children of the devil (3:8–10). But the approach of the author of 1 John is perhaps clearest in his presentation of the correct understanding of sonship. The opponents fail to see that the sonship of Jesus was unique.

The claim to the unicity of Jesus' sonship is expressed by the term *monogenes.* This word, frequently translated "only begotten," is more properly understood as "mono" (one) "genes" (class, type).[23] This adjective is used of Jesus in 1 John 4:9, and appeared in sections of the gospel which are frequently thought to be secondary (1:14,18; 3:16–18).[24]

The second element of the proper understanding of sonship regards the sonship of the Christian. For the Christian, sonship is a process, not a once-and-for-all happening. Divine sonship for the Christian involves yet another "both/and" position. "We are *both* sons (daughters) of God now, *and* it has not yet been revealed what we will be" (3:2). This revelation will take place at his second coming (2:28). But it is not simply a matter of waiting; the believer must

work to make himself/herself holy just as Jesus is holy (3:3). Thus
divine sonship for the Christian involves stages, and these stages are
related to the believer's efforts to grow in holiness.[25] So the Christian's
sonship involves "both" a true present reality "and" a need to strive
to bring that sonship to perfection. Thus the claim of the adversaries
to be "sons" in a perfect sense now is incorrect because they fail to
recognize the inchoative dimension of their sonship and so consider
themselves perfect and unable to sin in any sense (1:8,10).

The author devotes considerable space to the discussion of the
opponents' claim to sonship. The opponents are not true sons of God
but are sons of the devil (3:6–10). The one who commits sin (in a
sense different from that acknowledged by the author[26]) acts out of
lawlessness, because sin is lawlessness. The one who commits sin is
"of the devil" (born of the devil; a son of the devil) because the devil
was a sinner from the beginning (3:8). The one born of God does
not commit sin because the "seed" of God remains in him, and
because he is born of God (3:9).

Finally, as he is accustomed to do, the author of 1 John addresses
the ways one can *test* the claim to being begotten of God. In a general
sense one's being begotten from God is identified first of all by whether
one "does justice" (2:29) and "does not sin" (3:6,9; 5:18). But more
specifically the author gives two concrete "tests" by which it can be
determined whether one is a son of God or of the devil. First, does
the person love the brothers? (4:7; "Let us love one another, because
love is of God and everyone who loves is born of God"; cf also 3:
11). The author elaborates this in 3:11–18 where he compares the
actions of Cain and Abel. Cain killed his brother because his own
works were evil while those of Abel were just. But the believer has
heard from the beginning that he is to love the brothers and it is a
way by which the believer can know that he has gone from death to
life. Jesus' death is a model of this love, and it should exhibit itself
in not shutting oneself off from brothers in need.

The second test of one's begetting from God is one's confession
of faith. This is elaborated in 1 John 5:1–5. The two main affirmations
of the Johannine community frame the passage in a kind of inclusion.
The first affirmation is that Jesus is the Christ. This is said clearly in
5:1: "Everyone who believes that Jesus is the Christ has been born
of God . . ." Correct faith becomes the determinant of whether one

is born of God. In 5:4–5, after an elaborate "chaining" argument which interweaves the requirements of faith with those of love, the author turns to the second major faith affirmation: ". . . everyone born of God conquers the world. And this is the victory which has conquered the world, our faith. Who is the one who conquers the world if not the one who believes that Jesus is the Son of God?" Thus both correct action (love) and correct belief are necessary for one to be born of (and so be a "son" ["daughter"] of) God.

3. "Jesus Christ Come in the Flesh"

Not only do the opponents deny that Jesus is the (unique) Christ and (unique) Son of God, but they deny that he is come "in the flesh" (1 Jn 4:2; 2 Jn 7). This phrase is the author's way of expressing the opponents' conviction that "fleshly" actions are of no value in achieving salvation.[27] While the issue here is in some ways christological, it is more specifically soteriological, addressing the question of how we are saved. Basing themselves once again on a plausible reading of the Old Testament and the gospel, the opponents argue that their sins were not forgiven by the death of Jesus but by their reception of the Holy Spirit.

(a) The Spirit and the Forgiveness of Sin in Jewish Religious Thought

In the Old Testament the forgiveness of sins is reserved to Yahweh and was to be characteristic of the coming age. In Jeremiah 31: 31–34, the vision of the new covenant, in addition to other elements which we have seen paralleled in the disputed claims of the Johannine community (direct knowledge of God, no need for teachers), there is the conviction that Yahweh will forgive their sins: "All, from the least to greatest, shall know me, says the Lord, for I will forgive their evildoing and remember their sin no more." (NAB) In Isaiah also the pouring out of the Spirit (Is 32:15: "The Spirit from on high is poured out on us") brings about this forgiveness (33:24: "the people . . . will be forgiven their guilt").

There is also considerable evidence in the pseudepigrapha. Jub 1:23 provides evidence for the direct action of God through the Holy Spirit, bringing about forgiveness of sins, and a kind of "perfectionism." In addition the passage speaks of the believer as a "child of God" in those days:

> . . . and I shall create for them a holy spirit, and I shall purify them so that they will not turn away from following me from that day and forever. And their souls will cleave to me and to all my commandments. And they will do my commandments. And I shall be a father to them, and they will be sons to me. And they will all be called sons of the living God. (OTP trans.)

Also TBenj 8:2–3:

> He has no pollution in his heart because upon him is resting the spirit of God. For just as the sun is unpolluted, though it touches dung and slime, but dries up both and drives off the bad odor, so also the pure mind, though involved with the corruptions of earth, edifies instead and is not itself corrupted. (OTP trans.)

In the pseudepigraphical 4 Ez 6:26 we find still another description of God's action through his spirit: ". . . and the heart of the earth's inhabitants shall be changed and converted to a different spirit. For evil shall be blotted out, and deceit shall be quenched . . ." (OTP trans.)

Finally at Qumran the role of the Spirit in forgiveness of sins is equally clear. 1QS 3:6–9 (DSSE, 75) states:

> For it is through the spirit of true counsel concerning the ways of man that all his sins shall be expiated that he may contemplate the light of life. He shall be cleansed from all his sins by the spirit of holiness uniting him to His truth, and his iniquity shall be expiated by the spirit of uprightness and humility.[28]

(b) Basis of the Opponents' View in the Johannine Gospel

Not only is the opponents' view of soteriology in agreement with canonical and pseudepigraphical thought, but there are several dimensions of the gospel of John which could be said to favor such a view.[29]

(i) The Spirit and Forgiveness of Sin in the Gospel

Within the gospel of John, the forgiveness of "sins" (pl.) is directly related to the possession of the Spirit in only one text: 20:22–23. But that passage is one of particular importance since it is the only one to relate the actual giving of the Spirit in the gospel. There the giving of the Spirit is connected with the power to forgive sins.[30] Even though the text speaks of human agency (i.e. the disciples) in the process of forgiving sin, there can be no doubt that the primary focus is on the Spirit as the power of forgiveness. However beyond this there are several other elements of the gospel that could be seen to minimize the value of the death of Jesus.

(ii) The Relativizing of the External and Physical in the Gospel

Repeatedly in the gospel, there is a relativizing of what might be called the external, physical, fleshly dimension of religion. This would set the context for minimizing the value of the external, physical death of Jesus.

Relativizing of the external is evident, for example, in the words of Jesus to the Samaritan woman about worship (Jn 4:20–24). In response to the woman's question about the correct place of worship, Jesus first tells the woman that Jews worship what they know, while the Samaritans worship what they do not know. But then he goes on to say that the time is coming and is here now when true worshipers will worship the Father in spirit and in truth. This statement clearly relativizes the role of worship as it is conducted in the temple. And certainly a plausible interpretation would be that such "physical" worship (involved with external actions) is useless and unnecessary. True religious action takes place in the realm of the Spirit. Thus for those who take this literally there would be little place for a conception of the forgiveness of sin which was accomplished to the external, physical, death of Jesus as a vicarious sacrifice (not unlike what had been offered in the very temple which is so relativized in 4:21–24).

Such ambivalent assessment of the external is also evident from the development of the discourse on the bread of life. In the first part of the discourse (Jn 6:30–50), the emphasis is on the reception of Jesus as the bread from heaven and the only appropriate response is faith; however, in the second part, which shows definite signs of being a later addition,[31] the reception of the body and blood of Jesus is treated as just such an external, physical act.

This is confirmed by the words of Jesus: "That which is born of the flesh is flesh; that which is born of the Spirit is Spirit (3:5); "The Spirit is that which gives life; the flesh is of no avail" (6:63).

Not only do the words of Jesus to others seem to play down the role of the physical and material, but Jesus himself constantly exemplifies in his own life this detachment from and superiority to the material world. His foreknowledge constantly transcends the normal physical limitations of time and space (2:24; 6:6,64,70–71; 16:30; 13: 1,3). He has no need of human witness to himself (5:33–34) or to events (2:25). He controls his own fate so surely that his arrest is only at his own hour (7:8,30; 8:20,59; 9:4–5; 10:39; 11:9; 12:23,27–28), that even at the time of the arrest it is clear that he allows their action rather than being dominated by it (12:23; 18:6); Pilate has no power over him except that given him by the Father (19:11); he even dies only when he decides to (19:30).

Clearly the role of the external and the physical was an issue for the community and it undoubtedly affected the view one had of the importance of the fleshly, physical death of Jesus.

(iii) Death as Departure and Glorification

Related to the gospel's depreciation of the physical and external is the portrayal of the death of Jesus as a departure to and glorification with the Father rather than as a physical, atoning, sacrifice. It is commonly pointed out that the dominant view of the ministry of Jesus is that of a parabola or a pendulum arc. That is, the ministry begins with the descent of the Son into the world and it ends with his ascent back to the Father. It is precisely in these terms that the ministry is repeatedly described. The clearest statement is that of 16:28: "I have come forth from the Father and have come into the world; now I leave the world and return to the Father."

This element of the gospel's thought has been described in a number of recent studies. For example, in his commentary on the gospel Brown speaks of a great pendulum swing of the descent and ascent of Jesus.[32] In his discussion of the community's history, he suggests two reasons for thinking that the opponents lessen the salvific import of the public ministry. First, Brown suggests, "in Johannine theology the Word brought eternal life down from God to men and women on earth, but the secessionists may have thought that this eternal life was made available simply through the presence of the Word in the world and not through dependence on what the Word did while present."[33] Second, in the passion there is no victimizing of Jesus; he is lifted up in triumph. In the portrayal of Jesus' death "the notion of sacrifice has yielded to that of revelation."[34] Here Brown is dependent upon the work of T. Forestell who proposes that "The cross of Christ in Jn is evaluated precisely in terms of revelation in harmony with the theology of the entire Gospel, rather than in terms of vicarious and expiatory sacrifice for sin."[35]

More recently, G. Nicolson has indicated his view of this issue even in the title of his *Death as Departure,* a study of the "lifting up" sayings in the gospel.[36] According to Nicolson, "the interpretation of the death of Jesus which he [the evangelist] achieves is rather subtle: Jesus' death is really his return to the Father; Jesus came to return rather than to die; the focus of attention lies just beyond the cross in the moment of return—the 'hour' of the glorification of Jesus."[37]

This view of the death as departure is also completely consistent with the gospel's emphasis on realized eschatology. In the interpretation of the opponents, the life given by the Spirit becomes the (exclusive) means of eternal life for the Christian. After death, the Christian departs from this world and enters immortality in the realm of the Spirit with God who is Spirit.

(iv) Expiatory Death in the Gospel?

In spite of the dominance of the portrayal of the death of Jesus as departure and glorification, there are passages where there is evidence of the death of Jesus as expiatory, but these are minimal.[38] They would include the famous 1:29, where Jesus is identified as "the Lamb of God who takes away the sin of the world." 3:15 also carries evidence of atonement theology: ". . . it is necessary for the Son of Man to be lifted up so that everyone who believes in him may have eternal life." Although belief is important, so is the death of Jesus. There is also evidence of atonement theology in 6:51b ("And the bread which I will give is my flesh for the life of the world"); 10: 17 (". . . and I lay down my life for my sheep"); 11:52 (". . . but because he was high priest that year, he prophesied that Jesus was to die for the nation . . ."); and 15:13 ("Greater love than this no one has, that someone lay down his life for his friends"). Once again the interpreter is faced with the question of how the opponents would have interpreted these: Were they simply neglected or minimized or were they not part of the original gospel? This is not the place for an examination of the texts, but it is noteworthy that two of the texts (10:17; 15:13) occur within commandment passages, passages whose secondary character we have noticed above.[39]

(c) Position of 1 John on Forgiveness of Sins

If the opponents see sins as forgiven through the gift of the Spirit, how does the author understand forgiveness of sins? He argues repeatedly that sin is forgiven through the expiatory sacrifice of the death of Jesus. That this is the position of the author is clear. But in addition there are hints that he affirms that the Spirit is also a principle of forgiveness. It may be that the author simply intends that these two stand in reciprocal relationship to one another. When he speaks of the forgiveness of sin, he emphasizes the death of Jesus; when he speaks of the life which follows that forgiveness of sin, he speaks of the Spirit. The Spirit was the principle of life but one could not have the Spirit without possessing the Son (1 Jn 5:11,13). Thus once again it seems that the author may be presenting another of his "both/and" interpretations of the tradition.

The author's opinion of the means by which the believer is freed from sin is quite clear: our sins are taken away by the death of Jesus. Thus for the author the role of Jesus is essential. In 1:7 the author states: ". . . the blood of Jesus his Son cleanses us from all sin." In 2:2, Jesus is called an expiation for sin.[40] This is also expressed in 2:12 ("Your sins are taken away through his name") and in 3:5 ("That one [Jesus] revealed himself to take away sins"). In 3:16 we read: "This is how we know his love for us, that he laid down his life for us." 4:10 says: "God loved us and sent his Son as an expiation for our sins." This sacrificial shedding of blood is finally emphasized in 5:6 where Jesus is said to have come "not in water only but in water and blood" (5:6).

These passages are sufficient to indicate the difference between the view of the author and that of his opponents. He proposes that the death of Jesus was an atonement for sin. However in the author's interpretation of the forgiveness of sins, there is no *explicit* evidence of the "both/and" he takes elsewhere. Here we are in the same situation as we found ourselves when we attempted to discover how one was to become a child/son of God. That is, although there is explicit evidence about the origin of sonship in the gospel, there are no explicit references in the epistle. So it is with the question of forgiveness of sin: although there are statements in the gospel that would support a "both/and" interpretation (both through the atonement and through the gift of the Spirit), there are no explicit statements that would support this in the first epistle.

But it is likely that in fact there is implicit within the author's presentation a belief that the Spirit did have a role in forgiveness. I am inclined to this position because of the position of the gospel. As John 20:22 shows, the power of the Spirit was given for the forgiveness of sins. There is no evidence that the author of 1 John ever denies the traditions found in the gospel although he frequently modifies them. If the forgiveness of sin is at least part of the function of the Spirit (as John 20:22 indicates), the association of the giving of the Spirit with the sacrificial death of Jesus, expressed in 19:39 by the reference to water and blood, would seem to indicate that the tradition held that both played a role in the forgiveness of sin.[41] At the very least John 19:39 indicates that the death of Jesus was responsible for both the giving of the Spirit and the atonement for sin. Whether that giving of the Spirit entailed forgiveness of sins could be assumed, but on the basis of 20:22, rather than on the basis of 19:39. Thus, it is at least possible that in fact the author of 1 John holds to a "both/and" here too. Thus he would be arguing that it is not a matter of a one-sided understanding of the forgiveness of sin ("Spirit only") but rather the "both/and": both through the Spirit and through the atoning death of Jesus.

4. Conclusions Regarding Christology and Anthropology

We have seen in what precedes a new view of the opponents' understanding of the role of Jesus. I have tried to show how each of the elements of the opponents' position was a plausible reading of the Old Testament evidence as well as a plausible interpretation of the gospel. Finally I have tried in each case to show how the position is mirrored in 1 John and refuted by its author.

In addition to explaining the differing claims made for Jesus, this explanation of the opponents' position also provides a more satisfactory explanation of several other facets of 1 John.

(a) "Doing Away with Jesus"

The author describes the opponents' action in 4:3 as "doing away with" (*lyein*) Jesus.[42] We can get a sense of the meaning the author attributes to this word from its use in 3:8. There *lyein* is the verb the author uses to describe the effect of the ministry of Jesus on the works of the devil: "It was to do away with the works of the devil that the Son of God was revealed" (*eis touto ephanerōthē ho huios tou theou, hina lysē ta erga tou diabolou*). The author says that the opponents do to Jesus what Jesus did to the works of the devil! The absoluteness of the term and the way it is used in 3:8 make it difficult to correlate this with a theory of "relativizing" or "minimalizing" the role of Jesus. Rather it seems that the opponents are totally doing away with Jesus by denying any permanent, effective role in salvation. If the Spirit is the effective agent of all of the eschatological blessings, then Jesus truly is "done away with." If it is the opponents' recourse to the Spirit which leads them to deny an effective role for Jesus, the author's words are intelligible on a literal level (4:3): "Every spirit which does away with/destroys Jesus is not of God."

I have shown an alternative to this position which seems to do more justice to the statements of 1 John. The opponents have been believers in Jesus but have moved beyond (2 Jn 9).

(b) The Similarity of the Claims Made by the Two Groups

The second confirmation that this position is correct is the fact that the central claims for the Johannine Christian are so similar to those made for Jesus himself. Both groups claim to be born of God and to have an anointing, and these are two of the essential claims made by the tradition about Jesus (cf Jn 20:30–31).

Twice in the first epistle, the author explicitly and at length contrasts claims of the two groups: the claims to sonship (3:1–10) and the claims to possession of a (the) Spirit (4:1–6). The fact that these two elements are chosen to be contrasted indicates the importance of the two claims for the community. And although the comparisons distinguish possession of the Spirit (anointing) and sonship on the level of the believer, this undoubtedly was intended to echo the dispute about the anointing (by the Spirit) and the sonship of Jesus.

All of these claims are based on one's possession of the Spirit.

In every case the author does not deny the possibility of the claim but the way it is to be realized for Jesus and for the believer. He counters the one-sided interpretation of the adversaries with his moderate "both/and" position and he provides an external test.

(c) How Could a Christian Group Deny Jesus?

Those who argue other interpretations of the opponents find it difficult at times to account for the fact that such a group could have ever been Christian. However the founding of the opponents' claims on the possession of the Spirit accounts well for the fact that a person who has acknowledged that the eschatological outpouring of the Spirit has taken place through the ministry of Jesus could later on claim that Jesus himself, whatever his actual identity, was no longer important. This is of course what the opponents of 1 John do. If their position is "new," it is because the Spirit has told them something new.

(d) The "Antichrist"

Also it will be recalled that the opponents are described by the author as "antichrists." This term which has become familiar in modern religious language is used for the first time in the New Testament here. Scholars have argued that the author of 1 John probably coined the term. Such a combination of *anti* plus the key word would be parallel to many similar uses elsewhere in contemporary Greek literature to designate an opponent of the concept in question.[43] Here the antichrist would be the person who is opposed to the messiahship of Jesus. But it is important that it is particularly his "Christ-ness" that is selected to characterize what they oppose.[44]

(e) The Title Paraclete for Both Jesus and the Spirit

Another indication that the struggle concerns the role of Jesus vis-à-vis the role of the Spirit is the use of the title of Paraclete for both Jesus and the Spirit. This seems to be a deliberate, although subtle, attempt to clarify the role of Jesus in relation to that of the Spirit. We see that Jesus in 1 John 2:1 is called the Paraclete because he is a propitiation for our sins. Yet we know that the opponents sought to do away with the role of Jesus and his role as propitiation for sins is under attack since they deny that he has "come in the flesh."[45] If the opponents seek to expand the role of the Spirit to do away with the role of Jesus, the one responsible for the Paraclete passages in the gospel (not, I would claim, the author of 1 John, but one from his theological persuasion and historical circumstances) refers to the Paraclete and "another" to remind the reader that the Spirit is not the first Paraclete—that there was another, Jesus, who came first, and that the forgiveness of sins (which the author of 1 John links with the Paraclete) is not the sole prerogative[46] of the Spirit but is brought about through the atoning death of Jesus also.

(f) The Relative Absence of "Revelation," "Soteriology," and Ethics in the Gospel

In addition, this view accounts for the absence of several topics from the gospel which are so notable: Bultmann spoke of a revealer without a revelation. This is understandable if in some sense the revelation is given in and by the Spirit. Weiss speaks of a "soteriological vacuum" in the gospel. This is paralleled by the common observation that the dominant view of the death of Jesus in the gospel is as a departure to the Father. This is explained if the cleansing from sin is accomplished by the Spirit. Brown notices the lack of ethical emphasis and says that "the Jesus of John gives little specific ethical teaching. . . ."[47] It is striking that all of these major characteristics are related to the action of the Spirit!

(g) How the Opponents "Go Beyond" and Neglect "What Was from the Beginning"

Finally, such an explanation accounts well for the description of the opponents as "going beyond" and not "remaining in the teaching of the Christ" (2 Jn 9). Both of these phrases seem to be literal descriptions of the author's view of the opponents' error.[48] Their inspiration by the Spirit leads the opponents to new positions not consistent with the tradition. They do not "remain in the teaching of the Christ" but ignore what they have heard from the beginning (1 Jn 1:1; 2:24; 3:11; 2 Jn 5,6).

At the beginning of this chapter, we saw a listing of statements from 1 John showing the competing claims of the two groups and their different positions regarding belief. It was clear that the role of Jesus had been called into question, but there remained the very important question of how that could have taken place in such a way as to make sense of all the statements of the adversaries and also account for the fact that both believe the eschaton had occurred and that both had believed in Jesus. The view of the Spirit presented here had provided a key to a realistic explanation of all these facets of the opponents' understanding of Jesus. We will now turn to an examination of the third complex of issues about which the two Johannine groups disagreed: ethics.

C. THE OPPONENTS' VIEW OF ETHICS

The opponents' interpretation of the role of the Spirit also had implications for the understanding of the ethical life in its various dimensions. First, the opponents believed that their possession of the Spirit (and hence divine life) was complete and perfect in the present and that therefore they could no longer sin. Because of this, the opponents believed they had no need of external ethical directives (such as the commandment to brotherly love); they were spontaneously guided by the internal direction of the Spirit. This internal direction of the Spirit both taught them how to act and also was itself the force within freeing them from the impulses which would lead to sin.

Second, the opponents believed that the forgiveness of sins had come about only through their reception of the Spirit and that the death of Jesus was not salvifically important. Third, because their possession of the Spirit gave them eternal life in the present and because their possession of life was complete and perfect, there was no "need" of a future judgment nor a role for a physical resurrection from the dead. Their death would be like Jesus': a return to the Father. Judgment would be only for those who did not believe.

As was the case in the previous sections, we will show how these positions of the opponents represent a legitimate interpretation of Jewish eschatological hopes, of one strain of the Johannine tradition, and how they are echoed within 1 John.

1. SINLESSNESS: THE OPPONENTS'
AND THE AUTHOR'S VIEWS

There are two related issues involved in the discussion of sinlessness (or as it is sometimes called, "perfectionism"): the meaning of sinlessness and how such sinlessness has come about. We have already discussed how sin was taken away in the previous section. Here we will concentrate on the opponents' view of sinlessness/perfection.

The author of 1 John reports that the opponents make claims to sinlessness: "We have no sin" (1:8) and again "We have not sinned" (1:10).[49] However the author of 1 John disagrees and says that in fact his opponents have sinned. Those who claim they have not sinned deceive themselves and the truth is not in them (1:8). Those who make the second claim make Jesus, "who is trustworthy and just so that he might do away with sins, a liar; and his word is not in them" (1:10).

Yet later the author himself states that the believer is free from sin and does not commit sin: 3:6 ("Everyone abiding in him does not sin"); 3:9 ("Everyone born of God does not commit sin, because the seed of God abides in him. And he is not able to sin because he has been born of God"); 5:18 ("We know that everyone born of God does not sin"). From these texts then we see that the issue is not simply that one group claims perfection; both do. Rather the issue is how that perfection is to be understood.

From the above texts, we see that the claim to sinlessness is founded on two convictions, both closely related. The first is the conviction that because the Christian was a child ("son") born of God, he/she was free from sin. This is true for the author as can be seen from 3:6,9; 5:18 (all cited in the preceding paragraph). It is almost certainly true for the opponents also.

The second basis for sinlessness is the Christian's possession of the Spirit. It was the Christian's birth from the Spirit which in fact made him/her a child of God. It was remarked above in the discussion of the sonship of Jesus that it was strange that nowhere in the first epistle is the *means* of becoming a son discussed. However in the gospel the means of this sonship is clear; it comes from the Christian's birth from God by means of the Spirit (Jn 1:13; 3:5–8). Therefore if the Spirit is at the basis of sonship, then (according to 1 Jn 3:9; 5:18 quoted above), it is the Spirit which is also at the basis of sinlessness. Although, as I said, this is nowhere stated explicitly within the first epistle, we do find something quite close in 1 John 3:9 where it is said: "The one who is born of God does not commit sin because the seed of God remains in him." This notion of the "seed of God," although used only once in 1 John, is generally considered to refer to the principle of divine life, i.e. the Spirit.[50] If this is true for the author of 1 John, it is also true for the opponents who focus on the role of the Spirit even more than the author. Both groups claim a state of sinlessness through the Spirit, but each understands it differently.

In what follows we will see that the opponents understand perfection as total and complete in the present moment—an absolute possession of sinlessness. Consequently they have no need of ethical directives nor will there be a need for judgment. Love of the brethren means nothing to them. Because they thus possess divine, eternal life within, their conduct is spontaneously correct. However, the author of 1 John disagrees and says that although Christians do have a kind of perfectionism, it is present only inchoatively.

(a) Background in Jewish Thought for Sinlessness in the Eschatological Age

We have seen above that in the Old Testament it was Yahweh who forgave sins, and in the last times (Jer 31:31–34). In Isaiah 32: 15,23, this forgiveness of sin is linked to the final outpouring of the Spirit.

But the passage which provides one of the clearest examples not only of forgiveness of sins through the Spirit but of the continuing state of perfection that would follow is found in Jub 1:23:

> ... and I shall create for them a holy spirit, and I shall purify them so that they will not turn away from following me from that day and forever. And their souls will cleave to me and to all my commandments. And they will do my commandments. And I shall be a father to them, and they will be sons to me. And they will all be called sons of the living God. (OTP trans.)[51]

From a review of these passages, it should be clear that the claim to sinlessness as a result of the coming of the eschatological age has a definite precedent in the Jewish religious writings both canonical and non-canonical.[52] Consequently it should not be assumed that the opponents who held this view had constructed something radically new. It seems rather they were basing their position on what could be seen as one among various strands of Jewish eschatological hopes.

*(b) The Opponents' View of Sinlessness, and Its Basis
in the Johannine Gospel*

In the gospel of John, there is also considerable material which could be construed as suggesting that the Christian could expect a state of sinlessness as a result of the power of the Spirit and belief in Jesus.[53]

(i) Sonship as the Basis of Sinlessness

We have seen above that divine sonship was a central concept for the Johannine community—as it applied both to Jesus and to the Christian. Although the conception of divine sonship is present elsewhere in the New Testament it is nowhere else so important. Yet once one takes seriously that one is made a child of God through the Holy Spirit, then the risk arises that the Christian will make, without the proper distinction, the same type of claims as had been previously made for Jesus who was also "Son" of God.

One of the claims made for Jesus was sinlessness. As Brown points out, the opponents could argue that they possess the same qualities as Jesus, who is sinless and who said in the gospel, "Can any of you convict me of sin?" (8:46).[54] In addition, the Johannine Christians were taught that they had received the Spirit which gives a power over sin (20:22–23). Therefore it would be plausible to see in such possession of the Spirit a basis for "perfection."

(ii) The Gospel's Conception of Sin as Unbelief

Secondly, within the gospel the dominant conception of sin is of sin as failure to believe in Jesus.[55] It has been suggested that the opponents thought of sin only in the terms that were dominant in the gospel: namely as unbelief.[56] If that is so, the opponents could perhaps be said to be sinless since they believe in Jesus.[57] However the content of the opponents' belief would be different from that of the author of 1 John. For the opponents, Jesus was the agent of the Spirit's outpouring. Belief "in the name of Jesus" would have meant that the Christian believed first in the Father and in his promise (in the scriptures) of the outpouring of the Spirit. Second, they believed "in Jesus' name" that Jesus' announcement of the imminent outpouring was correct and that it would take place soon after his return to the Father. For the author of 1 John it would have meant that and more, encompassing as we have seen a view of Jesus as the unique

Son of God who possessed the Spirit perfectly and without measure, and who had saved us from our sins.

(iii) The Lack of Ethical Instruction in the Gospel

A third element in the gospel tradition that would favor the opponents' understanding of sinlessness is the fact that there is so little specific ethical instruction within the gospel.

There are general references to the deeds of some being evil, and of these people avoiding the light lest their works be exposed (Jn 3: 19–20), but even here the references are so general as to be of little use in ethical instruction, and it may even be that the usage of "works" here seems to reflect the apocalyptic framework of work in which it refers primarily to doing the will of someone, and so to the larger issue of one's general allegiance rather than to specific deeds. Finally this passage is commonly said to be an editorial addition to the gospel from the final editor.

The frequently quoted passage relating "faith to works" (6:28–29) does not refer to ethical behavior as such but to the general orientation spoken of in the previous paragraph.[58] The words of Jesus in 7:7 that he witnesses to the world that its deeds are evil also seems to come from this background and to reflect a concern for ethics only generally, as do the references in 8:38–47, discussed above in chapter two.[59]

The only passages, it would seem, which deal directly with specific ethical issues are those which treat of the love command. Here we are in touch with definite moral directives although even these are quite general. And as we have seen in chapter four there is considerable evidence that these passages dealing with the love command also come from the final edition of the gospel.

Even the phrase "to do the truth," which in the Old Testament and at Qumran means to observe the prescriptions of the law, means in the gospel of John to remain faithful to the truth of Jesus.[60]

In addition, when compared with the synoptics, the gospel of John has none of the ethical teaching associated with, for example, the sermon on the mount in Matthew.[61]

This unique orientation of the Johannine gospel could easily have given rise to the conviction that ethical conduct is not important, especially if the texts of the love command were not yet part of the gospel.

(c) Position of 1 John Regarding Sinlessness

To counter the position of his opponents, the author of 1 John presents two types of "both/and" arguments. First, he argues that the Christian is "both" perfect "and" sinful. Although "perfect" through his possession of the divine life through the Spirit, the Christian does not possess this perfection in an absolute sense. Rather perfection is present inchoatively. That is, the Christian has sinned in the past and may well sin again. The believer is involved in a process that involves a gradual growth and that will culminate at the time of the parousia of Jesus.

The second type of argument presented by the author of 1 John is that correct ethical conduct involves "both" belief (in the sense of *correct* belief) "and" love for the brethren. All of these elements were of significance in refuting the position of the opponents.

(i) The Christian as Both Sinless and Sinful

According to the author, the Christian has sinned in the past and he may well sin in the future. This is evident from a number of his statements: 1:7 (where there is mention of the blood of Jesus cleansing us from sin); 1:8 (where the author says that if we say we do not have sin, we deceive ourselves); 1:9 (where the believer is exhorted to confess his sins and where he is promised that the sins will be taken away); 1:10 (where it is said that if we say we have not sinned, we make Jesus a liar).

He also argues that true Christians may sin again but that their sins will be forgiven through Jesus: 1:9 (discussed above); 2:1 (where the reader is exhorted not to sin but where the possibility of the Christian sinning is discussed); 5:16–17 (where it is said that the one who commits a sin which is not deadly should be prayed for and life will be given to him).

But in spite of this, the believer is sinless just as Jesus was: "Everyone who does justice is born of him" (2:29); "Everyone who abides in him does not sin" (3:6); "The one acting justly is just, as he [Jesus] is just" (3:7); "Everyone born of God does not commit sin . . ." (3:9); "We know that everyone born of God does not sin" (5:18).

How then is the position of the author to be distinguished from that of his opponents? The key to understanding the author's claim to sinlessness (which is in imitation of Jesus) lies in a proper understanding of the believer's sonship vis-à-vis that of Jesus. The sinlessness of the believer is a continuing process: one becomes gradually less sinful. In 3:2 the author distinguishes our state now as children of God from the future state which has not yet been revealed. And in 3:3 the author says that everyone who has this hope sanctifies himself/ herself toward that future day.[62] Thus the sanctifying is a process which requires effort and time. This sanctifying of oneself is a growth in sinlessness. The believer has been given the ability to become sinless through the "seed of God" which remains in him (3:9).[63] But the process remains something yet to be achieved in its fullness.

(ii) Ethical Conduct as Involving Correct Belief and Love of the "Brothers"

The second element of the author's argument is that ethical conduct is necessary and that this involves "both" correct belief "and" love of the brethren. Sin in the gospel was conceived of almost entirely as unbelief. When we turn to the first epistle, however, it is clear that it is a matter not just of belief (versus unbelief) but of *correct* belief (as well as of proper ethical conduct). The focus on *correct* (versus incorrect) belief in the first epistle is evident in a number of ways. First there is the emphasis on what was "from the beginning" (1:1; 2:24) and on what was heard from Jesus himself (1:5) in comparison with the position of the adversaries which "goes beyond," which does not remain "in the teaching of the Christ" (2 Jn 9). The Christian is to keep the word of Jesus (2:4–7; 3:23) (and not to go beyond it).

Second, the focus on correct belief is evident in the thoroughgoing analysis of the incorrect claims of the opponents. They claim to be believers but are in error. The believer "knows the truth" while the opponents are deceivers (2:21–22,27; 3:19). Third, as we have seen repeatedly, the author exhorts his followers to "test the spirits" (4:1–6). Not every spirit is necessarily of God. Fourth, belief is consistently associated with specific statements regarding Jesus—e.g. that he is Son of God (cf 2:22–23; 3:23; 4:15; 5:5,10,13), that he is the Christ (5:1; cf 2:22), that he has come in the flesh (4:2). Thus there can be no doubt that the emphasis on correct belief is fundamental to the epistle. This is the first Johannine commandment.

The second element of the author's argument for correct ethics is his emphasis on the necessity of correct conduct. This takes the form of general injunctions to "do righteousness" (e.g. 2:29; 3:7,10) and to "make oneself holy" (3:3), but the concern for correct conduct focuses on the fulfillment of the love command. Throughout, the author describes as a commandment which they have received from God (3:23; 4:21) the injunction to love one another (3:11,23; 4:7,12; cf 4:20), to love the brothers (2:9–11; 3:14), not to shut themselves off from the one who is in need (3:17), and to express this not just in word but in deed (3:18). And the need to make oneself holy is to find its meaning in the day of judgment when such conduct will be evaluated (2:28; 4:17; cf 2:17). This is the second of the Johannine commandments.

Thus also the author affirms the radical sinlessness of the Christian; it is clear that there is still a path of holiness to be achieved, and the true Christian is to distinguish himself from the opponents by his correct belief and his proper conduct before God.

2. Life After Death, Resurrection, and Judgment

We now come to the final complex of issues on which the author of 1 John and his opponents differed. These issues deal with how the two groups understand the implications of their possession of the eschatological fullness of the Spirit for existence after death.

The opponents had taken the claim to sinlessness in an absolute sense while the author of 1 John had argued that, although the Christian was "inchoatively" sinless, sin was still a possibility for the Christian. The understanding of the Christian's possession of eternal life is closely related to one's understanding of sinlessness since sinfulness and eternal life are as it were reverse sides of the same eschatological possession of the Spirit.[64]

Although the author of 1 John never explicitly states the position of the opponents on these matters, it is clear that there were differences. From the way in which he states his own position and from the way eschatology is treated in the gospel and in 1 John, it is possible to "fill in the gaps" and to estimate the opponents' interpretation of the tradition.[65]

It is most likely the opponents argued that, because the Christian has eternal life in its fullness now, the Christian, after his/her death, will simply continue in the state of eternal life beyond death and in a spiritual state move on to existence with the Father in heaven.[66]

Because the Christian is sinless and in absolute possession of eternal life, and because the material aspects of existence are not critical, a bodily resurrection or a future judgment would be meaningless.

The author on the other hand is consistent with his understanding of sinlessness and argues that, while the Christian truly and actually has eternal life in the present, the Christian does not yet have it in its fullness, and the fullness of life will not be finally achieved until the second coming of Jesus. At that time the Christian will be bodily resurrected and all people will undergo a final judgment. The ones who have struggled to make themselves holy will gain eternal life fully and their bodies will be resurrected from the grave to be with God in heaven.

As we shall see, both of these views find representatives within the canonical and non-canonical Jewish religious literature of the time as well as within the Johannine tradition. Finally we will see the way that the author of 1 John refutes the position of his opponents.

(a) Future Life, Resurrection and Final Judgment in Jewish Writings

A complete discussion of these topics is of course beyond the possibilities of the present occasion.[67] Here our purpose is to ask the question whether there is precedent for the views of the opponents (and for those of the author of 1 John) and to what extent these views are related to the eschatological outpouring of the Holy Spirit. I will attempt only to present a few representative samples.

(i) Life Beyond Death

Our quest for parallels yields different results than in the previous cases. First we find that the beliefs discussed here came to expression rather late within the period of the canonical scriptures. Most of the later developments usually are traced by scholars to the influence of Trito-Isaiah.[68] Because of this relatively late awareness concerning the life after death, we are forced to be more dependent upon the non-canonical writings than previously.

Second, we find that during this period there was great fluidity in the expression of the complex of ideas involving eternal life–judgment–resurrection. Frequently ideas that are found in one complex are absent in another formulation. As a result it is not possible to discover exact parallels with all of the conceptions grouped together. Yet there can be no doubt that all of the ideas represented in the Johannine eschatology find parallels during the period.

In our previous discussion, we have seen numerous references to the Old Testament belief that the Holy Spirit would be the principle of life in the new age, making persons live with the life of God and thus become children of God. Since these persons believed they possessed life in its fullness now, the future dimension would not add anything that was not already present.

(ii) Life Beyond Death Without Resurrection

I wish to call attention to two sources of parallels to the position of the opponents: the Wisdom of Solomon and the Qumran documents. In the view of the Wisdom of Solomon, unrighteousness leads to destruction and death and righteousness leads to life and immortality.[69]

Court not death by your erring way of life, nor draw to yourselves destruction by the works of your hands. (NAB) (1:12)

It was the wicked who with hands and words invited death, considered it a friend, and pined for it, and made a covenant with it because they deserve to be in its possession. (NAB) (1:16)

For God formed man to be imperishable; the image of his own nature he made him. But by the envy of the devil, death entered the world, and they who are in his possession experience it. (NAB) (2:23–24)

But the souls of the just are in the hand of God, and no torment shall touch them. They seemed, in the view of the foolish, to be dead; and their passing away was thought an affliction and their going forth from us, utter destruction. But they are in peace. For if before men, indeed, they be punished, yet is their hope full of immortality . . . (NAB) (3:1–4)

Yes, the hope of the wicked is like thistledown born on the wind. . . . But the just live forever, and in the Lord is their recompense, and the thought of them is with the Most High. (NAB) (5:14–15)

At death the righteous person is "assumed" into heaven not through resurrection of the body but through the assumption of the immortal soul. But the general "eschatological timetable" of the Wisdom of Solomon, into which this fits, is not completely clear. The key, according to Nickelsburg, to understanding the "timetable" is found in the author's understanding of death and immortality. These are realities present already within earthly life.

The eternal life that the righteous man anticipates is already present in his immortal soul. . . . It is now evident why it is so difficult to pin down our author as to his eschatological timetable. He has no interest in such a timetable, because he has radicalized eschatological categories. And since immortality is already the possession of the righteous man, his death is viewed as his assumption. Like Enoch, he is translated to heaven. God receives him into his presence (3:6). In similar fashion, the wicked, already moribund in this life, go to their prediction. The precondition for this sorting of souls is a judgment immediately upon death, to which 3:13,18; 4:6 seem to refer.[70]

But there does appear to be a second judgment referred to in 5: 17–23 (see also 3:7). But if this is so, then there would appear to be a double judgment of the wicked, the first at death by God and the second at some future moment by the righteous.

The position of the Wisdom of Solomon regarding eschatology is similar to the position of the opponents in several respects. First, eternal life is a possession in the present.[71] Second, there is no mention of a resurrection of the body. Third, because the unrighteous are said to bring death upon themselves even within their earthly life (1:16), there is a real sense in which they can be said to be judged already. And in addition the idea of judgment at the time of death is quite close to the view of the opponents that judgment takes place in the present moment. As Nickelsburg says, ". . . here judgment after death does not require a resurrection of the body because, in spite of the destruction of the body, the soul continues to exist and can be judged."[72]

Finally there is an aspect of the Wisdom of Solomon that is of particular importance: the relation between Wisdom and the Spirit. This relationship which is frequently noticed is quite close although never actually explicit. The possession of the eschatological Spirit is not directly said to be the basis of the immortality of the person (which is based rather on the fact that the individual was made by God to be immortal—1:14; 2:23). Yet Wisdom/Spirit is to be given to kings (those addressed by the Wisdom of Solomon—cf 1:1). Solomon prayed and "the spirit of Wisdom came to me" (7:7). He gained special knowledge through the Spirit: "Such things as are hidden I learned, and such as are plain; for Wisdom, the artificer of all, taught me. For in her is a spirit intelligent, holy, unique . . ." (7:21–22). In 9:17–18 we find several echoes of the opponents' view of the Spirit: "Or who ever knew your counsel, except you had given Wisdom and sent your holy spirit from on high? And thus were the paths of those on earth made straight, and men learned what was your pleasure, and were saved by Wisdom." Although it would be incorrect to take this metaphorical speech as a literal expression, the echoes of the opponents' position are striking in this description of the Spirit/Wisdom giving knowledge of God, straightening the paths of those on earth (making them live in a sinless way?), having their sins taken away (?) by the power of the Spirit.

Yet in spite of these parallels to the position of the opponents there are differences. Perhaps the most striking is the presence of future judgment in the Wisdom of Solomon. But the judgment in the Wisdom of Solomon is not universal in the same sense it is in Daniel, where *all* will undergo a judgment in which the good will be rewarded and the wicked punished. Second, it would seem that the Wisdom of Solomon speaks of such immortality and assumption as not being the prerogative of all the righteous but only of those who are persecuted and who are put to death for the faith (3:1–9).[73] But it would be only a minor development to extend this reward to all who, for example, believed in Jesus.

At Qumran also, hope of immortality is clearly evident, with both a present and a future dimension, without mention of resurrection of the body.

> I thank Thee, O Lord, for Thou hast redeemed my soul from the Pit, and from the Hell of Abaddon Thou hast raised me up to everlasting height. I walk on limitless level ground, and I know there is hope for him whom Thou hast shaped from dust for the everlasting Council. Thou hast cleansed a perverse spirit of great sin that it may stand with the host of the holy Ones, and that it may enter into community with the congregation of the Sons of Heaven. (1QH 3:20–22–DSSE 158)[74]

The sectaries at Qumran also believed that eternal life was both their present possession and to be continued in the future beyond death.

> And as for the visitation of all who walk in this spirit, it shall be healing, great peace in a long life, and fruitfulness, together with every everlasting blessing and eternal joy in life without end, a crown of glory and a garment of majesty in unending light. (1QS 4:6–8–DSSE 76)

In this there is a promise of eternal life with no mention of death. As John Collins points out, the community could not have thought that the members would not die. Rather they move through death to the eternal life immediately. As Collins says, "That such a conception was possible . . . shows that the most significant aspect of the future hope of second century Judaism was . . . the transition from one sphere of life to another."[75]

This state is a continuation of the present:

> I thank Thee O Lord, for Thou hast redeemed my soul from the Pit and from the Hell of Abaddon Thou has raised me up to everlasting height.

> I walk on limitless level ground, and I know there is hope for him whom Thou has shaped from dust for the everlasting

Council. Thou has cleansed a perverse spirit of great sin that it may stand with the host of the Holy Ones, and that it may enter into community with the congregation of the Sons of Heaven. Thou hast allotted to man an everlasting destiny amidst the spirits of knowledge, that he may praise Thy Name in a common rejoicing and recount Thy marvels before all Thy works. (DSSE 158)

At Qumran the possession of eternal life before physical death is viewed in terms of a present merging of the physical and spiritual worlds and expressed frequently in terms of the community members already worshiping with the angels in the assembly (1QSa 2:3–11) or in terms of already being raised up to the heights (1QS 3:8), quoted above.[76] In the Qumran documents, then there are also parallels to the view of the opponents of 1 John; the only element lacking is mention of judgment.

Conclusions

From this sampling of the intertestamental materials, it is clear that at this time there were a variety of expectations associated with life beyond death and its mode of being. As Perkins points out,[77] the early descriptions of eternal life were metaphoric attempts to come to grips with something which lay beyond normal human experience. As time went on, there were attempts (with varying degrees of success) to systematize these metaphors. Perkins points to books such as 4 Ezra and 2 Baruch as first attempts at this process. There seems to be some evidence of this struggle in the eschatological timetable of the Wisdom of Solomon also. But essentially such attempts were not fully successful, and throughout the period under review there remained a considerable variety of views regarding the details associated with eternal life, resurrection, and final judgment. Thus it is not surprising to find that none of the examples adduced from the intertestamental period fits precisely the view of the author's opponents in 1 John.

But we do find that the individual elements (except for judgment at the time of death) are found within the literature. The Wisdom of Solomon offers the closest parallels to the opponents' view of exaltation being the form that life after death will take. Not only is it a form of life without bodily resurrection, but there are at least minor indications of the Spirit being related to this life.

In both the wisdom materials and in the apocalyptic ones, life beyond death typically functions in a context of judgment resulting in the vindication of the righteous who have undergone persecution at the hands of the wicked in this life. What is peculiar about the Johannine situation is that both groups agree that there will be vindication beyond death for the righteous; they disagree only about the time and the form of that vindication. But rather than being a technical dispute about extra-mundane realities, the dispute probably was seen as crucial for its impact upon the necessity of an ethical code and for ethical conduct in this life. If possession of that future life were seen as perfect, then there would be no need for "striving to make oneself holy."

When, at the beginning of this discussion, we asked what could have accounted for the particular view espoused by the author's opponents, we were only able to speculate. Unfortunately we are not much better off at the end of our review. Yet what was suggested at the beginning does seem plausible. If the opponents had believed that they were children of God in the present time because of their possession of the Spirit in its eschatological fullness and were therefore sinless, they undoubtedly would have seen themselves (as did the Qumran sectarians) as already lifted up to an existence on the level of heavenly, eternal life. Since they were perfect and sinless, there would be no future judgment for them since (like the just of the Wisdom of Solomon or of the Book of Daniel) they could see themselves as not undergoing judgment themselves. And since it was the spirit that was of importance, there would be little use for a bodily resurrection. As part of their belief, it is likely that they simply did not hold to the belief in the "shifting of the ages" which formed part of the apocalyptic viewpoint.

(b) Basis in the Johannine Gospel Tradition

Within the Johannine gospel, the opponents' view of eternal life without mention of bodily resurrection or of future judgment finds clear expression in the "realized eschatology" of the gospel. While "eschatology" is sometimes taken to refer only to "judgment," it can be used in the broader sense to refer to the complex of events which are understood to transpire after the death of a person. In realized eschatology for example there are references to "not dying," to "not perishing," but also of "passing from death to life"; the believer is not judged because judgment is something that happens in the moment of confrontation with the opportunity for belief. Whether or not it was intended, this view is at least compatible with the view of personal immortality without resurrection that we saw in the contemporary Jewish thought.

The texts which support the view of the author of 1 John, the gospel's so-called "future eschatology," speak of life also but of a coming hour when "all in the tombs" will rise, some to a resurrection of life and others to a resurrection of judgment. In these texts, the mention of physical death occurs as well as the resurrection of the body, the mention of a "last day" and a judgment for all, not just for the evil.

Of all the diverse interpretations of the tradition, these two views of eschatology are probably the most commonly noticed and commented upon.[78] It is with regard to eschatology that scholars first debated the issue whether the two divergent views are to be harmonized and seen as the work of one author or distinguished and seen as the work of two. The present study seeks to view that discussion from the perspective of, and to situate it within, the larger context of the crisis of 1 John.

The contrast between the two types is probably clearest in chapter five. The realized view of eschatology is described in 5:24–25:

> (24) Amen, amen, I say to you, the one who hears my word and believes in the one who sent me has eternal life and will not come under judgment but has crossed over from death into life. (25) Amen, amen, I say to you that the hour is coming and now is when the dead will hear the voice of the Son of God and the ones who hear it will live.

Here the passing from death to life refers to spiritual realities in both cases, but the believer will not be judged. The hour which is "yet to come" in future eschatology is already present in 5:25. Again in v 25, the dead are the spiritually dead, and the coming to life is not out of a tomb but a rising from spiritual death to spiritual life. Whether the opponents would see in this statement a foundation for believing that the Christian died physically and was taken immediately to eternal life with the Father and that the body was no longer of concern is not clear. Such an understanding is more likely from a text such as 6:50–51b as we shall see.

Future eschatology is found immediately following the above statement (5:26–29):

> (26) For just as the Father has life in himself, so he has also given the Son the power to have life in himself. (27) And he has given power to him to perform judgment because he is Son of Man. (28) Do not wonder at this, that the hour is coming in which all those in the graves will hear his voice (29) and all will come forth, those whose deeds were good, to a resurrection of life, those whose deeds were evil, to a resurrection of judgment.

Here all the elements (life, death, judgment, the hour) are present, but with a different meaning and a different timetable. The "hour" is in the future and the "dead" are those who are physically dead. They will emerge from the tombs and will receive a bodily resurrection to eternal life (with a physical dimension which includes the body). The "judgment" in this case is applied literally only to the evil, but the fact of the "sorting" out on that day implies a judgment for all.

The two types of eschatology are also found in the bread of life discourse in chapter 6. Future eschatology is evident in 6:39–40, where it is said that the believer has eternal life in the present and will be raised up on the last day. The believer has spiritual life but will die physically. But this physical (bodily) death will be overcome on the last day. Four times in this discourse is there an affirmation of Jesus raising the person on the last day (vv 39,40,44,54).

The discussion of eternal life in 6:49–51 speaks of realized eschatology. Here (v 49) it is said that the fathers died (physically), but v 50 says that if someone eats of this bread he will "never die." V 51a–b then affirms the possession of eternal life for the one who eats the living bread.[80] The statement in v 51a–b that one who eats this bread "will live forever" (*zēsei eis ton aiōna*) is a strong one. Such a statement is perfectly compatible with the conception of personal immortality without resurrection of the body as found in the Wisdom of Solomon and at Qumran. It may be that the opponents, given their deprecation of the material and given this precedent, took the expression in just this sense. Such a reading could also be compatible with 5:24–25.

In 11:23–26 we again find the two views side by side. Vv 23–24 affirm a future eschatology. V 26 affirms a realized view. In vv 23–24 it is said that even if a person dies (physically), he will live (spiritually).[81] V 26 affirms that one who is alive (physically) and who believes in Jesus will never die (spiritually). Thus here we have the clearest expression of the relation of physical to spiritual death in the "system" of realized eschatology. It is evident that in the view of realized eschatology there was no concern for the physical body after death. Properly speaking this view of realized eschatology is described as one of "immortality" rather than "resurrection."[82]

Although the difference spoken of in these two views is one of "eschatology," in fact the issues are broader than that. In those passages where realized eschatology is present, judgment takes place in the present age (3:18–19; 5:24; 12:31,47–48; 16:11) and is something that the believer does not undergo (3:18; 5:24). Judgment in future eschatology takes place at the end of time and is something that all will undergo (5:27–29).[83] "Life" and "death" in the former passages primarily refer to *spiritual* life and death.[84] However in the latter passages, life and death refer primarily to physical life and death.

Thus we conclude that for realized eschatology the concern is entirely with spiritual ("eternal") life. The believer has eternal life in the present and has already passed over from death to life. Clearly this form of life is far more important than any form of physical life. "The hour is coming and now is when the dead will hear the voice of the Son of God and those who hear it will live" (5:25). This person does not undergo judgment.

In these passages there is no belief in a future universal judgment nor is there expressed concern for the future of the body beyond death. Nor is there mention specifically of the state of the body beyond physical death in these passages.[85]

In the passages dealing with future eschatology there was undoubtedly the belief that spiritual life was directly related to bodily life and that the fullness of spiritual life was not possible without some form of bodily life (cf esp. 6:40). Thus we find in these passages the consistent references to being raised up "on the last day" (6: 39,40,44,54; 11:24).

Once Again: The Relation Between the Two Views— The Literary Question

There is much discussion of the relationship of the future eschatology to the original edition of the gospel.[86] It is frequently said that they are the work of an editor. Brown and others would argue that dealing with these differences is more properly a matter of emphasis: the gospel emphasizes realized eschatology while the epistle emphasizes the future dimension of eschatology.[87]

Whether one chooses to deal with the two sets of texts in terms of the approach taken by Brown (the author of 1 John and his opponents emphasized different aspects of the gospel) or in terms of the approach taken by source critics who view some passages as editorial additions, the fact of two versions of eschatology within the gospel tradition remains clear. It is also clear that the predominant motif of the gospel is realized eschatology. Yet from the words of the author of 1 John it is evident that an interpretation of the tradition which allows only for realized eschatology is not, in the author's opinion, the correct one.

(c)   The Position of 1 John

When eschatology is spoken of in the first epistle, we find a different emphasis than in the gospel. 1 John takes pains to indicate that the correct answer to the problem of eschatology revolves around another "both/and": the Christian has eternal life "both" in the present "and" in the future.

In 1 John there are clear indications of realized eschatology: we already walk in the light (1:7; 2:9–10); the true light is already shining (2:8); we are children of God now (3:1); the evil one has been conquered (2:13–14); we have eternal life in us now (implicit in 3:15; 5:11–13,16. Yet in spite of this present possession of eschatological gifts, there is clearly a future element in the author's thought. This future element deals with what we will be at the second coming of Jesus.

In 2:28–3:3, the believer is exhorted not to shrink from Jesus (*mē aischynthōmen ap' autou*) at his coming but to "be bold" (*echō-men parrēsian*).[88] Then the author says that the one who does justice is born of Jesus, and goes on to say that "now" we are children of God, and that it has not yet been revealed what we will be, but that we will be revealed to be like him, and that everyone who has this hope makes himself holy as Jesus himself is holy. The believer clearly expects a future judgment, and he has hope that if he works at making himself holy, even though he is a child of God in the present, he will be revealed to be more like Jesus then.

In 4:17–18, the day of judgment is spoken of. This is of course the same as the *parousia* of Jesus. Again there is mention of *parrēsia*. This time it is love which will make possible the "boldness" by driving out fear. There is clearly a present realization of likeness to Christ since it is affirmed that "we are like him in this world" (4:17). Yet clearly there is also a matter of the Christian having a concern about the future; not everything has been achieved in the present. But love drives out fear, and the love of the disciple if it is perfect will give the disciple courage on the day of judgment.[89]

Thus we see once again that the author of 1 John argues for an understanding of eschatology which involves a more nuanced view than that of his opponents. The Christian, he argues, has eternal life "both" now "and" in the future. And while he can be said to in some sense avoid judgment in the present, he clearly must face judgment in the future.

3. CONCLUSIONS REGARDING THE POSITION OF THE ADVERSARIES

It is hoped that by now the reader can see the complex of inter-relationships between the opponents' convictions regarding possession of the Spirit and those regarding the possession of eternal life. The conviction of the opponents that they possessed the Spirit in its es-chatological fullness, based on their interpretation of various elements of Jewish eschatological hopes, had conditioned them to expect certain benefits from that reception of the Spirit. In addition, because they understood themselves to have the same life as Jesus and because they too had been "anointed" and were now "children of God," their claims could be brought to rival the claims made for Jesus. If the opponents possessed the Spirit (and therefore eternal life), they had the same sinlessness as Jesus; and that sinlessness and eternal life meant that there would be no future possession of eternal life that would be superior to their present state. They were perfect now and so they escaped judgment. But that sinlessness came about through their reception of the Spirit, rather than through some "material" act like an atoning death by Jesus.

With our journey through all the elements of the opponents' position complete, it is appropriate to look back at some of the more general questions raised about the opponents.

(a) Were the Main Topics of 1 John Christology and Ethics?

It is repeatedly said in discussions of the opponents of 1 John that the two main topics at issue were christology and ethics. While this is to a certain extent true, I think that a more proper statement is that the central issue was a proper understanding of the relationship between the role of Jesus and that of the Spirit. The issues of christology and ethics provide material for objective tests by which the theological orthodoxy of the believer could be tested. One could test objectively whether one is willing to confess Jesus as the Son of God or as the Christ, whether a person is willing say that Jesus was an atonement for sin. One can also test ethics by seeing whether one is willing to love the brethren. The struggle for the Johannine tradition involved both christology and ethics but it went beyond this. It involved a complex of ideas resting ultimately on their understanding of the Spirit—and upon the conceptual framework within which salvation was to be interpreted.

(b) A Struggle for an Interpretative Framework for Johannine Christianity?

From what has been said about the state of the Johannine community, that a struggle took place is obvious. First it was a struggle to determine the specific ways in which the unicity of Jesus was to be conceived and expressed.[90] Second, it was a struggle to define the relationship between Jesus and the Spirit. Third, it was a struggle to define the role of human ethical action within life. Allied with this last view is the struggle to define eschatology for the community. This part of the struggle was not without its parallels elsewhere in the contemporary Jewish matrix.

But one might ask whether the struggle of 1 John may have been in part a struggle to determine the framework within which the tradition was to be expressed: Was Christianity to be conceived of according to the apocalyptic model as it was expressed elsewhere in the New Testament or in what might be termed a "wisdom model"?

The combination of a belief in two temporal spheres (present–future) as well as two spheres of reality (physical–spiritual) typical of apocalyptic fits well the view of the author of 1 John and distinguishes his view from that of the opponents who, while acknowledging the distinction between the sphere of the physical and spiritual, give no evidence of recognizing the temporal distinction nor the ethical dualism of apocalyptic.[91]

Without entering into a discussion of the genres themselves, I would simply point to certain specific characteristics present *within some texts of the gospel (and 1 John) and absent from others.* Each of these groups of texts tend to have greater affinities with one rather than the other of these genres. *In general* the so-called apocalyptic sections *as they appear in the gospel and 1 John* are characterized by a "two spirits" worldview, humanity seen as "children of God or of the devil," as "children of darkness or light," possession by spirits, expectation of a "last day," resurrection of the body.

The worldview of the opponents has a dualism which is characterized primarily by an appreciation of the spiritual aspect and a devaluation of the material aspect of existence—a worldview in which Jesus is pictured against the background of wisdom motifs, a figure which descends from heaven to be with humanity and then returns to the heavenly realm. It is a worldview in which the dualism is "vertical" (this world/other world; physical/spiritual) but is much less "horizontal" (this period/that period of history), and which finds greater affinities in the Wisdom literature and certain strands of Hellenistic philosophy.

We have seen throughout that the author of 1 John used apocalyptic imagery and the apocalyptic worldview to confront his opponents. But there is no indication of apocalyptic within the position of his adversaries. It is not without significance that *within the Johannine gospel* the apocalyptic language, imagery and worldview occurs (exclusively?) in isolated passages, passages which bear close resemblance to the thought of 1 John.

(c) The Opponents and Gnosticism

There has been no discussion of gnosticism as a possible background for the errors of the Johannine secessionists. This is so for two reasons. First, there is the problem of using texts for such comparison which have come from a period considerably later than the Johannine texts. Second, the parallels within contemporary Jewish texts are so clear and so extensive that they by all rights must take precedence. But perhaps one further word about gnosticism and its relation to the Johannine writings might be in order.

The relation of the two "Johannine" groups to gnosticism is elucidated by two recent studies. K. Weiss has shown that several elements of what is later called gnostic thought can be found *in both the position of the author of 1 John and of his opponents.*[92] If this is so, then the categories of this so-called "incipient" gnosticism will be of little help in defining the differences between the two groups.

Of similar interest is the discussion in Brown of the elements in the positions of the opponents that are paralleled in later gnostic writings. Brown lists ten elements:[93] (1) a dualism between light and darkness, between truth and falsehood; (2) a claim to special union with God resulting in sinlessness; (3) a stress on the special privileges of the Christian; (4) the Christian is begotten by God; (5) an unction received from Christ teaches the Christian about everything; (6) God's seed remains in the one begotten by God; (7) a lack of emphasis on conduct; (8) some claim to be in light but do not love their brethren; (9) some love the world and its wealth and show no compassion for others in need; (10) the self-image of the adversaries is close to that of the gnostic self-image.

It is striking that all of the features of the list, except for the first, can be found within canonical Old Testament thought, associated with the Spirit and particularly within Wisdom materials.[94]

One element of the larger context of the opponents' position that is not accounted for by the many Old Testament parallels is the pervasive presence of a non-apocalyptic dualism in the gospel. We have repeatedly noticed that the position of the author of 1 John is couched in apocalyptic language and worldview, and that this appears in only isolated sections of the gospel. The remainder of the dualism is of a non-apocalyptic type, a worldview that is frequently associated with Old Testament Wisdom and Hellenistic philosophy. How do we account for this blend?

It is often said that the sectaries of Qumran had taken Deuteronomic thought and incorporated it within a framework of modified (apocalyptic) dualism. It may be that the opponents, on the other hand, had couched their understanding of the Spirit and the implications of their position, which had originally been derived from the canonical Old Testament also, within a framework of *non*-apocalyptic dualism.[95]

NOTES

1. At Qumran the situation is different and it does not seem likely that the opponents could have based their position on a view like that evidenced there. The possession of the Spirit is also linked with the knowledge of God: 1QS 4, "And he shall be plunged into the spirit of purification that he may instruct the upright in the knowledge of the Most High and teach the wisdom of the sons of heaven to the perfect of way." However the Essene view differs in two ways from the position of the opponents. First, at Qumran, the role of teacher was pronounced, and, second, the knowledge was both interior and through a teacher. Thus Qumran supports a view closer to that of the author of 1 John. However the author of 1 John never refers to himself as "teacher" but as "witness."

2. The meaning of *chrisma* is disputed. In some Old Testament texts it refers to the oil of anointing, in other texts it is the anointing itself. Bultmann (*Epistles* 37) and Brown (*Epistles* 342–43) among others argue that it means both the oil and by association the act of anointing. Schnackenburg (*Johannesbriefe* 152) takes it as "oil." All agree that it is intended as a symbol for the reception of the Holy

Spirit. This is likely to be an allusion to the initiation ceremony of the Johannine community, the occasion by which the believer came to receive the Spirit. Grayston (*Epistles* 83–87) claims that it is a term introduced by the opponents and more likely to be derived from a gnostic use. I find this unconvincing and unnecessary.

3. See below for similar "both/and" positions on sonship, sinlessness, and the possession of eternal life.

4. As Weiss ("Gnosis" 347) says: "Was der Geist lehrt, ist dagegen die von Anfang an vernommene Botschaft von Jesus dem Christus und der Verheissung des ewigen Lebens, in der es zu bleiben gilt." Also see Woll, *Johannine Christianity* 95.

5. In fact a third category might well be that of soteriology—how our salvation is effected. But it seems best to simply include this in the above categories.

6. Marshall (*Epistles* 150–51) expresses a similar understanding when he suggests that the opponents are termed antichrists because they are "people who stand in the place of Christ and claim that they are Christ."

7. For a detailed discussion of *chrisma* in this context, see I. de la Potterie, "Anointing of the Christian by Faith," in *The Christian Lives by the Spirit* by I. de la Potterie and S. Lyonnet (Staten Island: Alba, 1971) 79–143; Brown, *Epistles* 341–48; Grayston, *Epistles* 83–88; Schanckenburg, *Johannesbriefe* 150–54.

8. Mowinckel (*He That Cometh* 65–68, 79) gives a detailed treatment of the anointing of the king and the relationship between this anointing and the conferral of the Spirit. For further treatment see the texts referred to by Mowinckel.

9. G. Vermes in *Jesus the Jew* (Philadelphia: Fortress, 1981) 158–59, now followed by Harvey (*Constraints* 141–42), suggests that "anointed" eventually took on an extended meaning of "chosen, appointed, installed in office." Vermes suggests that this could have evolved from Jesus' own use of the term to refer to himself as appointed for a task as a charismatic figure. While this is true it does not touch on the question of whether the anointing continued to have a primary association with the conferral of the Spirit in a special way.

10. The connection of anointing and the Holy Spirit is also evident in the Psalms of Solomon 17:37 where the messiah is empowered by

the Spirit: ". . . for God made him powerful in his Holy Spirit and wise in the counsel of understanding, with strength and righteousness." See Mowinckel, *He That Cometh* 308–311.

11. The possession of the Holy Spirit is also associated with anointing in Acts 10:38 where Jesus is described as being anointed by God with the Holy Spirit and power.

12. Most recently Burge (*Anointed* 54–56) but also others have seen the gospel's use of *menein* as a further indication of Jesus' unique possession of the Spirit.

13. For example, Brown, who is generally quite conservative in source-critical matters, proposes that this is an addition by an editor (*Gospel* 29, 160). See also Schnackenburg, *Gospel* 1, 360–63 and others.

14. It will be recalled that when dealing with the issue of how the opponents interpreted passages such as John 3:34–35, we are faced with a dilemma. As was explained above Brown would interpret these as being reinterpreted by the opponents or simply not attended to. I would opt for a literary critical solution. This certainly is not the place for such a literary critical analysis. Consequently for the present the most that can be said is that within the gospel the dominant presentation of the Spirit is ambiguous, although passages such as 3:34 do make the role of Jesus more specific.

15. See, for example, O. Cullmann, *The Christology of the New Testament* (Philadelphia: Westminster, 1963); R. H. Fuller, *The Foundations of New Testament Christology* (New York: Scribner, 1969); F. Hahn, *The Titles of Jesus in Christology* (London: Lutterworth, 1969); G. Vermes, *Jesus the Jew.*

Brown (*Gospel* 139, *Epistles* 389) speaks of sonship in terms of the covenantal relationship. While this undoubtedly plays a part, the king and his anointing, his reception of the Spirit, his being described as "begotten" and as "son of God," form a more complete parallel than the more general sonship ascribed to Israel as a nation. In addition the Spirit which was given to (reserved to) the king is precisely what is promised to all in the eschaton.

16. This is the rationale which underpins the New Testament statements at the baptism of Jesus where once the Spirit has been seen to descend, he is proclaimed as "Son" by the voice (cf Mk 1:11; Mt 3:16–17; Lk 3:21–22).

17. DSSE 246–47. Vermes (*Jesus the Jew* 198–99) also discusses a fragment (1Q Ser 2:11–12) which is mutilated. According to one conjectured reading, the text runs: "This is the order of the session of the men of renown, called to the assembly of the common council when [God] shall beget the Messiah." Here "God shall beget" (YWLYD) may well be "God shall *lead*" (YWLYK). Thus this text is not helpful either in establishing a precedent outside of the Jewish literature.

18. Brown, *Epistles,* 73.

19. The uses of *teknon* in 2 John and 3 John are not included because those instances refer to the "children" in a community sense. This is also true of *teknion* in all its uses within 1 John.

20. Although it was common practice in apocalyptic to distinguish between various groups by describing them as "sons/daughters of God" or "of the devil," the use of this terminology in the Johannine tradition should not be construed simply as a figure of speech. The claim occurs too frequently in the gospel and epistles and is taken too seriously (e.g. Jn 1:13) to be simply a literary device. In 1 John, the author also takes these claims seriously, as can be seen from the extensive use made of the claim in his letters, and from his development of the topic throughout 2:29–3:10. This sonship even becomes the basis for the community's (and the opponents') claim to sinlessness, as will be seen below. Sonship in 1 John and in apocalyptic (as evidenced at Qumran) is closely related to being possessed by a Spirit however. See 1QS 3–4 passim (DSSE 74–78).

21. But in the view of the redactor, it also comes through the eucharist (6:51,54).

22. Brown, *Epistles* 388–89. Perkins (*Epistles* 39) suggests that the community had originally designated themselves "sons" of God but that they changed it to "children" when "son" came to be associated with the unique relationship between Jesus and the Father. There is of course no proof for this but such a statement indicates the ambiguity inherent in the concept of "being born of God" as applied to the believer as well as to Jesus.

23. See D. M. Smith, "God's only Son. The translation of John 3:16 in the Revised Standard Version," *JBL* 72 (1953) 213–19.

24. On the secondary character of the Prologue see, for example,

the discussion in Schnackenburg, *Gospel* 1, 221–231. On 3:13–21 see Schnackenburg, *Gospel* 360–363 and others.

25. So also Brown, *Epistles* 422–31.

26. See the discussion of sinlessness, pp. 162–69.

27. The meaning of this phrase is somewhat contraverted. Some, rather than seeing it as a reference to the importance of Jesus' earthly life, would see it as a reference to whether he was truly incarnate. For a discussion see Brown (*Epistles* 491–93) who holds the first view; S. Smalley (1, 2, 3 *John* 221–23) is a proponent of the second.

28. J. Schmitt, "Simples remarques sur le fragment Jo., xx, 22–23," in *Melanges en l'honneur de Monseigneur Michel Andrieu* (Strasbourg: Strasbourg University, 1956) 415–23, argues that this text is related to 1QS 3:7–8: "He shall be cleansed from all sins by the spirit of holiness," and to CD 13:9–10. The *mebaqqer,* the leader of the community, is to loosen all the fetters that bind them so that no one should be oppressed or broken in his congregation. This is a close parallel to John 20:22 as we shall see below. It is curious that although Qumran provides some of the clearest texts for the role of the Spirit in the forgiveness of sins, the Qumran texts clearly oppose a view that human life is perfect. We will see more of this below.

29. Weiss (" 'Gnosis' " 348–49) speaks of a "soteriological vacuum." He suggests that the opponents emphasize those elements of the tradition which have no "salvation history." Weiss speculates that perhaps the opponents link their possession of eternal life with their direct knowledge of God. While I would agree with Weiss' recognition of the lack of an historical element in their soteriology, I think their acquisition of eternal life can be more adequately linked with their possession of the Spirit since this can be shown to be a plausible interpretation of both the Johannine and the Jewish eschatological traditions.

30. So also Brown, *Epistles* 83; *John* 1041–45. The meaning of this passage is disputed. However most of the related issues are not directly pertinent to our discussion. One of the major issues has been whether this refers to an ability for each believer to forgive sins, or whether it is reserved to ordained ministers. In addition there is a question whether the passage refers to sins committed after baptism or whether it is a matter of preaching the forgiveness of sins and/or

admitting others to baptism. See Brown (*Gospel* 1036–45) for the range of the problems connected with the verse.

31. For a full discussion see the article *Wiederaufnahme* referred to above.

32. Brown, *Gospel* 146.

33. R. E. Brown, *The Community of the Beloved Disciple* (New York: Paulist, 1979) 117.

34. Brown, *Community* 119.

35. T. Forestell, *Word* 191. See also Brown, *Epistles* 76–79, 98–99.

36. G. Nicolson, *Death as Departure: The Johannine Descent-Ascent Schema* (SBLDS 63; Chico: Scholars, 1983).

37. Nicolson, *Departure* 167; see also 19 and 141–145. Other studies of this aspect of Johannine theology include those of S. Talavero Tomar, *Pasión y Resurrección en el IV Evangelio* (Salamanca: Universidad, 1976) 173–223, who speaks of the passion as the revelation of Jesus as king, and U.B. Mueller, "Die Bedeutung des Kreuzestodes Jesu im Johannesevangelium" *KD* 21 (1975) 49–71, who says that the death of Jesus accomplishes the revelation of the glory of Jesus.

38. C. H. Dodd, in his famous study of the theological relationship between the gospel and the epistles, concluded that in the gospel the death is not a sacrifice for the expiation of sin except for 1:29 (where Jesus is identified as the Lamb of God who takes away the sin of the world); see "The First Epistle of John and the Fourth Gospel," *BJRL* 21 (1937) 129–56. This position has been followed recently by Bogart (*Perfectionism* 37). However it seems that this framing of the question is faulty. If one looks only for texts in the gospel where expiation is explicit, then 1:29 stands out. However, the more correct posing of the question, in my opinion, is that followed by Brown, who asks about the passages where there is a salvific value attributed to the death. This is a broader category, and one which ultimately leads back to the notion of the death of Jesus as expiatory, but it allows for an understanding of the death of Jesus "for his own" as not simply a matter of an example of love and of humble service.

39. Another of the texts also (6:51b) occurs in a passage that is frequently judged to be secondary. I myself have examined this text elsewhere and found it to contain, in addition to the conflicting theological features normally pointed out, the editorial technique known as *Wiederaufnahme* ("*Wiederaufnahme*" 542–49).

40. The Greek word *iliasmos* is disputed. Some would translate it "propitiation," others as "expiation." For a thorough summary of the possible translations and bibliography see Brown, *Epistles* 217–22, 245–246.

41. Brown, *Epistles* 373–80; *Gospel* 948–52.

42. There is considerable textual discussion of the verb in 4:2. Most significant Greek and Latin manuscripts have *mē homologei*. But the patristic and Latin versions strongly support *lyein*. I would agree with Schnackenburg (*Johannesbriefe* 222), Bultmann (*Epistles* 62), and Brown (*Epistles* 494–96), who consider *lyein* the original reading. But Marshall, *Epistles* 207–08, and Grayston, *Epistles* 122, hold for *mē homologei* as the original reading. For a full discussion see the commentaries referred to above. If *lyein* is accepted as the correct reading, the verse would read: "Every spirit which does away with the need of Jesus is not of God." As Brown points out, *lyein* occurs only one other time in the Johannine epistles, at 1 John 3, where it is said that Jesus has come to "destroy" (do away with) the works of the devil." In both instances, the verb seems to communicate the notion of eliminating something which had had a prior existence. That is precisely the opponents' view of Jesus: they have come to do away with the role of Jesus as it was formerly.

43. Scholars have argued that there were parallels within apocalyptic literature for a mythological beast who would appear at the end times and oppose God. See, for example, B. Rigaux, *L'Antichrist et l'opposition au royaume messianique dans l'Ancien et le Nouveau Testament* (Gembloux: Duculot, 1932); H. Schlier, "Vom Antichrist—Zum 13. Kapitel der Offenbarung Johannes," in *Die Zeit der Kirche* (Freiburg: Herder, 1956); R. Yates, "The Antichrist," *Evangelical Quarterly* 46 (1974) 42–50. There is no need to see a specific forerunner to the figure of the antichrist in such mythology. Rather the author has simply taken over the position of his opponents as the ones who oppose the Christ and given them this name.

44. Weiss (" 'Gnosis' " 348) also argues for a literal reading of this term. Weiss however argues that the "soteriological vacuum" (i.e. that the opponents believed in a Christ whose incarnation, passion, cross and parousia were denied) must have argued for salvation as coming directly through the promise of eternal life for those who believed in Jesus (pp. 348–49).

45. See below III,C,2 for full discussion of this.

46. But according to John 20:22–23 it is part of the Spirit's function.

47. Brown, *Epistles* 98.

48. The meaning of the phrase *mē menōn en tē didachē tou Christou* ("not remaining in the teaching of the Christ") is disputed. Some take it to mean "teaching about Christ" (Bultmann, *Epistles* 113; Marshall, *Epistles* 72–73; Smalley, *Epistles* 332); others take it to mean "teaching of Christ" (Schnackenburg, *Johannesbriefe* 314–15; Brown, *Epistles* 674).

Absolute certainty is not possible. Where it occurs in the gospel (7:16–17; 18:19) it refers to the teaching *of* Jesus. In these cases the term is used with "outsiders" (with the Jewish questioners in John 7:16,17; and with Pilate in 18:19). The much more common phrase is to remain in his word (Jn 5:38; 8:31), or to have the word remain in the believer (1 Jn 2:14,24 [twice]), or to keep the word (8:51,52,55; 14:23,24; 15:20 [twice]; 17:6).

"Teaching *about* Jesus" would imply the presence of human teachers, something that 1 John clearly says is not appropriate. The community witnesses to the teaching of Jesus but does not itself teach. 1 John 2:27 says that the believers have no need for anyone to teach them, but the same verse goes on to say that the anointing they have from the holy one will teach them. But some vocabulary in 2 John 9 is unusual: *Proagōn* ("going beyond") occurs only here in this sense; *didachē* is infrequent; *tou Christou* as a name for Jesus occurs only here. This may indicate that v 9 represents a unique formulation of the concept.

Even the final phrase of the verse (*kai kathōs edidaksen hymas, menete en autō*) ("and just as he taught you, remain in it") does not resolve the ambiguity because *autō* ("it") could refer either to Jesus or to the *kathōs*-phrase. Of course, in terms of content to the teaching there would be no difference since the believers would claim that Jesus' teaching was that he was the unique "Christ."

The most likely position then is that this is simply another formulation of the notion of not remaining in the word of Jesus. But whichever position is taken on this, there is no dispute that these members (or former members) of the Johannine community have gone beyond and do not remain in what they have heard from the beginning.

49. Although it has been speculated that this perfection could be conceived of as possessed by nature (see Bogart, *Perfectionism* 33–35), it is most likely that it is thought of as stemming from the believer's initiation as a Christian (Brown, *Epistles* 82–83). There is considerable evidence that the opponents reached their position by interpreting the Johannine tradition, and in the gospel the notion of sonship is always linked to something that has happened since one's natural birth. Bogart argues that the anthropology of the group is gnostic and is such that they claim they never have sinned. He attributes this anthropology to either a part of the community which had become gnostic (by unknown means) or perhaps "by an influx of pro-gnostic gentiles who had never accepted the basic biblical doctrines of God and man" (p 135).

50. See the thorough discussion in Brown, *Epistles* 408–11.

51. See also TBenj 8:2–3; 4 Ez 6:26; 1QS 3:6–9 quoted previously.

52. Bogart (*Perfectionism,* 97–127) presents an extensive survey of material dealing with perfectionism in pre-Johannine literature, much of which is valuable as a background for understanding the claims to eschatological sinlessness. Much of this will be incorporated into what follows.

53. See also Bogart, *Perfectionism* 51–92.

54. Brown, *Community* 126.

55. In my consideration of sin in the gospel, I will exclude for the moment the possibility of violation of the love commandment in the gospel since there is evidence that this has been added to the gospel and is not part of the earlier stratum.

56. Brown, *Epistles* 81–83. Bogart (*Perfectionism* 74, 55–62) phrases it too strongly when he says ". . . there is no sin but unfaith in the Gospel of John" (74). There are other sins (e.g. 3:20) but they are not given the attention that unbelief is.

57. There can be no doubt that belief and unbelief are major topics of the gospel, indeed perhaps the major issue. How would the opponents have viewed this? I would think that they saw belief as being belief that Jesus was indeed the eschatological messenger of God, announcing the coming of the final definitive outpouring of the Spirit. Thus for them belief in Jesus as the agent would set them apart from the Jews and other unbelievers who did not think that Jesus was such an agent nor that the outpouring of the Spirit had been accomplished.

58. For a detailed discussion of these verses, see my article "Faith and Works" 304–315, and Bergmeier, "Glaube als Werk? Die 'Werke Gottes' im Damaskusschrift II, 14–15 und Johannes 6, 28–29," *RevQ* 6 (1967) 253–60.

59. See above.

60. I. de la Potterie, *Verité.* See Brown, *Epistles* 80.

61. See further the discussion in Brown, *Epistles* 80–81.

62. This is a common position—especially Brown, *Epistles* 431. For a contrary position, however, see Perkins, *Epistles* 39–41, who argues for a community which was "perfect" but individuals who were occasionally sinful.

63. The notion of the "seed of God" occurs only once in 1 John. In the gospel a somewhat similar phrase is used (8:33,37) by the Jews when they describe themselves as "seed" of Abraham. In the epistle the phrase means the divine principle of begetting and probably refers to the Holy Spirit which is the principle of begetting elsewhere in the Johannine tradition.

64. In order to put this topic in some perspective it may be helpful to recall that within the New Testament it is common to speak of eternal life as a possession that one will not obtain until one has experienced physical death. It is a purely future possession. However for the Johannine community there was no dispute that eternal life was a present possibility for the Christian. The only dispute was whether one's possession of it in the present was so perfect that the future would add nothing to it.

65. That there is a difference between the author and his opponents regarding eschatology is commonly recognized. For example, Weiss, " 'Gnosis' " 343; Brown, *Community* 135–38.

66. Closely related to this is the fact that the opponents deny any permanent role for Jesus in salvation, seeing him only as the one who gives the Spirit. This means that the opponents would deny any "second coming" of Jesus also. Jesus was not significant in the actual process of forgiveness of sin, nor would he be significant in judgment. So also Weiss, " 'Gnosis' " 343. Thus it would seem likely that related to the issue of christology is the issue of the worldview (apocalyptic or not) within which the tradition was to be cast.

67. There are several excellent studies. See, for example, H. Cavallin, *Life After Death: Paul's Argument for the Resurrection of the*

Dead in 1 Cor 15. Part I: An Inquiry into the Jewish Background (Lund: Gleerup, 1974); G. Nickelsburg, *Resurrection, Immortality, and Eternal Life in Intertestamental Judaism* (HTS 26; Cambridge: Harvard, 1972); P. Perkins, *Resurrection: New Testament Witness and Contemporary Reflection* (New York: Doubleday, 1984); J. Collins, "Apocalyptic Eschatology and the Transcendence of Death," *CBQ* 36 (1974) 21–43.

68. For example, in Isaiah 52:13–15 the plight of the suffering servant gives hints of reward beyond this life:

> See, my servant shall prosper, he shall be raised high and greatly exalted. Even as many were amazed at him—so marred was his look beyond that of man. . . . So shall he startle many nations because of him kings shall stand speechless. . . .

This passage finds echoes in later developments as we shall see.

There are earlier examples within the Old Testament which provide an even more remote hint of a concept of life beyond physical death—for example, the assumption of Enoch (Gen 5:24) and Elijah (2 Kgs 2:11). In Psalm 9, we hear of God: "You forsake not those who seek you, O Lord" (v 11). "The needy shall not always be forgotten, nor shall the hope of the afflicted forever perish" (v 19). This is an expression of the hope that God will not forsake the righteous.

69. I am dependent here on the analysis of G. Nickelsburg, *Resurrection* 48, 66–70. Nickelsburg (*Resurrection* 66) would see WisSol 2–5 as a reshaping of the tradition in Isaiah 52–53 referred to above. See also Perkins, *Resurrection* 40.

70. Nickelsburg, *Resurrection* 88–89.

71. But although WisSol speaks of the unrighteous inviting death, they too seem to live beyond death in some sense since they are said to undergo a judgment by the righteous at the future "eschatological moment."

72. Nickelsburg, *Resurrection* 88.

73. Nickelsburg, *Resurrection* 89.

74. That this passage speaks of the present possession of eternal life together with the hope of a further fulfillment in the future is proposed in similar ways by Vermes, *Scrolls* 187–188; by J. Collins,

"Apocalyptic Eschatology" 21–43, esp 35–36; by H. W. Kuhn, *Enderwartung und Gegenwärtiges Heil* (Studien zur Umwelt des NT 4; Göttingen: Vandenhoeck & Ruprecht, 1966); and by H. Ringgren, *The Faith of Qumran. Theology of the Dead Sea Scrolls* (Philadelphia: Fortress, 1963).

75. Collins, "Eschatology" 37.

76. See J. Collins, *The Apocalyptic Imagination* (New York: Crossroad, 1984) 134–138. See also his "Apocalyptic Eschatology" 34–37. The recognition of both a present and future dimension to eternal life at Qumran is also recognized by Kuhn, *Enderwartung* 44–112 and Ringgren, *Faith* 187–88.

77. Perkins, *Resurrection* 50.

78. See, for example, the discussion in Brown, *Gospel* cxv–xxi; Schnackenburg, *Gospel* 352–361, 426–437; the discussion and literature in R. Kysar, *The Fourth Evangelist and His Gospel* (Minneapolis: Augsburg, 1975) 207–214, but especially J. Blank, *Krisis. Untersuchungen zur johanneischen Christologie und Eschatologie* (Freiburg: Lambertus, 1964).

79. The position of the gospel on the question whether the Christian is judged is clearer than its answer to the question of whether Christ will judge. These latter statements are ambiguous and seemingly contradictory. Compare for example 3:17 and 12:47 with 5:22,27. The resolution of this problem is beyond the focus of the current study.

80. V 51c is part of the redactor's addition. See the discussion in my "*Wiederaufnahme*" 546.

81. There is some discussion whether the various uses of life and death in these verses refer in each case to spiritual or physical entities. The view followed here is that argued by Brown, *Gospel* 425.

82. Other texts where such versions of eschatology are presented at length include: realized eschatology in 3:16–21; final eschatology in 6:39–40,44,54; 11:23–27; 12:44–50. In addition, there are other passages which clearly imply one or other approach. These would include: realized eschatology: the believer already walks in the light (3:21; 8:12); the believer has eternal life in the present (3:36; 5:24; 6: 47,53–54; 10:28); future eschatology would include the references to raising up on the last day (6:39,40,44,54).

83. It must be said that the term "judgment" is literally applied only to those who do evil in these passages also and therefore it should

be said that the term judgment itself seems to have a negative connotation in both eschatologies. But in a larger sense the term is surely
intended to be used in a neutral sense as can be seen in 5:27.

84. Physical death is spoken of in 6:50 and 11:25, but the emphasis
is on spiritual death.

85. But presumably this present possession of eternal life would
be thought of as something extraordinary since eternal life normally
would be thought to be a possession attained only beyond physical death.

86. R. Bultmann is the most famous proponent of this. A conve-
nient summary of Bultmann's theory may be found in D. M. Smith,
The Composition and Order of the Fourth Gospel (New Haven: Yale
University Press, 1965) 217–219. For a survey of past analyses, see
R. Schnackenburg, *Gospel* 2, 114–119 and the bibliography
cited there.

87. Brown, *Epistles* 99–100. However it must be noted that Brown
in his commentary on the gospel considers 5:26–30 to be a duplicate
version of 5:19–25 but in terms of future eschatology (*Gospel* 219–
21). In addition, he proposes that 12:46–48 is a variant of 3:16–19
(*Gospel* 490–91). In both instances, however, Brown judges the material to be composed by the evangelist but added by the redactor.

88. The language here is somewhat ambiguous. The Greek has *ean
phanerōthē* ("*if* he revealed"). Grayston interprets this as an indication
that the apocalyptic hopes are more firmly held by the adversaries
than by the author (95). After a discussion of the possible meanings
of *ean*, Grayston concludes that the firmest evidence is from Johannine thought. However here he focuses almost exclusively on the
present element of the possession of Christ and of life. In my view
this does not do justice to the more nuanced view of the author.

89. It is curious however that the final eschatology of 1 John does
not discuss physical resurrection from the dead, as does the gospel.

90. Bogart, *Perfectionism* 120–21, sees the introduction of heretical
perfectionism through an influx of gnostic ideas. Thus we would
disagree about two elements here. First, I would conceive of the heretical perfectionism as occurring at an earlier stage and as being
derived from traditions indigenous within Judaism. I would agree
however that these heretical ideas have much in common with what
is later called gnosticism.

91. The fact that WisSol acknowledges a future judgment also prevents us from a too hasty *identification* of this worldview with that of the opponents.

92. Weiss, " 'Gnosis' "; also "Orthodoxie und Heterodoxie im 1. Johannesbrief," *ZNW* 58 (1967) 247–55.

93. Brown, *Epistles* 59–65.

94. Brown has long been a major proponent of the Wisdom background of much of the gospel. See, for example, Brown, *Gospel* cxxii–cxxv.

95. A search for materials in which there is evidence of such a combination of Old Testament eschatological hopes within a non-apocalyptic dualistic framework may bear some fruit for an understanding of the early stages of what came to be known as gnosticism. It is frequently suggested that gnosticism found its roots in Judaism, particularly within the Wisdom materials. If we recall that everything found in the parallels with gnosticism adduced by Brown can also be found in the Old Testament itself as a promise connected with the eschatological possession of the Spirit (except the dualistic framework), we may have a starting point for an understanding of what at a later stage gave rise to gnosticism.

Chapter Seven

CONFRONTING THE CRISIS: THE WRITING OF THE FIRST EPISTLE

Once we have gained some sense of the nature of the crisis that confronted the Johannine community at the time of the first epistle, we are in a position to understand various aspects of the author's confrontation with the opponents in the epistle itself. There are three aspects of the epistle that are particularly important for our purposes: the structure of the epistle, the theological approach of the author, and then finally a brief survey of the epistle itself showing the importance of the Johannine commandments for the epistle and for confronting the opponents.

A. The Structure of 1 John

The structure of 1 John is one of the most disputed aspects of this epistle.[1] As can be seen from the survey of recent opinion given at the beginning of chapter 5, and from the detailed survey in Brown's commentary, there is very little agreement about the structure except in the most general of terms.[2] Most scholars favor a division into three parts, with the second part beginning either at 2:18 or 2:29, and the third part beginning at either 4:1 or 4:7. A relative minority would see a division into parts ranging from two to seven.[3]

The situation is further complicated by theories that the letter is a combination of a source document which has been commented on by another author.[4] It must be said, however, that these source theories have not gained wide acceptance. The present discussion will be carried on with the presupposition that the letter is the work of one person.

The theory that I would propose is closely related to that adopted by Raymond Brown. This theory, originally proposed by A. Feuillet,[5] and followed by Brown in a slightly different form, has much to recommend it, especially since both of these scholars have demonstrated the existence of similar forms of this schema in the gospel as well as in the epistle.[6]

Feuillet proposes that the epistle is divided into two main parts (1:5–2:28 and 2:29–5:12) together with a prologue (1:1–4) and an epilogue (5:13–21). He parallels this with what he sees as the main lines of the structure of the fourth gospel: a prologue (1:1–19), two major sections (1:19–12:50 and 13:1–20:31) and an epilogue (21:1–25). Brown had proposed the same division for the gospel and proposes an only somewhat different division for the epistle. Instead of dividing the two major parts at 2:28 as does Feuillet, Brown suggests that the division occurs after 3:10.[7]

Feuillet points out that the major theme of the first part of the epistle is indicated by the antithetical use of light and darkness and their correlative themes of truth and falsehood. Yet these two antitheses do not occur from chapter 3 onward.

In the epistle, the theme of light (and its correlative, darkness) occurs in 1:5,6,7; 2:8,9,10,11, yet is absent from the second half of the epistle.

In the gospel, the contents of the first part (1:19–12:50) consistently focus on the theme of the light coming into the world. Within the gospel the theme of light first appears in the prologue (1:4,5,7,8,9) and continues throughout (3:19–21; 8:12; 9:5; 11:9–10; 12:25–26,46). This theme of the light is contrasted with the darkness in the Prologue in 1:5 and in the first part of the gospel in 3:19; 8:12; 12:35,46. Yet these themes disappear completely from the second part of the gospel.

In the second part of the epistle, however, the distinctive terminology becomes that of "love." Between 3:1 and 5:12 of 1 John, the verb *agapan* occurs twenty-five times as opposed to only three times in the first part of the epistle. The noun *agapē* occurs sixteen times in the second part of the epistle but only two times previously. When this is compared with the gospel it can be noted that *agapan* and *agapē* occur only six times in the first part of the gospel but thirty-six times in the second part of the gospel.[8]

In his comparison of the two parts of the gospel, Feuillet points out that this shift in terminology is accompanied by a clear shift in thought. In the first part, the gospel presents the disciples opening themselves up to the divine light which is Jesus and their belief in him. In addition, the remainder of the first part of the gospel centers on the efforts of Jesus to bring the rest of the world to belief. However, in the second, the theme is that of relationships between the disciples and within the community. This relationship is expressed primarily in terms of love of one another and in love of God (Jesus).

What is more important than the simple occurrence of these words in the two halves of the epistle is the fact that the thought of the two halves is dominated by these respective ideas. In the first half of the epistle, the major topic is that of the belief that is appropriate for the community member, while the development of the theme of mutual love occurs only in the second half of the epistle.

While Brown agrees in general with the division proposed by Feuillet, he locates the beginning of each half of the epistle more precisely in the parallel statements: "This is the gospel that we have heard from the beginning, that God is light" (in 1:5) which parallels the statement in 3:11: "This is the gospel which we have heard from the beginning, that we love one another." In part one of the gospel, there is the separation of the believing disciple from the unbelieving world, and in part one of the epistle there is emphasis on separation from the secessionists; in part two of the gospel and the epistle there is concentration on addressing the believers. In part two of the gospel, Jesus speaks of passing from this world; in part two of the epistle, the author speaks of passing from death to life. In part two of the gospel and the epistle, Jesus speaks of the Paraclete/Spirit of truth. Near the end of part two of the gospel, John speaks of the blood flowing from the side of Jesus and the seeming equation of this with the giving of the Spirit; in addition he speaks of the beloved disciple who witnesses to this. Near the end of part two of the epistle the author speaks of blood, water and the Spirit as witnessing.

Although Brown and Feuillet differ in several particulars, and although not all of the parallels between the gospel and the letter are convincing, the basic insight of the two scholars is impressive.

In my opinion one of the major pieces of corroborating evidence for this view of the structure is not only the thematic parallels between the gospel and the epistle but also the linguistic parallels by which both sections are introduced ("This is the gospel which we have heard from the beginning . . .").[9]

Once this structure of the epistle has been observed, it can be seen that the structure is intimately related with the two essential topics of the epistle. That is, the symbols of light (correct belief) and love (ethics) are used to structure the epistle around the two elements of the tradition which have been attacked by the secessionists: the correct understanding of the role of Jesus in salvation and the place of mutual love. Of course the correlation with each of the Johannine commandments should be obvious also, but we will see more of this below.

B. The Theological Method
of the Author of 1 John

There are two important aspects to the method of the author. First, in his refutation of the opponents, the author of 1 John makes several subtle but important shifts in his presentation of Johannine theology. Second, every claim put forward by both groups of Johannine Christians is evaluated by means of two "tests": that of belief and that of love. Because these tests are spread throughout the epistle, the consistency with which they appear is not easy to notice. However we will return to the list of claims presented at the beginning of chapter 6 and observe how every one is tested in these two ways. This is important since it confirms so clearly the theory that in the author's own mind the errors of the opponents manifested themselves in terms of incorrect belief and lack of love.

1. Shifts in Theology by the Author of 1 John

It is often noted that although 1 John reflects the thought of the gospel in many ways, it is strangely different from the gospel in other, sometimes significant, ways. Brown lists several of these: (1) attribution of important features to God rather than to Jesus; (2) stress on aspects of a lower christology; (3) a clearer presentation of the sacrificial and atoning death of Jesus; (4) less specific reference to the Spirit than in the gospel; (5) a shift in emphasis from a realized eschatology in the gospel to a future eschatology in the epistle;[10] (6) the absence of Old Testament quotations in 1 John.[11]

While some scholars suggest that these features are evidence of differences in authorship, I would contend (without at the same time denying that there are separate authors for the epistle and the gospel— or for that matter separate authors for the epistle and the redaction of the gospel) that the majority of these differences are due to the approach taken by the author of 1 John.[12]

The author of 1 John has a peculiarly difficult task before him in his letter. While he shares many of the convictions of his opponents, he differs considerably with regard to others. At times he insists that his opponents' claims are improper; at other times he says that they do not fulfill legitimate claims. He attempts to refute and to encourage, to explain his own position, and to point out the deficiences of his opponents. And finally he establishes certain "tests" by which one can determine the correctness of their position.

Not all of the differences listed by Brown (and others) are of equal importance. The alleged stress on lower christology could perhaps be argued. Brown points to the use of "word" to refer to message in 1 John as opposed to its use to refer to Jesus in the prologue of the gospel. He also mentions the absence of any reference to the "glory" of Jesus in the epistles while it was used thirty-nine times in the gospel. Nevertheless, one could point to the more frequent (proportionately) use of the phrase "Son of God" (*huios tou theou*) (eight times in the gospel, seven times in 1 John).[13]

It is significant that final eschatology is clearly more dominant in the epistles than in the gospel, yet it is not correct to say that the gospel contains only realized eschatology, as Brown readily recognizes. The reasons for this shift have been discussed above,[14] as have the reasons for the emphasis on the sacrificial, atoning death of Jesus.[15]

The lack of Old Testament quotations in 1 John is a clear change from the gospel. Brown proposes that this may be because the epistle is not shaped by debate with the Jews.[16] It may well also be that the author felt that the Old Testament evidence was ambiguous. If the position of the opponents was founded on an interpretation of Old Testament evidence, as I have suggested throughout, it would have been perilous to seek to defend claims simply on the basis of the Old Testament. There can be no doubt, however, that the author knows the Old Testament and in fact uses it to structure his argument (cf the development of the comparison of Cain and Abel in 3:12–18). What is lacking is the recourse to citations as proof texts.

The two other differences listed by Brown (the attribution of claims to Jesus in the gospel and to the Father in the epistle, and the differences in the presentation of the Spirit) require somewhat more detailed discussion and will be treated below.

2. *Attribution of Qualities to Jesus and to God*

First, in the first epistle, the author attributes certain features to God in 1 John that are attributed to Jesus in the gospel. For example, in the gospel Jesus is the light (Jn 1:4,9; 8:12; 9:5, etc.) while in the epistle God is the light (1 Jn 1:5). The commandments are said to be "of God" in 1 John (2:3–4; 3:22–24; 4:21; 5:2–3; see 2 Jn 4–6), while in the gospel they are said to be "of Jesus" (13:34; 14:15,21; 15:10,12). In the gospel the word which is spoken is said to be "of Jesus" (5:24; 8:31,37,43,51,52; 14:23,24; 15:3,20 [twice], while in 1 John it is the word "of God" (1:10; 2:5,14).[17]

The gospel had been written to describe the role of Jesus (and the Spirit!) in salvation, Jesus who was the *Son* of the Father. It was written at a time when the community's fellow Jews did not believe that God's eschatological action had yet come about. Consequently the gospel intends to explain the role and the importance of this person Jesus vis-à-vis the Father and to show that through him the outpouring of the Spirit has taken place. But even in the gospel, it must be remembered that there is never any doubt that Jesus is totally dependent upon the Father in spite of all the high christological claims made for him.

Second, the author of 1 John puts the place of Jesus within salvation in a larger context and framework by describing the work of Jesus within the larger framework of his relationship with the Father. 1 John was written to confront the crisis caused by those who had come to believe that the life of Jesus was only of temporary significance. For them, the Spirit, not Jesus, was of ultimate importance. In the gospel the author could identify the commandments as "of Jesus," but in the epistle the role of Jesus is in doubt and so the author of the epistle goes beyond Jesus to what is not in dispute: the Father. And the author reminds his readers that these commandments are in fact commandments of the Father. The author of 1 John would thus be arguing on the same basis as his opponents, who claimed to know God. If the opponents claimed to know God, they should know that it was God who had commanded them to keep his commandments which he had given through Jesus. Thus it is the purpose and circumstances of 1 John which account for the shift.

3. The Spirit in 1 John and the Gospel

Another significant way in which the first epistle differs from the gospel is in its presentation of the Spirit. It is commonly said that the role of the Spirit is less developed and less important in the epistle than in the gospel. However these differences can be accounted for more satisfactorily as deliberate changes because of the author's purposes.

There are two elements of the presentation of the Spirit in 1 John which are striking. First, the role of the Spirit in relation to the obtaining of eternal life is not as clear in 1 John as it is in the gospel. Second, the author of 1 John at times makes oblique references when speaking of the Spirit rather than referring directly to him. This will involve some repetition of material regarding the Spirit from the previous chapter but the review is necessary to properly perceive the approach of the author.

(a) The Role of Jesus and of the Spirit in the Obtaining of Eternal Life

The essential question for the Christian and the one that the Johannine gospel and epistles hold in the forefront is how one can obtain eternal life. The answer to this in the Johannine gospel is twofold: life comes through Jesus and it comes through the Spirit. However in the first epistle, although the life-giving role of the Spirit is implicit, there is no explicit mention of this, even in the discussion of topics where it was explicit in the gospel. But, by contrast, the role of Jesus in the giving of life is much more explicit in the first epistle than it was in the gospel.

In the gospel the role of Jesus in giving life is clear. The words of Jesus are said to be "spirit" and "life" (6:63,68). The dead will hear the voice of the Son of God, and those who hear will live (5:25). Jesus is life (11:25; 14:6); he is the bread of life (6:34,48,51) come down from heaven and giving life to the world (6:33; 10:10,28). It is the one who believes in Jesus who will have eternal life (1:12–13; 3:15,16,36; 5:40; 6:40,47; 20:31). It is the eating of his flesh and drinking of his blood that will give life (6:51b,53,54,57,58). Thus there can be no doubt about his role according to the Johannine tradition.

Nevertheless when one asks how one understands the message of Jesus, how belief becomes possible, how one obtains life, how one is born of God, it is the role of the Spirit which comes to the fore. Even Jesus is said to speak the words of God because God gives the Spirit without measure (Jn 3:34–35). One is not able to see the kingdom of God "unless one is born from above" (3:3); one is not able to enter the kingdom unless one is "born of the Spirit" (3:4). It is the living water that Jesus will give which will become a spring welling up to eternal life (4:14), yet this water is defined in 7:39 as the Spirit, and the Spirit will not be given until Jesus is glorified (7:39).

It is only after the glorification (12:16) and resurrection of Jesus (2:22) that the disciples are said to believe in the deepest sense, and it is only then that they receive the Spirit (7:39; 20:22). Even the Paraclete passages (which may originate from approximately the time of 1 John) speak clearly of a sequence: first, Jesus; then the Spirit. The Paraclete passages clearly indicate that it is the Paraclete who will remind them of the words of Jesus, and who will make all things clear and who will teach them what they could not learn while Jesus was with them. Although there is an explanation of the relationship between Jesus and the Spirit as the source of life, there can be no doubt that the relationship between the Spirit and Jesus as the source of eternal life is ambiguous and is held in tension within the gospel.

On the other hand, nowhere in the first epistle is eternal life linked with the Spirit as it is in the gospel. Even though Christians are repeatedly spoken of as being "born of God" (a process which takes place through the Spirit in the gospel), it is nowhere said in 1 John how this comes about. Rather in the first epistle what are spoken of are the manifestations of the fact that one is truly born of God (i.e. one does justice—2:29; one shows love—4:7; 5:1; one believes—5:1), or its consequences (one does not commit sin—3:9; 5:18; one conquers the world—5:5). Perhaps the closest connection between being begotten of God and the Spirit is the reference in 3:9 where it is said that one who is begotten of God does not sin because God's seed remains within him. Although the meaning of "God's seed" here is much discussed, it is likely that it refers to the Christian's possession of the Spirit.[18] This then represents at best an indirect reference to begetting by the Spirit.

However, the author of 1 John frequently speaks of life (eternal life) as coming through Jesus. Jesus is referred to as the "word of life" (1:1) and the "life" (1:2; 5:20);[19] life is "in him" (5:11);[20] the one who has Jesus has eternal life (5:12); the message which he brought is eternal life (2:25); God gave eternal life and it is in Jesus (5:11).

But *how* does Jesus give eternal life? There are two passages which shed light on this question. The clearest statement is given in 1 John 4:9–10. In 4:9 it is said: "In this has the love of God for us been revealed, that he has sent his only Son into the world in order that we may live through him." This is then elaborated in v 10 where it is said that God sent his Son as a propitiation (*iliasmos*) for our sins. We live through Jesus, who takes away our sins. This clear statement that Jesus was sent to be a propitiation for our sins then becomes the key for understanding the other statements regarding the purpose of Jesus' coming: "We know that he was revealed so that sins might be taken away" (3:5); he cleansed us from sin by his blood (1:7). He is the Paraclete (2:1), the propitiation (2:2): "For this purpose was the Son of God revealed, that he might do away with the works of the devil" (3:8). Thus there can be no doubt that the giving of life by Jesus is linked to his death for our sins.

The second passage is 5:16. This verse reads: "If anyone sees his brother sinning a sin not unto death, he will pray and he will give him life, to those not sinning unto death." Here the giving of life is associated with sin. The petitioner who prays for his brother will gain the forgiveness of the brothers' sins, and Jesus will give him life. This verse corroborates the view of 4:9–10 that the giving of life through Jesus is connected with the forgiveness of sin.

The reader need only recall the various statements in the gospel that the Spirit was not given until after Jesus had been glorified. This would correlate with the position described here in 1 John, namely that even though the Spirit was the principle of divine life, the Spirit was given by Jesus and it was given only after the sins of the world had been taken away by the death of Jesus.

I would then see the author of 1 John taking a position on this matter that is similar in form to that he had taken in several other instances in the gospel, namely he opposes a one-sided interpretation of the Johannine tradition. Both Jesus and the Spirit are essential to the gaining of eternal life.

(b) Implicit Rather Than Explicit References to the Spirit

Another of the changes in the presentation of the Spirit in 1 John is the fact that references to the Spirit are often implicit in the letter whereas they were explicit in the gospel. The Spirit is a major factor in the argument of 1 John six times: 2:20–27; 3:24b–4:6; 4:13; 5:6–10,19. In these passages, the author refers to the Spirit in various ways. He speaks explicitly of the Spirit in 3:24b–4:6, 4:13, and 5:6–10. However at other times he speaks of the Spirit in a variety of oblique ways also where he seems to want to avoid the implications that the term Spirit would have for his opponents' position. In 2:20 he speaks of the "anointing" which his readers have; in 4:4 the Spirit is referred to as "the one within you" (*ho en hymin*); in 5:19 the possession of the Spirit is implicit behind the reference to the fact that "he has given us awareness" (*dedōken hēmin dianoian*).

The author says that the members of his community have an "anointing from the holy one" (2:20). This enables his readers to have knowledge. Then in 2:27, the author returns to the subject of the anointing and describes it as being "from him." This anointing means that they have no need for anyone to teach them. The anointing teaches them about all, and this is true, not false. He finally urges them that what he has taught should be allowed to remain in them. Clearly what is at stake is the conviction that the Spirit will bring about the believers' knowledge of the truth, and that because of their possession of the Spirit they will have no need for anyone to teach them. This is of course true, in the main, for the opponents too. They reject the teaching of the very tradition which the author of 1 John upholds.

Yet nowhere in this passage is the Spirit mentioned specifically.[21] Rather the effect of the Spirit is what is emphasized. Why does the author avoid speaking directly of the Spirit? I would suggest that he considered it dangerous to use the same language as his opponents.

The Spirit teaches the Christian, and it gives the Christian knowledge. In the last analysis, the author must acknowledge that his readers rely upon the same principle for their direction as the opponents do: anointing by the Spirit. The only control for the author is "what they have heard from the beginning" (2:25), and so he exhorts them that "what he has taught" (2:27) should remain in them.

The Spirit is mentioned explicitly in 3:24, but immediately after this (4:1–6) the author launches into a detailed description of how to distinguish between spirits. In the gospel it had been simply a question of whether one possessed the Spirit or not. In the epistle both groups claim to possess the Spirit, and so the question becomes one of distinguishing properly between the correct and the incorrect spirit. Some who claim to have the Spirit have the spirit of deception (4:6), the spirit of the antichrist (4:3). Again the author provides a test: the Spirit which confesses Jesus Christ come in the flesh is of God (4:2). The test is ultimately tied to the tradition they have received about Jesus.

The author then returns to the mention of the Spirit directly in 4:13 where he says that the possession of the Spirit is an indication that God abides in the believer and the believer in God.

The next time the author speaks of the Spirit explicitly is 5:6–12. Here the topic is witnessing. The Spirit witnesses that Jesus came in water and blood. There are three that witness: the Spirit, the water, and the blood; and the three are one. The author makes an important, although somewhat redundant, point here. Jesus has come in water and in blood. That is, he has come to give the Spirit ("in water") and he has come to die in order to take away sin ("in blood"). The Spirit's witness is to the fact that Jesus did not come in water alone (only to give the Spirit) as the opponents claim. Once more the presence and activity of the Spirit is tied to the tradition about Jesus.[22]

Finally the author returns to a paraphrase for the Spirit in 5:20. "We know that the Son of God has come, and he has given us 'insight' (*dianoia*) so that we know the true one." Although there is no explicit reference to the Spirit here, within the context of the Johannine tradition such gift of insight or perception would be immediately recognized as a veiled reference to the Spirit.

Thus the Spirit does not play less a role in the thought of 1 John, but the references to it are expressed in a greater variety of ways, sometimes explicit, sometimes implicit, but always in a way which would guard against "giving ammunition to the enemy."

4. Dual Testing for Claims

At the beginning of chapter five we saw a series of claims that were made by the two groups in the first epistle. We will now return to that list and observe how the author tests these claims. It will be apparent in what follows that the author tests each claim two ways. He asks whether the claim is backed up by correct belief and whether it is manifested in correct love. Although the statements are scattered throughout the epistle, this dual testing occurs with great consistency. In fact every claim listed in chapter six is so tested except those which speak of "communion" either with the Father or with the Son. (The numbers in square brackets in the following list refer to the order in the original list in chapter six.)[23]

(a) [2] "knowledge of God"

The author of the epistle argues that the claim to "know God" can be fulfilled only if one keeps the word of Jesus, that is, has correct belief, and only if one truly loves the brothers. In 2:4–7 the argument is somewhat complex but nevertheless clear: "The man who claims, 'I have known him,' without keeping his commandments, is a liar; in such a one there is no truth. . . . It is no new commandment that I write to you, but an old one which you had from the start. The commandment, now old, is the word you have already heard." The failure to keep the word of Jesus is expressed in terms of failure to keep a commandment, and the person who does not keep the commandments does not know God.

With regard to love, the author is much more brief and direct. 4:7d–8b says: ". . . everyone who loves . . . knows God. The man without love has known nothing of God, for God is love . . ." Thus the author explicitly related the fulfillment of the claim to the test of correct belief and to love.

(b) [3] "abiding in God"

"To abide in God" is "*menein en tō theō.*" In what follows, it is variously translated "to remain in," "to abide in," "to dwell in." In the epistle it is used in two senses. First, it is used to describe the state of indwelling which exists between God/Jesus and the believer. Second, it is used to describe the fidelity that the believer ought to exhibit toward the tradition as he has heard it from the beginning. In this second sense it is one of the major forms of exhortation that the author of 1 John uses to encourage his readers.

However for the present it is the first of these senses that we are interested in: the claim to mutual indwelling with God. The author of 1 John tests this claim the same way as before. 4:15 states: "When anyone acknowledges that Jesus is the Son of God, God dwells in (*menei*) him." Also 2:5-6 agrees: "The way we can be sure we are in union with him is for the man who claims to abide in (*menein*) him to conduct himself just as he did." The "conduct" then is interpreted (2:7) in terms of keeping the commandment which is the "word which they have already heard." A third text confirms the above: "As for you, let what you heard from the beginning remain in your hearts. If what you heard from the beginning does remain in your hearts, then you in turn will remain in the Son and in the Father."

About love and abiding, 4:12 cannot be clearer: "Yet if we love one another, God dwells (*menei*) in us." So also 4:16: "God is love, and he who abides in love abides in (*menei*) God, and God in him."

(c) [4] "being in the light"

"Being/walking in the light" is also subjected to the dual verification. The claim to be in the light is tested by their adherence to the word of God. In 1:7 correct belief is the issue: "But if we walk in light, as he is in the light . . . the blood of his Son Jesus cleanses us from all sin. If we say that we have not sinned or that his blood does not cleanse us from sins, we make Jesus a liar and his word is not in us." (NAB)

The claim to be in the light is tested by the practice of love in 2:9: "The man who claims to be in light, hating his brother all the while, is in darkness even now. The man who continues in the light is the one who loves his brother." (NAB)

(d) [6] being "of God"

The claim to "be of God" or "to belong to God" (*einai ek tou theou*) is also a prominent claim in the first epistle. Yet it is to be tested by both love and belief. Belief and belonging are tested by means of the Spirit. 4:1-2 deal with this: "Beloved, do not trust every spirit but put the spirits to a test to see if they are of God . . . every spirit that acknowledges Jesus Christ come in the flesh belongs to God, while every spirit that fails to acknowledge him does not belong to God (*ek tou theou ouk estin*)." This is then followed by 4:4a: "You are of God (*ek tou theou este*), you little ones . . . for there is One greater in you than there is in the world."

In 3:11 we find the test of love: "No one whose actions are unholy is of God, nor anyone who fails to love his brother."

(e) [7] "begotten of God"

The attainment of the status of being begotten of God (*ek tou theou gegennētai*) is also linked by the author to both love of one's brothers and to belief in Jesus. Thus 4:7c says: ". . . everyone who loves is begotten of God (*ek tou theou gegennētai*) . . ." 5:1 says the same of belief: "Everyone who believes that Jesus is the Christ has been begotten of God (*ek tou theou gegennētai*) . . ." Also 5:4–5: ". . . everyone begotten of God (*pan to gegennēmenon*) conquers the world, and the power that has conquered the world is this faith of ours. Who then is conqueror of the world? The one who believes that Jesus is the Son of God."

(f) [8] "having eternal life"

Both correct belief and mutual love are necessary to have "eternal life."

The link between the possession of eternal life (*echein tēn zōēn*) and belief in Jesus is explicated within the argument of 5:10–13, a passage which deserves to be quoted in its entirety:

(10) The one who believes in the Son of God has the witness in himself. The one who does not believe in God has made him a liar, because he has not believed in the witness which God bore about his Son. (11) And this is the witness, that God has given us eternal life, and this very life is in his Son. (12) The one who has the Son has life (*echei tēn zōēn*); the one who does not have the Son of God does not have life (*tēn zōēn ouch echei*). (13) I wrote these things to you, to you who believe in the name of the Son of God, so that you might know that you have eternal life (*zōēn echete aiōnion*).

3:15 provides the correlation of life with love: "Everyone who hates his brother is a murderer, and you know that no murderer has eternal life abiding in him (*ouch echei tēn zōēn aiōnion en autō menousan*)."

(g) [9] "being of the truth"

"Being of the truth" (*einai ek tēs alētheias*) also is tested by belief and by love. After the author discusses those who have enough of this world's goods yet close their hearts to their brothers, he exhorts the reader to love in deed and not merely talk about it (3:17–18). The exhortation ends: "This is our way of knowing we are committed to the truth (*ek tēs alētheias esmen*) and are at peace before him . . ."[24]

Being "of the truth" is made dependent upon belief in 2:21–23. "My reason for having written you is not that you do not know the truth (*oidate tēn alētheian*) but that you do, and that no lie has anything in common with the truth (*pan pseudos ek tēs alētheias ouk estin*). Who is the liar? He who denies that Jesus is the Christ. . . . Anyone who denies the Son has no claim on the Father."

(h) [10] "loving God"

If we claim to love God we should keep his word and we should love one another. In 2:5 we hear: "The one who keeps his word, in this one the love of God is brought to perfection." And in 5:2 it is stated: "Everyone who loves the father loves the child he has begotten."

(i) "from the beginning"

In addition to the previous eight examples of tests involving correct belief and love of the brethren, both of these tests have been heard from the beginning of the community's existence. Love of one another is a message the community has heard "from the beginning" (*ap' archēs*) (3:11). And belief in the word of Jesus is a commandment. This commandment is "an old one which you have heard from the start" (*ap' archēs*). Once again this parallel statement is a description rather than a proof. But both are elements of the community's theology which have been with the community since its inception; they are not new ideas introduced by the "progressives."

(j) "the two commands"

Finally, this parallel statement, while not strictly a test, nevertheless provides a further instance of a description which indicates the parallel way in which the two commands were perceived. The content of the first commandment which the faithful are to obey is that they are to remain faithful to the word of Jesus (cf 2:5): "The commandment, now old, is the word which you have heard" (*hē entolē hē palaia estin ho logos hon ēkousate*) (2:7). And the second command is that they love one another: "The commandment we have from him is this: whoever loves God must also love his brother" (*kai tauten ten entolen echomen ap' autou, hina ho agapon ton theon agapa kai ton adelphon autou*). This usage parallels the other eight examples of dual testing of claims but now identifies belief and love as commandments given by God.

(k) Conclusions

This listing of claims and tests for them is revealing and illustrates a number of things about the thought of the epistle. The fact that there are so many pairs of parallel statements shows that the errors of the opponents manifested themselves in two major, discernible ways. This would seem to be a very powerful kind of evidence against the position that there was only one error within the community. Second, it shows that correct love and correct belief were both used as "tests" for the position of the author's adherents and of his opponents. Third, the repeated use of such pairings of belief and love also indicates beyond a reasonable doubt that the author's language about commandment was also intended to revolve around two specific commandments: belief in the message of Jesus and "brotherly" love.

A SURVEY OF 1 JOHN

We are now in a position to gain a sense of the overall thought of the first epistle and how the commandment passages contribute to that thought.

It is the thesis of what follows that the epistle is structured into two major sections, and that in the first the theme of light is meant to symbolize the topic of correct belief and that it is within this section that the commandment material dealing with remaining faithful to the word of Jesus appears. In the second half, the theme of "love" predominates and the discussion centers around the theme of correct ethical behavior: love of one another within the community. It is in this section that the focus is on the commandment to love one another. Thus the themes and topics of the epistle parallel the distribution of commandment texts within the epistle.

It cannot be said, nor do I intend to say, that the topic of belief occurs in the first half exclusively and love in the second half; rather the point is that the dominant themes in each half are respectively belief and love, and where the other topic appears there is a reason. There are two texts which should be noted in advance. 2:3–11, although it starts with the discussion of the commandment to correct belief, ends with an extended discussion of mutual love. A similar process takes place in 4:7–5:12. The beginning of this section deals with the commandment to love. But this love is then shown to involve correct faith, and the discussion of love ends with perhaps the longest discussion of correct belief in the epistle. This is important for understanding the way the author develops his thought. These are not exceptions to the plan I have suggested above but affirm it as well as affirming that in the author's view the two commandments are ultimately intertwined: one cannot really keep one of the commandments without keeping the other.

For the purposes of the following discussion I will use the subdivisions (i.e. those divisions within each of the two major parts of the epistle) of the epistle proposed by Brown in his commentary.[25]

THE PROLOGUE

1:1–4

These verses serve as a prologue to the tract and the parallels between them and the prologue of the gospel have been frequently noted. The prologue affirms three things. First, what the author will say about the word of life he has heard and seen and touched from the beginning. Second, the word of life he talks about and witnesses to and announces was with the Father and was revealed to "us." Third, the author writes his letter so that his readers might be joined in community with him and with the Father and his Son Jesus so that the author's joy might be fulfilled.

THE FIRST MAJOR DIVISION
OF THE EPISTLE (1:5–3:10)

1:5–2:2

The author immediately begins with the affirmation that God is light and that there is no darkness in him. Then the author introduces three false claims made by the secessionists. The first claim is that they are in communion with God; the second is that they are free of sin; the third is that they have not sinned.

Each of these is treated as a distortion of the message of Jesus. The one who makes the first claim and yet walks in darkness is said not to act in truth. The one who holds the second is said not to "have the truth in him." The one who holds the third is said to make God a liar and God's word is not in him. Thus the three boasts which deal with conduct (sinfulness) are all answered ultimately in terms of being lies, and as being evidence that the "word" of God is not within them. Rather, as the author asserts, he hopes that they will not sin, but if they do, they have Jesus as a paraclete, a propitiation for their sins and for those of the whole world. This is the "word" which they have seen and received.

2:3–11

In the second section[26] the author begins by saying that the true way of knowing God is by keeping his commandments. Again he switches to three false claims: the claim to "know" God, the claim to "abide" in him, and the claim to be "in the light." This is the first of the three sections in the epistle to deal with commandments. The author says that the claim to know God can be tested by seeing whether the person keeps the commandments (general exhortation, as we have seen above). The one who does not keep them is a liar, and the truth is not in him, but the love for God is brought to perfection in the one who "keeps his word." Keeping the word is the basis of true abiding.

The person who claims to abide in him (the second claim) is tested by the criterion of whether the person walks as Christ walked. This is then defined in terms of the "new" and "not so new" commandment. This commandment is then further defined as the word of God. The reader is commanded to keep the word of God. It is a "new" commandment in that the true light is shining.

Finally the claim to be "in the light" can be tested by seeing whether the person's beliefs issue into mutual love. This is the only instance of mutual love being discussed in the first part of the epistle. But close inspection shows that the basic topic is not really mutual love, but rather the importance of walking in the light. Mutual love is discussed only as a test whether the community member really is walking in the true message of Jesus. This then is the first instance of one commandment being used to "establish" the other. Mutual love is a proof that one believes correctly, that one is in the light!

2:12–17

In the third section of the first part the author reassures the members of his community that they have the correct belief. Their sins are forgiven, they know God, they have conquered evil, and *the word of God remains in them* (2:14). Consequently they are urged to retain their love for the Father and not for the things of the world. The things of the world pass away but the one who does the will of God remains forever.

This section deals mainly with a poetic exhortation, but it is marked by the recollection that the members of the community have *the word of God remaining in them.* That is, they believe correctly. Therefore they should not love the world or its allurements.

2:18–27

In the fourth section, after the description of the secessionists as antichrists and after their departure from the community has been mentioned, mention is made of the anointing which the readers have. It is an anointing which gives them knowledge. The faithful readers are reminded that they know the truth, but the one who does not know the truth is a liar, and the liar is the one who denies that Jesus is the Christ. Whoever denies Jesus is said not to have the Father either, because the one who denies the Son denies the Father. The author exhorts his readers to hold fast to *what they have heard from the beginning.* What they have heard from the beginning is of course, the "word," the message of Jesus. The others, the secessionists, are attempting to deceive them. But because of their anointing the faithful have no need for others to teach them. Rather they should remain in "what his anointing taught them," i.e. the message of Jesus.

2:28–3:10

In the fifth and final section of the first half, a comparison is made between the children of God and the children of the devil. At the beginning the readers are urged to abide in Christ and are told that if they know that he is just, they will also know that the one who acts justly is born of him. The author then takes up the topic of birth and begins to talk about sonship. The author reminds his readers that they are sons now, and what they will be in the future has not yet been revealed, but everyone who holds this hope of his future coming makes himself holy just as he is holy. On the other hand the one who commits sin has not seen God nor does that person know God. The one who does not commit sin is "just," as Jesus is just. The one who commits sin is of the devil. This then is the way to tell the children of God from the children of the devil; those are not of God who do not do justice—and who do not love the brothers.

Here again there is a discussion, in general terms, of the relationship between belief and conduct. The principal assertion is that one's status as a child of God or of the devil can be determined by one's conduct. The major topic is one's sonship (i.e. one's status), not conduct. However this section again shows that the way one acts follows from the orientation one has. This transition is particularly clear in the awkward reference to "loving the brothers" found at the end of v 10 which "chains" this section with the following. Thus we have a second clear instance of love being a test of one's belief.

THE SECOND PART
OF THE EPISTLE: 3:11–5:12

3:11–24

Beginning the second major part of the epistle, the author reminds his readers that the announcement they have heard from the beginning is that they should love one another. This statement begins the shift toward a concentration on the need for love within the community even though there is a continued discussion of the content of, and the need for, correct belief.

After a series of exhortations in which the Christian who loves the brother is contrasted with Cain who killed his brother (v 12), it is said that Christians can tell that they have passed from death to life by the fact that they love one another (vv 13–17). Then in vv 18–21 we are told that it is precisely in the exercise of mutual love that one can tell that he/she belongs to the truth. If one loves, then one knows that that person belongs to the truth. Thus we see, in both of these statements, that conduct is used as a test for claims regarding belief.

Then in vv 22–24 we come to the second of the sections dealing with commandment. Here in a carefully worked out chiasm,[27] the author urges his readers to general keeping of the commandments at both the beginning and the end of the section (v 22b and v 24a) and then in the middle defines the two commandments as believing in the name of his Son, Jesus Christ, and loving one another.

4:1–6

In 4:1–6 we find a return to the theme of correct belief. This is treated through a discussion of two spirits. The Spirit which belongs to God confesses Jesus Christ come in the flesh and does not negate the importance of Jesus. The "little children" belong to God and have conquered the world, and those who belong to God listen to them.[28]

4:7–5:4a

In the third passage of the second part, we see a development of the love commandment. Although it is not identified precisely as a commandment here, there is no doubt that this is what is intended. It begins with an exhortation to love, followed by the statement that the one who does not love knows nothing of God because God is love. God's love is exemplified in his sending of his Son. In turn this sending is used as an example of the way mutual love is to be expressed within the community. Since no one has seen God, it is by loving one another that we will have God abide in us.

Then in vv 13–16, the topic of belief returns briefly but in relation to love. V 12 had said that if we love one another, God abides in us. If God abides, then we have the Spirit. It is the Spirit that confesses that God has sent his Son as savior. But as v 15 explains, confessing the Son is necessary because otherwise God does not abide (confessing the Son is necessary in addition to loving one another—cf v 12). And of course it is only if we believe that Jesus is the Son that we are able to see the *love* that God had by sending the Son as savior!

In vv 16–21 the theme of love continues and the importance of remaining in love and the importance of expressing love of God in terms of love for community members.

This then leads into the third of the commandment sections of the epistle (4:21–5:4). Although the actual mention of the commandment takes place in this section, the development of it spills over into the next section. In addition the author follows the same format as he did in the discussion of the first commandment. That is, he uses a general exhortation to keep the commandments (vv 5:2c–3), a statement of the commandment itself (4:21–5:2a), and then a linking of this (the love commandment) with correct belief (5:4b–10).

Here the commandment spoken of is the commandment to mutual love. The commandment is to love not only God but also one's brother. If one loves God, then one should also love one's brother because the brother believes that Jesus is the Christ and therefore is also begotten by God. This love of the brothers then also involves correct faith. This leads immediately into the next section.

5:4b–12

Toward the end of the previous section, a chaining process had begun (the begotten . . . is victorious; the victory . . . is faith; the victor . . . is one who believes that Jesus is the Son of God; Jesus . . . came through water and blood) but the theme returns to a discussion of faith. Throughout this section there is the language of truth (v 6d,e) and of testimony (6d,7,9a,11c). But here again we see that the commandment to love has served as the foundation for this discussion of faith, again intertwining the two.

It is the one born of God who is to be loved. But in 5:4 we find that it is the one who is born of God who conquers the world (5:4), and specifically it is the person's faith that has conquered the world. This in effect defines the one who is to be loved: the one born of God, but only one who believes correctly can be said to be born of God. Then in a complex section various essential elements of belief are treated: that Jesus is the Son of God (5:5); that Jesus came through water and blood (5:6); that the Spirit testifies to all this (5:6b–9); that the one who believes in the Son of God has this witness inside himself (5:10); that God has given us eternal life and this life is in the Son and that therefore the one who has the Son has eternal life (5:10–12). Thus again the discussion begins with a mention of the commandment to love but is linked to the need for correct belief, and so what would otherwise appear to be a discrepancy in the distribution of the material on love and belief is in fact accounted for by the author's technique.

EPILOGUE

5:13–21

Finally, in the epilogue there is no direct mention of either correct belief or love. Rather the theme is one of hope, of sinfulness, and of the importance of belonging to God and that it is the Son who has come who has given us the insight to know the one who is true.

CONCLUSIONS

The conclusions to this chapter in relation to the Johannine commandments and the Johannine crisis may be stated briefly. Throughout the epistle there is a consistent identification of two objectively testable faults as the root of the opponents' errors. We see that the commandments were undoubtedly formulated in order to deal with these two basic facets of the opponents' position. Further the distribution within the epistle itself of the passages dealing with these two commandments echoes (1) the structure of the epistle (2) the dominant motifs of the epistle (light and life), (3) and the discussion of correct belief and correct love. Thus it should be evident how central the thought of the commandments is to the thought of 1 John and to the refutation of the opponents.

NOTES

1. Although 1 John is traditionally called an epistle, form-critical studies of the ancient letter tradition indicate that 1 John is not a true letter. The first epistle does not have the opening typical of a letter in which there is mention of the sender or the addressee; there is no trace of a greeting, a health-wish, nor is there a concluding formula of farewell and the typical greetings for the community.

1 John is more properly called a tract, that is, a piece of literature organized more or less systematically for the purpose of setting forth an author's views on a topic. The problem with this term is that, at least as Windisch originally described it, it was seen to be intended for all Christians. This is not the case with 1 John. It speaks too clearly of a specific set of problems, a specific group of opponents, and a specific tradition within Christianity. Nevertheless, the term "tract" is close to describing the reality of 1 John.

2. See Brown, *Epistles* Appendix 1, 764.

3. For a full discussion, see Brown, *Epistles* 116–129.

4. Among the more well-known commentaries, Bultmann favored a theory of compilation, while Grayston's recent commentary proposes a theory of moderate editing of a previous document.

5. A. Feuillet, "The Structure of First John: Comparison with the

4th Gospel," *BTB* 3 (1973), 194–216; Houlden, *Epistles* 24–25, suggests similarity with the gospel of John but does develop it extensively.

6. Brown, *Epistles* 123–129.

7. Brown and Feuillet differ on several other matters also, notably authorship. On the basis of the similarity in structure between the gospel and the epistle, Feuillet would argue for identical authorship for the epistles and the gospel. Brown would not agree; nor would I.

8. This contrast can be sharpened even more when it is pointed out that *agapan, agapē* in the first part of the gospel does not refer to mutual love between the members of the community but to love of God or Jesus.

9. Beyond the determination of the general structure of the epistle, I would agree with Brown (*Epistles* 128) that it is best to use the various literary and rhetorical techniques present within the material as a means of subdividing the material.

10. The wording of Brown's statement here is somewhat misleading. He does not, as can be seen from his development of the topic (*Epistles* 27–28), claim that the two views are actually different, but rather in the gospel the impression is dominant that the period of darkness is totally gone, whereas in the epistle the note of "gradualism" is much clearer. The same is true for the description of eschatology. In the gospel the element of realized eschatology is dominant. Status as "children of God," possession of life, seeing and knowing God, and judgment are all elements which are clearly defined in the epistle as having both a present and a future element. Indeed, it is this tension between the perfect and the gradualist possession of various qualities resulting from the divine sonship of Christians that is in many ways at the heart of the struggle for the Johannine tradition.

11. This list is taken from Brown, *Epistles* 26–28. I have discussed the differences in eschatology above. All of the other topics in the list will be discussed in what follows, except for (6). I have no explanation for the absence of Old Testament quotations in 1 John. Nor, in my opinion, is that absence necessarily of major significance.

12. Brown (*ibid.* 25–28) himself does not think that such differences necessarily *prove* separate authorship.

13. This is a counting only of this precise phrase; there are numerous other instances where "Son" (*huios*) is used independently. This is

of course not a full accounting of the christology, but the phrase "Son of God" in 1 John clearly is a high christological title.

14. See above, 180–181.

15. See above, 157–58.

16. Brown, *Epistles* 28.

17. In the gospel there is of course no doubt that the word which Jesus speaks is ultimately that of the Father. There are times when Jesus specifically refers to the word of his Father (5:38; 8:55; 17:6,14,17). However Jesus refers to it most frequently as "his own."

18. See the detailed discussion and presentation of various opinions in Brown, *Epistles* 408–411.

19. The grammar of this reference is obscure. See the discussion in Brown, *Epistles* 625–26.

20. It is also possible that 5:16 speaks to this. The subject of the verb "give" is uncertain. I would be inclined to the position that the subject is God or Jesus. See the discussion in Brown, *Epistles* 611–612. I will discuss this text further below.

21. "From the holy one" is probably a reference to Jesus who gives the Spirit. See Marshall, Brown.

22. There are four commonly proposed explanations of the phrase "in water and blood": (1) that they refer to the sacraments of baptism and the eucharist; (2) that they refer to the incarnation; (3) that they refer to the baptism and death of Jesus; (4) that they refer to the death of Jesus. The only other time the phrase occurs in the Johannine writings is in John 19:34, where blood and water flow from the side of Jesus. There the two refer to the giving of the living waters of the Spirit (cf 7:39) and of the death of Jesus as a sacrificial victim. These are not unrelated. The Spirit which Jesus gives is the source of life, and the death of Jesus was the means by which sin was taken away, thus making the reception of the new life possible. Thus I would see this as another example of the "both/and" approach: the death of Jesus and the giving of the Spirit are related as the negative and the positive elements of the process of obtaining eternal life.

23. The idea of "tests" being present in 1 John was evidently first proposed by R. Law in *The Tests of Life. A Study of the First Epistle of St. John* (Edinburgh: Clark, 1909). Law proposed that the epistle was to be divided into three sections, each of which was structured by three tests for the position of the opponents: that of justice, of

love and of belief. It was commonly recognized that Law's division of the epistle was flawed in the third section by the fact that the term "justice" did not occur there. I do not claim that the two tests here determine the epistle's literary structure, but that they do account for much of the theological orientation. In addition, it will be clear that the two tests I propose clearly are used to test all of the claims made by the two groups. Thus these are both more widespread and more explicit than the use of the testing concept by Law.

24. Admittedly the text here is very difficult to determine. (See the extensive discussion in Brown, *Epistles* 453–60). If the phrase "This is our way . . ." is taken to refer back, then it clearly refers to love. If it is taken to refer forward, then it refers to the double statement of love and belief (3:22–24). In either case the linkage is clear, if not the text itself.

25. For a summary of Brown's division, see *Epistles* xx–xxi.

26. I will use the term "section" throughout to refer to the secondary divisions of thought within the two halves of the epistle.

27. For a discussion of the chiasm, see above, 53.

28. In terms of the dual structure presented by Brown, this section is a surprise in that it does not develop the theme of mutual love as we would be led to expect.

Chapter Eight

THE COMMANDMENTS IN CONTEXT: A SEARCH FOR SETTING AND GENRE

With our analysis of the Johannine commandments and their relation to the crisis of 1 John complete, it is time to ask several larger questions of the Johannine commandment tradition. First, what is the theological background of the use of commandment itself within the Old Testament and other Jewish religious literature? Second, what is the relation between the two Johannine commandments and other contemporary "two commandment" traditions. These other "two commandment" traditions include most immediately and most importantly, the "two great commandments" of the synoptic gospels but also include other "two commandment" traditions elsewhere in the contemporary literature. Finally there is the question of the function of the commandments within the Johannine tradition. We have seen that they were intended to specify two external observable areas of community tradition by which the true believer could be distinguished. But we may ask whether they in fact had a more precise function within the life of the community.

A. PARALLELS TO THE JOHANNINE USE OF "COMMANDMENT"

1. Commandment in the Jewish Canon: Deuteronomy

The obvious source to examine for parallels to the notion of commandment is the Old Testament. Commandment in the Old

226

Testament has a rich background and has been the subject of thorough study.[1]

Commandment is first used to refer to the commands of God simply as expressions of the divine will which derive from the fact of God's election of and covenant with the nation. The relation of commandment to covenant and election is evident in the first four books of the Pentateuch but especially clear in Deuteronomy, where commandment occurs most frequently and where it gets its characteristic stamp.[2]

In Deuteronomy the word commandment is used in a variety of ways, but the most prominent use is with regard to God's relations with the chosen people where his commands constitute the laws of Israel. In this sense the term is frequently combined with the terms "statutes and decrees" (*dikaiōmata kai krimata*) (Dt 4:1; cf 4:40). The commandments are the creation of God, and the people are not to add or subtract from them (4:2; 5:32).[3]

The primary motive of the covenant relationship of which commandment is an expression is the love that people should show to God (Dt 5:10; 10:12; 19:9; 28:69). In fact, love itself is commanded (10:12). This is a central feature of the presentation of Deuteronomy. It is only after the basic description of the covenant and of its blessings and curses (5:1–11:32) that the specific injunctions are narrated (12:1–26:15).

Nevertheless there is an essential relation between this love and keeping the commandments: Dt 5:10; 10:12; 11:1,13,22; 19:9; 30:16. In fact, loving God becomes almost synonymous with keeping the commandments. One cannot be said to love if one does not keep the commandments (Dt 7:9–10). Failure to keep the commandments will result in punishment: 8:11–20; 28:15–69. But observance of them will result in obtaining the blessings promised by God: 4:40; 5:16,32; 6:2,24; 7:12; 11:8,14; 15:5; 28:1–14.

One of the clearest summations of the Deuteronomic theology of commandment within its larger context is found in Deuteronomy 7:9–11, where almost all of the elements discussed above occur:

> Understand then, that the Lord, your God, is God indeed,
> the faithful God who keeps his merciful covenant down to
> the thousandth generation toward those who love him and

keep his commandments, but he repays with destruction the person who hates him; he does not dally with such a one, but makes him personally pay for it. You shall therefore carefully observe the commandments, the statutes and the decrees which I enjoin on you today.

Here commandment is directly related to the covenant obligations and is seen as an act of love. It speaks of punishment and reward, and it speaks of the necessity of keeping all the commands.[4]

2. Comparison of Commandment in Deuteronomy and in John

As can be seen from this brief survey, there are several notable parallels between Deuteronomy and the Johannine use of commandment. In both the Deuteronomic and in the Johannine use, commandment is closely connected with love. We have seen the Deuteronomic use above. In the gospel, love dominates the passages dealing with the commandments, both those given to Jesus and those given to the disciples. It is the motive of Jesus' fulfillment of the Father's commands (14:31). And keeping the command of the Father is the basis for Jesus' continuing in the love of the Father (10:17–18; 15:10).

Almost all commandment texts[5] in the gospel and epistles occur in passages which relate such commandments to love for the disciples also. Keeping the commandments is evidence of loving Jesus (14:15,21) and of loving the Father (1 Jn 2:5; 4:20–21; 5:1–3; 2 Jn 6). Specifically keeping the word of Jesus is evidence of loving him (14:23,24). Keeping the commandments is also the basis for being loved by Jesus (14:21; 15:10,14) and by the Father (14:21,23). The love which Jesus has shown is given as the model for our love (13:34; 15:12–13; 1 Jn 4:19). And negatively the one who does not love Jesus does not keep his words (14:24). Thus all of the Johannine commandment passages (except 12:50 and 1 John 3:22–24) are explicitly related to the theme of love! In addition to this general correspondence, just as love itself is commanded in the gospel ("Remain in my love"—15:9) so in Deuteronomy (10:12) the people are commanded to love God.

I have already noted that the Johannine conception of commandment has a conditional quality: "If you keep my commands, I will love you and my Father will love you." This presentation finds a close parallel in the conditional covenant language in Deuteronomy, evident in the blessings and curses.

Thus it is within the covenant tradition that the Johannine conception of the commandments has been formulated.[6] The believers' obligations are presented not as something separate from their past but closely linked with them and now the fullest expression of those traditions.

Much of what has been said above applies to all instances of the Johannine commandment texts. However, within the epistles, where there is no evidence that the commandment texts are secondary additions, the commandment texts occur in a framework of modified dualism. This dualism is not found at all within the canonical scriptures. The occurrence of the commandment texts within such dualism raises the question whether closer parallels occur where the Deuteronomic outlook is present within a dualistic framework.

3. Commandment in The Testaments of the Twelve Patriarchs

When we turn to an examination of The Testaments of the Twelve Patriarchs we are immediately struck by a major difference from its use in Deuteronomy. There is no mention of the Deuteronomic background of commandment which was essential to the Old Testament view. There is no mention of the covenant per se, but there is repeated mention of the keeping of the commandments "of the law." Consequently the question arises whether the view of the covenant is perhaps intended to be implicit since several aspects of the Deuteronomic view are present.

There is mention of the motive of love of God ("I tell you this, my children, from experience, so that you might escape hatred and cling to love of the Lord"—TGad 5:2) and mention of love by God ("So be wise in the Lord and discerning, knowing the order of his commandments, what is ordained for every act, so the Lord will love you"—TNaph 8:10). The conditional character of love is also evident here: if one keeps the commandments one will be loved by God. But the concern for love does not receive the emphasis it does in Deuteronomy.

A possible explanation of the lack of explicit Deuteronomic exhortation is the fact that The Testaments of the Twelve Patriarchs as a whole shows little theological depth and confine themselves mainly to ethical reflection and exhortation. Yet even when the motives of conduct are discussed, they are expressed in non-covenantal terms (e.g. TGad 5:1-11).[7] When God sends sickness as a punishment there is no mention of this in terms which would evoke images of covenant theology. Yet in spite of these differences, there are several striking parallels in The Testaments of the Twelve Patriarchs to the Johannine use of commandment.

Even though there are strong indications that the commandment passages are secondary additions to the last discourses in the gospel of John, it is striking that the author chose to put at least some of the commandment passages within the last discourse section of the gospel. All of the Twelve Patriarchs are in such testamentary form.

The Testaments of the Twelve Patriarchs also parallels the Deuteronomic use in its concern for the concept of commandment as evident in the sheer frequency of its occurrence. The noun occurs thirty-four times in The Testaments of the Twelve Patriarchs and appears only fifty times in the entire Old Testament. This is a clear indication of the importance of the concept for The Testaments of the Twelve Patriarchs.

Finally, The Testaments of the Twelve Patriarchs is set within an apocalyptic framework of modified dualism that is very close to the framework of 1 John. Some of the major elements of this dualism are (1) the presence of a cosmic struggle between God and Satan; (2) the conviction that this struggle is made manifest in the world by means of opposing spirits of good and evil which seek to dominate humanity; (3) description of life in terms of "two ways" and of "doing the works of God/Beliar."[8] This is of course a major element of the worldview of 1 John that is absent from the Deuteronomic presentation of commandment.

In addition there is evidence of a "two commandments" tradition within The Testaments of the Twelve Patriarchs as well as of a love described as "love of one another." These features are also present within the Johannine commandment tradition.

4. Commandment at Qumran: The Damascus Rule

The term *mishpat* is used rather infrequently at Qumran except in the Damascus Rule (CD).[9] Nevertheless there is fertile ground within this document for comparison with the Johannine and other uses. The Damascus Rule exhibits both the Deuteronomic theology of commandment and other parallels to the Johannine use found nowhere else in the same combination.

At Qumran, the concept of commandment is closely related to the covenant as it is in Deuteronomy. In fact, Deuteronomy 7:9 is quoted explicitly in the Damascus Rule in the context of the listing of the commandments for the Qumran community (CD 7:5, DSSE 103).

In addition the covenant in the Damascus Rule is clearly cast in a conditional form as it was in Deuteronomy. It speaks of the rewards and punishment that accompany obedience or rejection of the commandments.[10] There is also evidence that God's *love* for humanity is conditional:

> Hear now, all you who enter the Covenant, and I will unstop your ears concerning the ways of the wicked. God loves knowledge. Wisdom and understanding He has set before Him, and prudence and knowledge serve Him. Patience and much forgiveness are with Him towards those who turn from transgression; but power, might, and great flaming wrath by the hand of all the Angels of Destruction towards those who depart from the way and abhor the Precept. (CD 2:2–6—DSSE 98)

One way that the Damascus Rule differs from Deuteronomy however is in the place given to love. Although it is mentioned in the Damascus Rule (CD B 7:5—DSSE 103; 8:15–16—DSSE 105–06) and 1QS (1:1–4—DSSE 72), it occurs repeatedly only within Old

Testament quotations and the concept does not hold the place that it does in Deuteronomy. Rather the emphasis seems to be on anger and fear, elements which were present also in Deuteronomy but not in the same proportion.

The format of the Damascus Rule is not unlike that of Deuteronomy where the general injunction to obey the commandments, and the consequences of blessings and curses which follow on obedience or disobedience prefaces the listing of the specific commandments (Dt 12:1–26:15). So too in the Damascus Rule, a general description of the alternative consequences of obedience and disobedience in historical review are presented (CD 1–8, including chapters 15–16) (DSSE 97–110). Then there follow specific codes, for urban communities (CD 9:1–12:21; DSSE 110–115) and then for camp communities (CD 12:22–14:22; DSSE 115–117). This format of general description followed by specific listing corresponds *somewhat* to the pattern we have seen in the Johannine writings where a general exhortation to keep the commandments is followed by mention of specific commandments.

The notion of commandment occurs in a dualistic framework at Qumran just as it did in The Testaments of the Twelve Patriarchs. The world is presented in the same terms:

> He [God] has created man to govern the world, and has appointed for him two spirits in which to walk until the time of His visitation: the spirits of truth and falsehood. Those born of truth spring from a fountain of light, but those born of falsehood spring from a source of darkness. All the children of righteousness are ruled by the Prince of Light and walk in the ways of light, but all the children of falsehood are ruled by the Angel of Darkness and walk in the ways of darkness. (1QS 3:17–21—DSSE 79–80)

This dualism is of course very similar to that which informs the first epistle of John.

5. *Conclusions*

Our examination of the background of commandment to this point has provided us with a clear direction but yet with no simple answers. Each of the bodies of literature that we have examined has exhibited parallels to the various aspects of the Johannine commandments, but nowhere are all of the features present in the same way as they are in John.

While it is true, as was said at the outset, that the background of commandment finds close parallels in the Deuteronomic literature of the Old Testament, it is nevertheless true that this same theology appears at Qumran. The scrolls incorporate the Deuteronomic outlook insofar as it applies to the use of commandment. That is, they speak of commandments as related to the covenant. They speak of the covenant as conditional and as an expression of and demonstration of love. They see the performance of the commandments as necessary for obtaining the blessings of the covenant. And while the Damascus Rule makes use of Deuteronomic theology, Deuteronomy itself does not have the dualistic framework that is apparent at Qumran and in The Testaments of the Twelve Patriarchs.

Deuteronomy and The Testaments of the Twelve Patriarchs share a concern for commandment and put it within a last discourse genre. But even this is not decisive because not all of the Johannine commandment texts occur in such last discourse format, and those that do show signs of being editorial additions. Thus at this point the most we can say is that the closest parallels to the overall use of commandment exist within the Qumran materials. It is not possible to be more precise about the history of religions background of the Johannine use until we turn to a discussion of the various "two commandment" traditions which show signs of paralleling the two Johannine commandments.

B. OTHER "TWO COMMANDMENT" TRADITIONS

During the intertestamental and New Testament period there were other forms of "two commandment" traditions besides the Johannine type. The fact that there are two commandments in the Johannine tradition leads naturally to the question whether the Johannine commandments are a variant of this other form of commandment tradition or whether they were intended to be unique.

Although the two great commandments of the synoptic gospels are the most well known of these two commandment traditions, two commandment traditions also appear in the Jewish intertestamental literature. There are in fact two types of "two commandment" traditions in addition to the Johannine: the so-called "double commandment" and the "two great commandments."

1. The Double Commandment

In New Testament studies the term "double commandment" is with some regularity used to refer to the two commandment tradition in the synoptics.[11] According to the usage of the terms in the intertestamental period, however, this is not completely correct. The term "double commandment" refers to what was seen as a double aspect of every commandment: namely that proper obedience required executing an action at the proper time, and also that true obedience required abstaining from the same action when that was appropriate.

This double commandment is evident in TNaph where in 8:7 it is said:

> The commandments of the Lord are double, and they are to be fulfilled with regularity. There is a time for having intercourse with one's wife, and a time to abstain for the purpose of prayer.

Here the double aspect is clear: to do and to abstain. That this is intended as a separate aspect is clear from the fact that this double aspect is contrasted immediately with the "two" commandments, as the text continues:

> And there are the two commandments. Unless they are performed in proper sequence they leave one open to the greatest sin. It is the same with the other commandments. So be wise in the Lord and discerning, knowing the order of his commandments, what is ordained for every act, so that the Lord will love you. (TNaph 8:9–10)

Although the "two commandments" are not explicitly defined in this context, this second set of commandments is intended to refer to something distinct from the "double commandment." Most likely this is intended to refer to what is properly termed "two great commandments."[12] Thus the obligation to have intercourse would exemplify the obligation one had toward a "fellow human being" (spouse), and the obligation to abstain for purposes of prayer would exemplify the obligation one had toward God. But the two obligations must be performed "in proper sequence," i.e. the obligation to God takes precedence over the obligation to one's fellow human.[13] If they are not performed in sequence they leave one open to "the greatest sin," i.e. putting a human being above God.

The Johannine commandments are clearly not an expression of this double commandment tradition.

2. The "Two Great Commandments"

The second commandment tradition evident within the intertestamental period is the tradition of various attempts to summarize the law. These summaries took the form of "two great commandments," one commandment specifying one's obligations to God and a second one expressing obligations toward one's neighbor. Although the "two great commandments" are perhaps most widely known from their appearance within the New Testament, there is clear evidence of their existence within the intertestamental literature before the beginning of the New Testament period.

(a) The "Two Great Commandments" Before the New Testament

There are no attempts to summarize the law in the Old Testament itself even though the texts quoted in the gospels of Matthew, Mark and Luke are from the Old Testament (Dt 6:4–5; Lev 19:18). There are clear examples in the pseudepigrapha, however.[14] The first of these is in Jubilees 36:3–7:

And I am commanding this, my sons, that you might perform righteousness and uprightness upon the earth so that the Lord will bring upon you everything which the Lord said that he would do for Abraham and for his seed. And

among yourselves, my sons, be loving of your brothers as
a man loves himself, with each man seeking for his brother
what is good for him, and acting together on the earth, and
loving each other as themselves. And regarding the matter
of idols, I command you and admonish you to scorn them
and hate them and not to love them because they are full
of error for those who worship and bow down to them.
Remember, my sons, the Lord, the God of Abraham, your
father, and (that) I subsequently worshiped and served him
in righteousness and joy so that he might multiply you and
increase your seed like the stars of heaven with regard to
number and (so that) he will plant you on the earth as a
righteous planting which will not be uprooted for all the
eternal generations. And now I will make you swear by the
great oath—because there is not an oath which is greater
than it, by the glorious and honored and great and splendid
and amazing and mighty name which created heaven and
earth and everything together—that you will fear him and
worship him. And (that) each one will love his brother from
now and forever all the days of your lives so that you will
prosper in all your deeds and not be destroyed. (OTP trans.)

There are two references to the two great commandments in
this paragraph. At the beginning is a long description of the need for
the brothers to love one another. Then the author addresses the matter
of idols, i.e. correct worship of God. At the end, in a solemn oath
they are told to fear and worship the Lord, and to love one's brother.
In both instances within the passage there is a focus on two "basic"
responsibilities, and their enunciation is solemnized by their context
within an oath.

In TIss 5:1–2 we find the two commandments but as part of a
larger list:

Keep the Law of God, my children; achieve integrity; live
without malice, not tinkering with God's commands or your
neighbor's affairs. Love the Lord and your neighbor; be
compassionate toward poverty and sickness. Bend your back

in farming, perform the tasks of the soil in every kind of agriculture, offering gifts gratefully to the Lord.

Although there are no exact parallels to the great commandments at Qumran, there is a passage which focuses responsibilities into two areas: God and neighbor. Near the beginning of the Community Rule (1QS), in the description of the purpose of the community and the manner of its life, we are told:

> He [the Master] shall admit into the Covenant of Grace all those who have freely devoted themselves to the observance of God's precepts, that they may be joined to the counsel of God and may live perfectly before him in accordance with all that has been revealed concerning their appointed times, and that they may love the sons of light, each according to his lot in God's design and hate all the sons of darkness, each according to his guilt in God's vengeance. (IQS 1:7–11—DSSE 72)

This passage is different from the examples we have seen already in that there is no mention of love of God but only of observance of his precepts. Nor is there any evidence of a tendency to collapse the multiple obligations of the law into one or two commandments. However there is evidence of a categorical distinction between the focus on responsibility to God and to one's fellow Essene, and so there is a sense in which the passage can be said to witness to the tendency to focus responsibilities into these two areas.

(b) The Two Great Commandments in the New Testament

The two great commandments appear in three versions in the synoptics: Mark 12:28–34, Matthew 22:34–40, and Luke 10:25–29. The two "great commandments" and the "love commands" in the New Testament are a topic that have brought forward an enormous literature.[15] My purpose here is not to repeat such study. Rather, since they are the closest expression of two commandments within the Christian context, we will try to clarify the relationship between them and the Johannine commandments.

In each of these synoptic passages there is a concern to summarize the law. In each the first commandment speaks of one's obligations toward God (and in two of the passages this first one is said to be the "greatest"). Then a second is added urging love of one's neighbor. In all three gospels the two commandments are couched in quotations from Deuteronomy 6:4–5 and Leviticus 19:19.

(i) The Synoptic Version of the First Commandment

In all three passages we find a similar presentation of the commandment dealing with love of God, although each of the accounts shows evidence of editing in order to fit within the theological purposes of the individual evangelists.[16] The version in Mark is longer and more repetitive, containing a fuller quote from the Shema (Dt 6:4–5). This may be due to Mark's concern for a Gentile audience where it was important to stress worship of only one God. This concern for a Gentile audience may also be present in the relativizing of Jewish ritual evidence in the comparison with "burnt offerings and sacrifice."

Matthew's version is shorter and contains various expressions with legal connotations. His version is intended to make clear that such a summary is a Christian interpretation of the law, based on Jesus' eschatological fulfillment of the law. It represents the foundation and intention of the whole law.[17] Luke on the other hand focuses more on these commandments as a way to salvation than as a summary of the law. This is not surprising since Luke has a tendency to downplay Jewish/Christian comparisons. In the Marcan and Matthean accounts of the great commandments there is evident a priority assigned: the love of God is the greatest of the commandments.

(ii) The Synoptic Version of the Second Commandment

The second of the two great commandments, love of neighbor, is based on Leviticus 19:18. Yet in each of the synoptics the concern to define the neighbor is somewhat different.

In Mark the exact definition of who the neighbor is is not of concern. There is no attempt to elaborate the meaning of the term. The chief concern seems to be to relate the two commandments to one another. This is evident from their placement at the center of the so-called Judean controversy section (11:27–12:44), where the various controversies all hinge on the question of the relation between one's responsibility to God and the responsibility to one's neighbor.[18]

In Matthew, although the exact definition of who one's neighbor is is not specified in the text of the great commandment itself, two other passages provide clear indications: Matthew 5:38–42 and 5:43–48.

Matthew 5:38–42 was meant to be a progression over the understanding of retaliation in the Old Testament. It is of course meant to be taken within the context of the remainder of chapter 5 of Matthew which provides a series of new ethical ideals commensurate with the realized kingdom. But the passage clearly extends the love of neighbor even to circumstances where the neighbor is the enemy. Thus it prepares for the other statement essential for understanding Matthew's interpretation of love of neighbor: Matthew 5:43–48.

Matthew 5:43–48 addresses explicitly the issue of love of enemies. It clearly points to the limitless boundaries of Christian love. And it gives two motives for this. First, this is the way that God the Father acts, and we are to imitate him. And, second, it is this that will distinguish Christian love from the simply reciprocal relationships of friendship. Everyone is capable of reciprocal friendship; pagans and tax collectors do that much. The Christian is called on to imitate the Father and to love all, just as the Father does.

In Luke the definition of neighbor is also of primary concern. In fact, it has been said that the great commandment statement in Luke is really a preface to the question of who the neighbor really is. The identity of the neighbor is settled by the story of the good Samaritan (10:28–37). In this story, the true neighbor is the one who helps the injured man.

Thus although there are differences of detail and emphasis, the synoptic examples of the two great commandments belong to the same general tradition exemplified by TNaph 8:9–10; Jub 36:3–7; TIss 5:1–2. But do they represent a variation of the Johannine commandments?

(c) The Johannine Commandments and the Two Great Commandments

(i) The First Commandment: The Johannine Tradition

In all of the great commandment accounts, the first commandment is love of God. This commandment of love of God does not occur in the Johannine listing in any specific way. Nevertheless it is also true that the command to love God could be said to be implicit within the first Johannine commandment since that commandment orders us to keep the word of Jesus (of God). But this is hardly helpful since keeping fast to the word of Jesus was not intended to be a summary but to be a comprehensive statement urging faithfulness to *all* that Jesus said and preached.

In another sense, it is certain that the love of God was important for the Johannine community since, as is said repeatedly in connection with the Johannine commandment passages, unless one keeps the commandments, one cannot be said to love God (or to be loved by him). Why then is love of God not the first of the Johannine commandments?

Although we can only speculate about the answer to this question, some possibilities present themselves. As we have seen in detail above, the Johannine commandments took their form primarily in response to the circumstances that the community was facing at the time of their incorporation into the community's writings. At that time there was no dispute over the question of whether one should love God (or know him or abide in him); both groups within the community claimed to do this. The issue was how this love was made manifest. The author of the commandment passages responds by saying that it is evident in keeping the word of Jesus rather than by neglecting it in favor of a simple dependence on the inner direction of the spirit.

What would appear to be at first sight a "peculiar" formulation of a commandment is actually very understandable in the context of the history of the Johannine community. The schism of 1 John had precisely brought the value of the words/message of Jesus into question. The formulation of the "first" commandment therefore deals directly with this issue. Keeping faithful to the word of Jesus was of paramount importance. The first Johannine commandment therefore should not be looked upon as a Johannine version of the summation of the law, and in spite of the fact that it represents another "two commandment" tradition within the New Testament, the proper parallel for the first commandment is not the two "great commandments" tradition.

(ii) The Second Commandment: The Johannine Tradition

When we compare the Johannine and the synoptic traditions of love of others, we are again struck by what would seem at first to be considerable similarity between the Johannine version and that of the great commandments. However on closer analysis we find three major differences. First, the love of others is developed at greater length and is given a greater role within the writings, especially within 1 John. Second, the love is given a new model and a new motive. Third, the love is restricted to the members of the community and not given the universal extent evident in Matthew and Luke.

The first of these differences is obvious. Although in terms of extent the love command in the gospel is somewhat restricted, appearing as it does only in 15:9–17, the impact of the love command is extended by the modeling of it on the love of Jesus in dying for his own (10:15,17; 14:31; 15:12–13) and by its relation to the love of God who sent his only Son into the world that everyone who believes might not perish but might have life (3:16).

In addition, this love has a witness value. Jesus does what the Father commands as a witness to the world that he loves the Father (14:31); so the mutual love of the disciples will be a witness to the world that they are disciples of Jesus (13:35). Thus even within the gospel the love command assumes an importance greater than one might at first realize.

Within the first epistle, the love command occurs to such an extent that this epistle represents a prime place for the description of love within the entire New Testament. The identification of God as love (4:8) is unique to the Johannine picture. Thus one who loves imitates God; the one who does not love does not know God (4:8). We see the love God has shown us: by calling us sons of God (3:1), by sending his Son (4:9). It is not that we loved God first but that he loved us and sent his Son as a propitiation for our sins (4:10).

We see the love of Jesus in his death for us (3:16). We too should love. It is the proclamation that we have heard from the beginning (3:11). It is evidence that we walk in the light (2:9–11), that we are in the life (3:14). It is the evidence that we love God, for no one has ever seen God, but if we love one another, God remains in us (4:12). The reader is questioned how one could still have love of God if the person had enough of the means of life and yet shut himself off from the brother (3:17). This means that love is not simply to be spoken but to be put into action (3:18). We are to lay down our lives for the brothers (3:16).

The lack of love is described also: the one who does not love walks in darkness and is blinded (2:11). The killing of Abel by Cain is given as an example of what happens when one does not love his brother (3:12). The one who does not love is a murderer (3:15).

Secondly, in the Johannine literature the model for love of one another is unique: Christians are to love *as Jesus has loved them*. This is different from the synoptic tradition in several ways. First, it is different from the model of the "golden rule" in that the model is no longer oneself and what one would want for oneself, but rather Jesus and what Jesus would want for us—and is to extend to the same limits of dying for others as he did. But it is also different even from the model for love of enemies given in Matthew. In Matthew the model was the Father, who loves the just and unjust, and who makes his rain fall on all. In John the model is more concrete: Jesus and his human life and human death out of love. The love is made concrete and the unlimited bounds of that love are presented in the death of Jesus for his friends.

The third characteristic of Johannine love is perhaps the most startling: Johannine love is restricted to the members of the community. We have seen that, while the boundaries of love were not an issue in Mark, in the gospels of Matthew and Luke love is clearly extended to all: Gentile and Jew, friend and enemy. Does the restriction of the love commandment to "one another" diminish its idealism?

Perkins[19] suggests that however restricted the love commandment is in itself, other elements of the Johannine tradition would presumably be balanced off against the more restrictive and narrow passages we have been considering. For example Perkins and Schnackenburg[20] whom she quotes, see in 1 John 4:21 suggestions of a somewhat more universal scope of love. This formulation seems to retain the connotations of the neighbor as anyone with whom one has dealings. This is not altogether convincing, however. Second, the image of God-as-love in the Johannine writings is unique; it is not paralleled elsewhere.[21] And it is clear from other elements of the Johannine tradition (e.g. Jn 3:16; 1 Jn 4:9–10,14) that God's love is directed toward the salvation of the entire world. Thus she would suggest that the love command within the Johannine tradition is not as restricted as it would seem at first.

More likely as a factor in the formulation of Johannine love is the particular set of historical circumstances within which it came to expression. The community had already experienced expulsion from the synagogue at the time of the gospel; now it experienced something of the same but now in terms of the expelling (or the simple departure) of other members of the Johannine Christian community. But another factor may be of equal or greater importance.

The fact that such a formulation of love is found at Qumran is also of considerable significance. Both the Johannine and the Qumran communities were sectarian groups; both saw themselves gathered together in the face of an opposition that in their eyes included the rest of the world.

The community at Qumran possessed a dualistic worldview which led them to think of humanity as being ruled by the spirit of God or of the evil one.[22] Such a dualistic worldview clearly infuses the thought of the Johannine epistles. Consequently since one is led to look upon others as doing the works of the devil and as ruled by the spirit of the devil, one cannot love that person. The community which seeks to retain its purity against the contamination by the world will naturally be led to draw strict boundary lines. This is evident at Qumran, and the close similarities with the Johannine community suggest that it is also the motivation for the Johannine group.

Several times before in this book we have had occasion to call attention to the conditional form of covenant theology and its connection with the commandment traditions of both the Johannine community and the Qumran community. Both in Deuteronomy and at Qumran we have found examples of love coming from God which was limited by obedience to the commandments. If one did not obey the commandments, one would not be loved by God. What the Johannine and Qumran communities say about themselves in relation to God is also said about their own relation to others who do not obey the commandments. This sort of situation is clearly in evidence within the Johannine tradition. I find no difference in what the community says about its relations to others and in what it says about God's relations to disobedient humanity. In the Old Testament, this theology of a conditional covenant is balanced by other theologies. So too in the Johannine tradition, other theological statements serve to balance the view which would seem to limit God's love too much.

This theology also had a social function.[23] The community was almost constantly under pressure either from without or from within. This tends to develop the same sort of sectarian mentality which has a suspicion of outsiders and of the enemy. Within the New Testament however this view is balanced not only by the other statements of the Johannine tradition but also by the other descriptions of Christian love within the canon, especially by the Lucan and the Matthean versions which present other dimensions so eloquently.

But it remains for the Johannine literature to have plumbed the depths of the intensity and profundity of Christian love in a unique way by pointing out to its own community and through the canon to all ages that this love that is called for is of the very heart of God— God is love—and also by pointing out that the model of our own life is not only how we would love ourselves (which indeed can have many imperfections) but to love as Jesus himself loved us by giving his life for us that we might live.

(iii) Summary

We have seen that the first Johannine commandment was a response to the historical circumstances of the community. As was said above, what was at issue was not whether one loved God but how that love was correctly to be manifested. For the Johannine community this love involved a correct understanding of the role of Jesus and an adherence to his words. Consequently it cannot be said to be a form of the first synoptic great commandment.

The same can be said of the "second" Johannine commandment. Although this commandment bears more resemblance to the second of the two great commandments than does the first, there is no evidence that the intention involved in the formulation of this commandment was to provide a summation of the law. Rather it was intended as a response to the specific historical circumstances of the community. The opponents failed in love not because of the traditional reasons for failure in love but because in theory and in practice they no longer believed such love was necessary. In this sense, the issue is considerably different from that of the summary commandment tradition.

C. The "Double Scrutiny" and Community Initiation: At Qumran and in the Johannine Community

We have seen that in form and in intention the two Johannine commandments do not resemble the two great commandments of the synoptic tradition to any significant extent. Forged as they were within the crucible of the community's theological struggles, they took on a form which was suited to their need. Yet in spite of this undoubtedly unique history, we do find a surprisingly close parallel to the several important aspects of the Johannine commandments within the initiation rite of the Qumran community.

1. The "Double Scrutiny" at Qumran and Parallels in the Johannine Community

The understanding of the initiation process for the community at Qumran is still somewhat disputed.[24] However it would appear that there were two distinct phases of initiation. The first involved a promise to follow the covenant as the community interpreted it. The second involved entry into the community itself. This second initiation was composed of three parts. The first was a probation in which the applicant was not able to partake of the meal of the congregation. At the end of the first year, the applicant was re-examined and then allowed to give his possessions and earnings to the congregation. In addition, he was allowed to partake of the meal but not of the drink of the congregation. At the end of the second year, the applicant was again reviewed and, if found acceptable, he was allowed to join the community in full and to partake of the meal and the drink. In addition he was allowed to offer his judgment in matters of the community. Thereafter members of the community were reviewed annually and they were promoted or demoted in rank in the light of that review.

In each of these steps, the criteria that are set up are a "double scrutiny" of the person's understanding of the law as the community interpreted it and of the person's actual conduct with regard to the law.

The initiation process together with repeated reference to these two criteria is described in 1QS. We will quote it at some length:

Every man, born of Israel, who freely pledges himself to join the Council of the Community, shall be examined by the Guardian at the head of the Congregation concerning *his understanding and his deeds.* If he is fitted to the discipline, he shall admit him into the Covenant that he may be converted to the truth and depart from all falsehood; and he shall instruct him in all the rules of the Community. And later, when he comes to stand before the Congregation, they shall all deliberate his case, and according to the decision of the Council of the Congregation he shall either enter or depart. After he has entered the Council of the Community, he shall not touch the pure Meal of the Congregation until one full year is completed, and until he has been examined concerning *his spirit and deeds;* nor shall he have any share of the property of the Congregation. Then when he has completed one year within the Community, the Congregation shall deliberate his case with regard to his *understanding and observance* of the Law. And if it be his destiny, according to the judgement of the Priests and the multitude of the men of their Covenant, to enter the company of the community, his property and earnings shall be handed over to the Bursar of the Congregation who shall register it to his account and shall not spend it for the Congregation. He shall not touch the Drink of the Congregation until he has completed a second year among the men of the Community. But when the second year has passed, he shall be examined, and if it be his destiny, according to the judgement of the Congregation, to enter the Community, then he shall be inscribed among his brethren in the order of his rank for the Law, and for justice, and for the pure Meal; his property shall be merged and he shall offer his counsel and judgement to the Community." (1QS 6:13–23—DSSE 81–82). (emphasis added)

As can be seen from the italicized words in the passage above, each of the stages of initiation into the community is judged according to two essential concerns of the Qumran community. These concerns repeatedly emphasize the necessity of correct understanding of the community's interpretation of the law, and the correct adherence to "deeds, rules, observance."[25]

In the second of the passages which describe the double scrutiny, we find some repetition of the above process, but in addition there is the new element of the annual review according to the two criteria.

> But when a man enters the Covenant to walk according to all these precepts that he may join the holy congregation, they shall examine his spirit in community with respect to his *understanding and practice of the Law,* under the authority of the sons of Aaron who have freely pledged themselves in the community to restore His Covenant and to heed all the precepts commanded by Him, and of the multitude of Israel who have freely pledged themselves in the Community to return to His Covenant. They shall inscribe them in the order, one after another, according to *their understanding and their deeds,* that every one may obey his companion, the man of lesser rank obeying his superior. And they shall examine *their spirit and deeds* yearly, so that each man may be advanced in accordance with *his understanding and perfection of way,* or moved down in accordance with the offences committed by him. (1QS 5:20–24— DSSE 80) (emphasis added)

Thus within these two passages we find seven references to this double scrutiny. This repetition confirms beyond a doubt that these two categories were not simply a casual reference but represented a deliberate categorizing of the essential concerns of the community. This double scrutiny played an essential role not only in the initiation of the member into the community but throughout his life within the community. It was the means by which his rank within the community was determined.

The Qumran community saw itself as the true Israel and the true interpretation of the law over against the larger Jewish society, which the community saw as corrupt. Consequently such a concern for proper understanding and propriety in deeds took on some importance as a means of distinguishing the Essene interpretation from that of other forms of Judaism.

2. The Johannine Commandments and the Double Scrutiny

Of course, this double scrutiny at Qumran echoes quite closely the two concerns of the Johannine community: (1) adherence to the word of Jesus (the word of God); i.e. the correct understanding of the tradition as the community interpreted it ("that which they had heard from the beginning") and (2) adherence to correct conduct: love of one another. Thus although the specific content of the scrutiny is different in each community, the Johannine commandments are in general orientation similar to the Qumran scrutiny.

There are other similarities between the Johannine commandments and this scrutiny at Qumran. In addition to the type of concerns expressed, there is also a clearly expressed association of the scrutiny with a covenant context at Qumran. This parallels the Deuteronomic covenant theology which surrounds the Johannine commandment tradition.

In addition, there is the conditional element present at Qumran which we have seen in the Deuteronomic covenant. At Qumran covenant love has a conditional element expressed in terms of admittance or rejection of the candidates on the basis of their adequacy in terms of the double scrutiny, and in terms of their promotion or demotion within "ranks" again in terms of the scrutiny by the Council of the Community. The conditional element of the covenant is also evident in 1QS 5:12—DSSE 79, where it is said of the sons of falsehood, "Therefore Wrath shall rise up to condemn, and Vengeance shall be executed by the curses of the Covenant."

One difference is of course that there is no strong evidence that the Qumran community thought of the double scrutiny itself in terms of commandment. Certainly the statement of 1QS 5:22 (DSSE 80) that the one who joins the community pledges himself "to heed all the precepts commanded by Him" presumably would refer implicitly to "the understanding and the deeds" that the community observed as part of the law, but there is no explicit statement of this. Nevertheless, it would be only a very short move to see them as such.[26]

There is even a verbal parallel between the examination regarding "his spirit" in the second of the passages above which recalls 1 John 4:1–6, where the author exhorts his readers to "test the spirits": "In this we know the Spirit of God. Every Spirit which confesses Jesus

Christ come in the flesh is of God; and every spirit which destroys Jesus is not of God." The scrutiny regarding spirits was clearly present in both communities, and it is clear that in the Johannine community it was concerned with the correct understanding of Jesus.[27]

In addition it may also provide a key to an understanding of what may be one of the major functions of the commandments within the Johannine community: a scrutiny connected with initiation into the Johannine community.

3. The Initiation Rite at Qumran and the Johannine Commandments

The parallels between the Qumran "double scrutiny" and the Johannine commandments suggest a further function for the Johannine commandments. The material of the double scrutiny is clearly part of the initiation rite at Qumran. The parallelism between the Johannine commandments and the Qumran scrutiny suggests that the Johannine commandments may have formed part of such a scrutiny for the Johannine community, functioning, in some form, as an element of the initiation/conversion ceremony. This would be in addition to (but not totally distinct from) its more obvious function as the criteria by which the community defined its understanding of Jesus and of proper behavior over against the interpretation of the opponents.

(a) Previous Notice of Motifs in 1 John Dealing with Christian Initiation

It has been suggested often in commentaries that the first epistle exhibits evidence of influence from the Johannine "conversion exhortation."[28] This thesis has been developed primarily by comparison with the Qumran initiation ceremony quoted above, and also by comparison with descriptions of Christian baptismal ceremonies found in the Didache (1:1–6:2) and in the Epistle of Barnabas (18: 1–21:9).[29] This theory of baptismal influence, observed by many scholars,[30] has been developed perhaps most notably by W. Nauck[31] and M.-E. Boismard,[32] but also by B. Thiering.[33] It is also developed extensively by Brown in his commentary, particularly in relation to 1 John 1:5–2:2; 2:12–14; 2:20; 2:29–3:10; 4:7–10.[34]

(b) Elements in 1 John Which Are Commonly Called Baptismal

The first passage which is thought to contain baptismal overtones is 1:5–2:2. Here the dualistic language is linked with the "two ways" exhortation that is found at Qumran and in the later Didache (1:1–6:2) and in Barnabas (18:1–21:9).[35] Other elements include the confession of sinfulness, the exhortation to walk in light rather than in darkness, the contrast of truth and lies; the reference to a figure who will bring the sons of righteousness to walk in light; atonement; *koinonia*. Brown concludes that this "association of ideas is not accidentally similar to that found elsewhere in contemporary Jewish and Christian initiatory practice."[36]

In 2:12–14 some see the address to the older and the more recent members of the community as an allusion to their status within the community and in relation to baptism. All those who were converted to the community had become "children." One of the two groups which make up the children are the "fathers," those who had been Christians for a longer time. These are reminded that they have known God "from the beginning." This reference to the beginning then would refer to the time when they first heard the good news about Jesus at the time of their own conversion.

The "young men" were the more recent converts. They are told that they are strong, that the word of God abides in them and that they have conquered the evil one. This exhortation then recalls what effect their conversion has had on their lives.

The unusual language of 2:20 leads some scholars to associate it with a baptismal context. It is unusual that the author uses the term *chrisma* ("anointing") for the possession of the Spirit. The anointing seems to refer to a particular ceremony, most likely the community's initiation ceremony. The initiation most likely involved some form of anointing in which the descent of the Holy Spirit upon the individual was effected.

Another passage said to contain evidence of baptismal motifs is 2:29–3:10. This has been the object of detailed study by both W. Nauck, who claimed that behind 1 John was a written source whose context was originally baptismal, and by M.-E. Boismard. Boismard studied this passage in relation to similar passages in 1 Peter 1 and in Titus 2–3. Although not all ideas are found in all three, 1 Peter contains ideas found in both 1 John and in Titus but not found in each other. Fourteen ideas which occur in the three are listed by Brown: revelation, unveiling, appearance of Christ; begetting anew or regeneration by God; love or mercy of God for us; a future yet to be revealed or unveiled; hope; the Christian is to be pure or purified; the Christian is to be pure or holy as Christ and God are; assurance that the believer "knows"; the taking away of sins, the lack of sin in Christ; mention of *anomia* ("lawlessness"); appearance or revelation of Christ for a salvific purpose; love of brother; begetting by a seed which abides.[37] Because of this remarkable number of similarities, Brown suggests that the passage echoes a process of entry into the Johannine community.

In 4:7–10, the theme of begetting returns and is connected with the theme of God sending his only Son to save us and of having life through the Son. These themes are also closely joined in Ephesians 2:4–5 ("But God is rich in mercy because of his great love, for us he brought us to life with Christ when we were dead in sin. By this favor were you saved"—NAB) and in 2 Timothy 1:9–10 ("God has saved us and has called us to a holy life, not because of any merit of ours but according to his own design. . . . He has robbed death of its power and has brought life and immortality into clear light through the gospel"—NAB).

There are also other passages that are discussed with regard to the theme of baptism, but the ones listed give a representative sample.

(c) Evaluation of the Evidence for a Baptismal Background to 1 John

The establishment of a baptismal context for 1 John is difficult for a variety of reasons, and not all scholars would agree that such a context exists. It is made difficult first because of the paucity of comparative information. As I have already pointed out, we do not have a fully developed model in the New Testament of any Christian initiation rite as we do from Qumran. Much of our knowledge of the Christian baptismal rite is gathered from hints throughout the New Testament and from such documents as the Didache and the Letter of Barnabas. This makes it more difficult to determine whether the alleged features really were truly characteristic of the baptismal ceremony.

Second, some of the elements are simply ambiguous. For example, the repeated references to what they have heard "from the beginning" may well refer to what they have heard from the beginning of their own membership within the community, but they may well equally refer to what has been said since the beginning of the community as a whole.

The third problem is that the material that is identified as having baptismal connotations to it in 1 John (and elsewhere in the New Testament) is also found in contexts that are non-baptismal. This is because of the fact that many of the motifs that are proposed as baptismal are central to the thought and to the thought-world of the epistle as a whole.

The discussion of "two ways" is inherent to the framework of apocalyptic dualism. This was simply the prism through which they viewed reality. Incorporation of the symbols of light and darkness, love and hate, walking in light and not in darkness, cleansing from sin, *koinonia,* etc. play a role in all of the thought of the community. How then can we be sure that the presence of these elements in 1 John is evidence precisely of a baptismal background? The parallels from Qumran show how ambiguous such information can be.

At Qumran, there is clear evidence that the double scrutiny was an essential feature of the multiple initiation processes of the community. Yet we also have clear evidence of its use within the annual review of the members apart from any direct connection with the initiation. In short, the evidence for baptismal motifs tends to be founded on similarities in content without sufficient formal characteristics. Consequently, until such a time as it is possible to define form-critical parallels, it seems that great caution is called for in assessing the precise function of these similarities in language, symbols, and worldview. Nevertheless, from a review of the texts above, it does seem fair to say that the collective impression left by the texts is that some allusion to the initiation process of the community is intended and echoed within the language.

D. QUMRAN AND THE LIFE SETTING
OF THE JOHANNINE COMMANDMENTS

What does our knowledge of the double scrutiny at Qumran add to the discussion of a possible baptismal context of some Johannine language? I have already indicated one important conclusion.

It seems certain from the comparison with Qumran that in the double scrutiny we find a much more adequate parallel to the Johannine commandments than we do within the tradition of the two great commandments. In every aspect of their content and function, the double scrutiny provides a closer parallel than do the great commandments.

Second, given the constant presence of the double scrutiny in the various initiation rites at Qumran, and given the various other suggestions by Johannine scholars about baptismal motifs in 1 John, it seems likely that the Johannine commandments functioned at least partially as such a scrutiny for the Johannine community. As such, the parallels of the Johannine commandment tradition with Qumran and its location within the "two ways" exhortation in 1 John (especially in 1:5–2:2) form another type of argument for establishing a baptismal context for the first epistle.

Third, in spite of the possible associations of the commandments with a baptismal context, it would be inaccurate to associate the Johannine commandments solely with such a context. The double scrutiny at Qumran functioned, outside of the community initiation procedures, as a part of a continuing evaluation of the members of the community. We have already seen that the Johannine commandments functioned to correct the two most objective external features of the errors of the opponents within the community. Thus they had a larger function than any use within the baptismal context. As such they identified what the community considered to be, at the time, the correct understanding of the community tradition and the correct enactment of the tradition within their own conduct.

In spite of the considerable formal similarities pointed out above, the dual concern evidenced at Qumran is different from the Johannine in three important ways. First, the content of the "understanding" is unique to the Johannine circle. The first Johannine commandment requires that the believer hold fast to all that Jesus had said. Thus the tradition about Jesus functions as a controlling factor in the life of the community. The content of the Qumran scrutiny was obviously of an entirely different character.

Second, the conduct required of the community member was different. Although mutual love was a part of the conduct required of the member at Qumran, the Qumran scrutiny was never "reduced" to this alone. However the second Johannine commandment does focus entirely on love of one another. In addition, the motive and model of love within the Johannine community is focused on the example given by Jesus and so is radically different from anything at Qumran.

Third, at Qumran this "double scrutiny" is not specifically elevated to the status of commandment as it is in the Johannine community. This is an important difference. In both communities, the concept of commandment was of the utmost importance. It was the expression of the covenant will of God. Each community attempted to live out this covenant will as it understood it and sought to preserve it in its integrity. For the Johannine community to claim that adherence to the word of Jesus and that expression of mutual love were commandments meant that these two requirements were at the very heart of the religious life of the community. They beyond all else expressed the will of God in their regard.

Thus we see that the Johannine community's commandment tradition, as was the case with so much else in the community's interpretation of the Jesus traditions, chose to go its own way. Where it borrowed, it also transformed. But at root, the Johannine commandment tradition remained a clear witness both to the community's unique history and to its struggle to define and preserve their tradition about Jesus.

NOTES

1. The most detailed studies of commandment in relation to New Testament usage are in G. Schrenk, "*entellomai, entolō*"; O'Connell, "Commandment"; and S. Pancaro, *Law* 431–38.

2. O'Connell, "Commandment" 351. O'Connell points out that this would include a study of Deuteronomy and the psalms, especially Psalm 112. O'Connell sees the Deuteronomic usage as the background of the commandment texts except John 12:49–50 where he would see a prophetic background.

I find his study of the prophetic background as a parallel unconvincing. The texts that O'Connell refers to are not numerous and as he points out are largely restricted to Jeremiah. The prophecy of Jeremiah contains a greater degree of "compulsion" than is found in the Johannine description of Jesus' speaking the word of God. It will be argued later that the purpose of describing Jesus' speaking the word of God as a commandment was in large part to provide a basis for the author to speak of the disciples' faithfulness to the word of God also as a commandment. Thus the prophetic use of *entellesthai* does not seem to provide a sufficient background for the Johannine use.

3. In Deuteronomy (as well as in the earlier traditions) the word *entolē* is not used to refer specifically to the ten commandments. For this *ta deka hrēmata* (Dt 4:13) or *ta deka logoi* (Dt 10:4; cf Ex 34: 28) occurs. M. J. O'Connell proposes that this is the only evidence of *dabar* (Gk: *logos* as a "legal term") and that in these instances the stress was on the revelational character of the decalogue.

4. In the past, the link of the commandment passages with the last discourse form has been pointed out by among others Pheme Perkins. Since not all of the Johannine commandments occur in such a genre (e.g. all the instances of 1 John) and those which do occur (i.e. those of chapters 14 and 15 of the gospel) show evidence of being editorial additions, this may be less significant than previously thought.

5. Here I refer not to texts which enjoin brotherly love, but to those which refer to love for God manifest in keeping the commandments.

6. The covenant background of 1 John is well known. See, for example, M.-E. Boismard, "La connaissance dans l'Alliance nouvelle d'aprés la Première Lettre de Saint Jean," *RB* 56 (1949) 365–91; *idem,* " 'Je ferai avec vous une alliance nouvelle' (Introduction à la Première Epitre de Saint Jean)," *LumVie* 8 (1953) 94–109; J. Chmiel, *Lumière et charité d'après la Première Epitre de Saint Jean* (Rome: Gregorian University, 1971) 137; Brown, *Epistles* 279–81, 319–322, 470–472.

7. The discussion of the testaments by H. C. Kee in his introduction to the translation in OTP is helpful in this regard (pp. 779–780).

8. This dualism is discussed in detail in Kee's Introduction, OTP 779.

9. CD 2:18,21; 3:2,6,8,12.

10. CD 2:14–3:12—DSSE 98–99; CD 5:17–6:1—DSSE 101; blessings and curses, e.g. 1QS 2:1–10—DSSE 73.

11. For example, P. Perkins, *Love Commands,* Chapter One, "The Double Love Commandment" 10–26; R. H. Fuller, "The Double

Commandment of Love: A Test Case for the Criteria of Authenticity" in *Essays on the Love Commandment* (ed. R. H. Fuller; Philadelphia: Fortress, 1978). Both Perkins and Fuller refer to them as the "double commandment *of love*" which is of course true in a sense, but the more accurate term is "two great commandments."

12. Kee, OTP, 814, note c.

13. This represents a similar ordering of the two great commandments similar to the question posed to Jesus about which is the "greatest of the commandments."

14. Perkins (*Love Commands* 15) states, following K. Berger, *Die Gesetzesauslegung Jesu. Teil I: Markus und Parallelen* (WMANT 40; Neukirchen-Vluyn: Neukirchener, 1972) 120, 162f, that there are only two examples in Hellenistic Judaism of the attempt to summarize the commandments in the twofold love of God and neighbor: Jubilees 36:3–7 and TIss 5:1–2. However the number of parallels one finds is determined somewhat by the decision about what constitutes a satisfactory parallel. I would not limit examples to those which explicitly state that the two commandments are intended as a "summary" of the law but would include other texts where such an intention is evident. Secondly, I would not limit the parallels to those passages where the relationship is described as one of "love" (rather for example "fear and worship of God" or "compassion" upon the neighbor). If we are content to show that there was a *de facto* summarizing of the commandments into two basic obligations (as I would propose) and if the wording of these obligations is allowed to vary, then we find other examples of the interest in the "two great commandments" in Jewish literature, e.g. TIss 7:2–6; TJos 11:1.

15. A sense of this literature can be gained from a glance at the bibliography listed at the rear of the book.

16. Nor does there seem to be evident within the synoptic accounts a common literary tradition. The Matthean and the Lucan accounts show some indications of stemming from a different origin than simply that of the gospel of Mark (see Perkins, 22).

17. For example, Perkins, *Love Commands* 23; Fuller, "Double Commandment" 44. Matthew gives another summary of the law in 7:12 in the golden rule, "Treat others as you would have them treat you: this sums up the law and the prophets." In addition, Matthew

speaks at greater length about the form and extent of love when he gives the new law of retaliation and of love of enemies.

18. The section is arranged chiastically with the two great commandments as the center. Immediately on either side of the two great commandments there are questions dealing with the understanding of (God's) scripture and its impact for understanding of *human* obligations (Mk 12:18–27; 12:35–37). On either side of that there are passages dealing with the proper use of money in a way which balances obligations to God and to fellow humans (Mk 12:13–17; 12:38–44). The great commandments then provide the principles by which these problems are to be dealt with.

19. Perkins, *Love Commands* 120.

20. Schnackenburg, *Johannesbriefe* 121–22.

21. Perkins, *Love Commands* 120; Schnackenburg, *Johannesbriefe* 231–37.

22. For a discussion of the Qumran view see the Appendix.

23. Most famous among these is W. Meeks, "The Man from Heaven in Johannine Sectarianism," *JBL* 91 (1972) 44–72.

24. See, for example, M. Delcor, "Le vocabulaire juridique, cultuel et mystique de l'initiation dans la secte de Qumran," *Qumran-Probleme* (ed. H. Bardtke; Berlin: Akademie Verlag, 1963) 109–34; Vermes, *Perspective* 94–96.

25. This is also behind the beginning statement of 1QS: "The Master shall teach the saints to live according to the Book of the Community Rule, that they may seek God with a whole heart and soul, and do what is good and right before Him as He commanded by the hand of Moses and all His servants the Prophets; **that they may love all that he has chosen and hate all that he has rejected; that they may abstain from all evil and hold fast to all good;** *that they may practise truth, righteousness, and justice upon earth and no longer stubbornly follow a sinful heart and lustful eyes committing all manner of evil*" (1QS1:1–6—DSSE 72).

The words in boldface reflect various ways of describing the correct understanding necessary for membership, and the words in italics indicate the necessity of correct conduct as well.

26. Pancaro (*Law* 436) points out that commandment is used at Qumran to refer to something other than that which is directly con-

tained in the law. As he points out this is the first time in Jewish literature that this is evident. Commandment in the Johannine literature is used the same way. However in both traditions, the members would undoubtedly see their tradition as being contained within the law in the sense that both were rooted in what they saw to be God's revelatory word to them.

27. There is also a parallel in 1 John 3:11–15 with the interest in examining one's works at Qumran. In such dualistic literature, it was possible to speak of certain works being the consequence of a proper inner orientation. But it was also possible to speak of previous actions determining one's future actions. It is said that Cain killed his brother "because his (own) works were evil while those of his brother were just" (3:12). In the Johannine literature the dualistic use of "works" (as distinguished from the use to describe the ministry of Jesus—cf chapter two) are repeatedly used to show one's orientation. Cain's actions were evil; that is why he killed Abel. In addition, these works were evidence of one's "father" as in John 8:38–47 and thus evidence of one's orientation.

28. The term "conversion exhortation" is Brown's (*Epistles* 242). I agree with Brown that it is not possible to determine more precisely whether this material reflects instruction before baptism, a baptismal liturgy, or a homily at baptism, or a homily about baptism.

29. There are also other passages in the New Testament that are proposed as having echoes of the baptismal ceremony, but these are much more fragmentary. These include Acts 26:18; Galatians 5:17–24; Colossians 1:13–14; Ephesians 5:6–11; Hebrews 10:19–21; 1 Peter 1:1–2:25; Titus 2:1–3:15.

30. For example, Schnackenburg, *Johannesbriefe* 80, 82, 209–10; Perkins, *Epistles* 12–20, 38–40; Grayston, *Epistles* 87–90. Those opposed to baptismal imagery include, among the more recent commentaries, Marshall, *Epistles* 153; Smalley, *Epistles* 106–07.

31. W. Nauck, *Tradition.*

32. Boismard, *Quatre hymnes baptismales dan la Première Epitre de Pierre* (LD 30; Paris: Cerf, 1961).

33. B. Thiering, "Inner and Outer Cleansing at Qumran as a Background to New Testament Baptism," *NTS* 26 (1979–80) 266–77.

34. See the extensive list of references to "Baptism (conversion/

initiation or entrance setting)" in the Subject Index to his commentary on the epistles.

35. See, for example, Perkins, *Epistles* 12–20.

36. Brown, *Epistles* 245.

37. Brown, *Epistles* 432.

Chapter Nine

THE JOHANNINE COMMANDMENTS AND THE JOHANNINE CRISIS: A LOOK BACK

We have now completed our study of the individual elements of the Johannine commandment tradition and are in a position to draw together the findings of our study.

We have come to see that the proper starting point for the understanding of the Johannine commandment tradition is the theological crisis which the Johannine community faced at the time of 1 John. That crisis was caused by an interpretation of the Johannine tradition which emphasized the role of the Spirit to the point that a permanent role for Jesus was considered unnecessary. Because of their understanding of the Spirit, the opponents also came to believe that there was no need for exhortation to proper ethical conduct. As a result, the author of 1 John focuses on those two issues in his rebuttal of the opponents. He argues that the role of Jesus is a permanent and essential one. Not only did Jesus speak the word of God in a way that the Spirit will not surpass, but he died for our sins. In addition, his love is a model for the love that Christians are to show one another. The author, expressing these two basic requirements in the language of covenant obligations, calls them "commandments." The first commandment is to keep the word of Jesus and the second is to love one another.

When viewed from the perspective of the ministry of Jesus, it can be seen that these two commandments correlate with the two commandments given to Jesus by the Father. Just as Jesus was commanded to speak the word of the Father as he had heard it, so the believer is commanded to keep the word of Jesus and to remain faithful to it. Just as Jesus laid down his life for his own out of love, so the believer is to love the other members of the community in imitation of the love that Jesus had shown.

When viewed from the perspective of the community's theological crisis, the commandments confront the two major "observable" issues of that crisis. The first commandment asserts that the "content" of the tradition is contained within the words of Jesus and that any inspiration from the "Spirit of truth" must conform to that word. The second commandment insists that ethical action is of importance and that it is most clearly summed up in the requirement of mutual love.

The author of 1 John chose for the larger framework of his commandment theology the covenant tradition which Christianity had inherited from Judaism. However, the Johannine community modified this Deuteronomic theology by situating it within the framework of apocalyptic dualism, a framework very much like that of the sectarian documents at Qumran. Within this Deuteronomic (conditional) understanding of the covenant, the commandments were presented as the expression of the basic obligations due to God. Obedience to the commandments was necessary both in order to demonstrate one's love of God, and in order to continue being loved by God.

The function of the commandment tradition was varied. Certainly it was designed to meet the crisis of the community by describing the ways in which the opponents erred and specifically by defining "tests" whereby the opponents could be both identified and refuted. That was its general function. But as we have seen, the Johannine commandment tradition is not unlike the double scrutiny of the Qumran community. This double scrutiny was part of the process used in the community's initiation to determine the understanding of the community's interpretation of the law and to examine the conduct of the person being examined. Just as the double scrutiny at Qumran asked about the content of the tradition, i.e. the proper understanding of the community's unique interpretation of the law, so the first Johannine commandment was concerned with the content of the tradition as the Johannine community perceived it. Just as the second part of the scrutiny at Qumran was concerned with proper conduct, so the second Johannine commandment was concerned with proper conduct: mutual love.

These two scrutinies from Qumran so closely parallel the categories of the two Johannine commandments that they give us a clue to one of the more specific functions of the Johannine commandment tradition: that is, just as the double scrutiny played a part in the initiation rite at Qumran the Johannine commandments probably functioned as part of the initiation exhortation of the Johannine community. The fact that there are numerous other indications of baptismal/conversion language in 1 John makes it all the more likely that the Johannine commandments were associated with a baptismal context. However, in both communities, the concern for proper understanding and conduct certainly extended beyond the time of entry into the community, and so it is likely that within the Johannine community the two concerns continued to play a role within the community life even though it may not have been as formal as the yearly "review" that was conducted by the Council at Qumran. Thus the study not only has been able to define the content of the commandment tradition and relate it to the historical circumstances of the community, but, thanks in part to the close parallels at Qumran, we are able to suggest two of its functions within the religious life of the Johannine community.

One of the other important aspects of the study of the commandments has been an examination of the relationship between the Johannine commandment tradition and the gospel of John. The commandment tradition was not a part of the original text of the gospel but was added at a later time. There were three major reasons for this conclusion. First, the commandments as they describe the ministry of Jesus run parallel to the conception of his ministry as a "work," yet these two conceptions are not integrated or interrelated. Second, it is clear from the gospel that the commandment tradition there focuses on the obligations of the disciples and develops these rather than being concerned with being a major conceptualization of the ministry of Jesus. At the same time it is clear that the "work" theology in the gospel focuses on Jesus and hardly at all on the disciples. This is a further indication that the two conceptions are not intended to be complementary to one another and that they are not the work of the same person. Finally, we found that all of the passages where commandment occurs showed considerable evidence of being secondary additions to the gospel. Thus we have been able to get a picture not only of the function of the commandment tradition but also of its literary history.

As we began this study, one of the major unresolved questions was the uncertainty among scholars about the most basic of issues: the actual number of commandments within the Johannine tradition! Throughout the study, as we have examined the various aspects of the commandment material, the final determination of this question of necessity remained one of the most essential. It may be helpful here to review the reasons that have been given for seeing two commandments within the tradition. First there is the terminology itself. While the term "word" is ambiguous and could conceivably be simply a synonym for "commandment," there is an indisputable history of its being used to refer to the entirety of the revelation of God in the Old Testament. Furthermore "word" is used with this same meaning frequently within the Johannine gospel, so much so that it can be said to be the common meaning of the term in the gospel. Consequently it is at least possible and indeed even likely that the term is used in the commandment texts with this more inclusive meaning. Second, there is the fact that the commandments given to the disciples correlate so closely with the two commandments given to Jesus. Not only are there two commandments given to each, but the commandments given to the disciples are explicitly related to those given to Jesus by the Father.

Third, there is the parallel structure of the two passages in the gospel where the commandments given to the disciples are described and developed in most detail (14:15,21–14; 15:9–17). The manner in which each is developed shows a parallelism which clearly points to the content of each as a definition of a specific commandment. Fourth, there is the discussion of commandments in the epistles. There are some texts where it is incontrovertible that there are two commandments within the Johannine tradition (e.g. 1 Jn 3:22–24). This fact then makes it clear that there were two commandments within the tradition! Fifth, there is the way that the content of the two commandments relates to the issues of the community's theological crisis; each confronts one of the two observable manifestations of the errors of the opponents.

Sixth, it also became clear that the two commandments have a close relation to the structure of the epistle, mirroring the images of light and love which the author had chosen to structure the two halves of his epistle. Furthermore the commandment texts mirror this structure by the way the commandment texts are distributed within the epistle: the commandment to believe located in the first half (where the theme of "light" appears) and the commandment of mutual love located in the second half (where the theme of "love" dominates), and with the double statement of the commandments near the center of the entire work. And, finally, it is not insignificant that the commandments also echo the tests of correct belief and correct love that are used to test each of the eight claims to special status as Christians. Thus it would seem that there can be little doubt that there are two commandments within the Johannine tradition.

When we started, there had been not only no settled opinion on the number of commandments within the tradition, there had been no clear picture of how commandments fitted into the whole of Johannine theology. There had been in fact no sense that there *was* a developed theology of commandment within the Johannine tradition. Hopefully, the material presented here will help change that.

The concept of commandment is of course closely bound up with the notion of covenant. The concept of covenant is in turn at the very heart of the Judaeo-Christian tradition. Consequently while it is difficult to say that any one concept within the Johannine theology is the "major" concept, it certainly seems fair to say that commandment, by its close relation to the concept of covenant, is one of the major and most basic elements of the theological tradition underpinning the first epistle. It is the concept of commandment that the author chose to express the basic responsibilities of the community.

As we have seen, it is often thought also that the Johannine commandments reflect a variant form of the "two great commandments" traditions found in the synoptic gospels as well as in The Testaments of the Twelve Patriarchs. However detailed analysis has shown that the first Johannine commandment does not really parallel the first of the great commandments. The first Johannine commandment is more specific than the first of the great commandments, and a study of it in relation to the community context and to the issues it confronts shows that its intention was considerably different. The same is true of the second Johannine commandment. There is similarity between the second of the great commandments in that both are directed to love of fellow man, but they are different in the way that love is expressed and different in the purpose of the formulation.

This study confirms the view that the Johannine conception of love is less universal than that of some of the synoptic presentations. In addition it confirms the opinion that the Johannine view of love is very similar to the view of love found at Qumran. Thus this view of love reinforces all of the other parallels we have discovered between the Johannine commandment tradition and the thought of the Qumran documents.

It has also been said that the concept of commandment is part and parcel of the testamentary genre, and that the commandments therefore are closely bound to the last discourse sections of the gospel. This conclusion is based primarily on the parallels between the Johannine commandment texts and The Testaments of the Twelve Patriarchs. The commandments within The Testaments of the Twelve Patriarchs and the commandments within the last discourse section of the gospel do occur within testamentary forms of literature. In addition the fact that there are two commandments in the Johannine tradition and in The Testaments of the Twelve Patriarchs (at least in some instances) would seem to strengthen that parallel. However our study has shown that this is an incorrect conclusion. First, the commandment passages in the Johannine tradition do not all appear in testamentary literature as happens in The Testaments of the Twelve Patriarchs. Where the Johannine commandments do appear within the testamentary form, we have shown that they are editorial additions. While the editor may have sensed an appropriateness for them within this genre, the numerous other instances of the commandments outside of the testamentary form at least weaken somewhat this argument. Second, our study has shown that the commandments in The Testaments of the Twelve Patriarchs were part of a tradition that attempted to summarize the law under two great commandments. There is no clear evidence that the Johannine tradition was attempting to do that. While it is true that there are similarities between the Johannine commandments and the commandments found in The Testaments of the Twelve Patriarchs the parallels with Qumran are closer and more persuasive.

A further gain from the study of the commandments is the increased awareness of the ways in which the Johannine literature seems to reflect both the worldview but also the theology of the Qumran. We have seen that many of the images as well as the deeper levels of apocalyptic thinking found at Qumran pervade 1 John but appear only in certain sections of the gospel. These sections also contain much of the material which most supports the position of the author of 1 John. This has not been the place to explore the relationship between the epistle and the gospel in all its facets, but the conclusions reached here would seem to suggest that those theories which suggest that the redaction of the gospel was performed to meet the issues confronted in 1 John would seem to be at least partially correct.

A word also should be said about the relationship between the author of 1 John and the one responsible for the commandment passages in the gospel. The study of the commandment tradition has shown that the commandment passages are secondary additions to the gospel. Throughout the study there have been hints that the commandments were not the only additions, but rather that they may have been part of a larger redaction. It is unlikely that the person responsible for the epistle is the same person responsible for the redaction of the gospel. This may be possible, but it would be in any case very difficult to prove that the same person did both. Nevertheless, given the similarities between the two bodies of material, it certainly seems appropriate to speak of the redaction of the gospel as being done from the same theological viewpoint and by someone who attempted to both confirm the theological position of the author of 1 John and who wrote to deal with a similar set of historical circumstances.

The Johannine community had been born in a time of crisis, and the first epistle witnesses to a continued struggle to define and preserve that tradition. Within that struggle the Johannine commandments played a major role, reminding the Johannine community that whatever form the community might take, it must remain true to the words of Jesus and it must persevere in mutual love toward the members of the community. In many respects this commandment tradition was borrowed—the covenant tradition it took from Judaism; its form and number it took from a worldview similar to that at Qumran. But for the remainder, the Johannine community's commandment tradition, as was the case with so much else in the community's interpretation of the Jesus traditions, chose to go its own way. Where it borrowed, it also transformed. But at root, the Johannine commandment tradition remained a clear witness both to the community's unique history and to its struggle to define and preserve their understanding of Jesus.

Appendix

VARIOUS DIMENSIONS OF THE LOVE OF ONE'S FELLOW HUMAN BEINGS

In the Jewish tradition, love for one's fellow human beings was defined in various ways. There was love of one's kin, of one's neighbor (generally conceived of as one's fellow countryman), of the stranger in the land (because the Israelites too had been strangers in a foreign land) and of all other human beings; at times this specifically included those who were enemies. A review of such types of love provides helpful background for understanding both the second great commandment and also for understanding the second Johannine commandment.

Love for One's Kin

That love should be directed to one's kin (i.e. one's brother) is clearly illustrated by most of the passages quoted above. Within The Testaments of the Twelve Patriarchs, love of one's brothers, defined as the fellow members of one's tribe, is the most common form of love.

In addition to this there are numerous passages from The Testaments of the Twelve Patriarchs where such love is exhorted.[1] Examples are frequently adduced of the effects of hatred between Jacob and Esau and among the sons of Jacob, especially toward Joseph.

Love of Other Members of the Sect

At Qumran there are passages where the love is directed toward the community as a whole. However at Qumran, this love is clearly *limited* to the members of the sect itself, and it is even said that those outside are sinners and are to be hated.

At the beginning of the Community Rule we see the following:

> The Master shall teach the saints to live according to the Book of the Community Rule, that they may see God with a whole heart and soul, and do what is good and right before Him as He commanded by the hand of Moses and all His servants the prophets; that they may love all that He has chosen and hate all that He has rejected; . . . That they may love all the sons of light, each according to his lot in God's design, and hate all the sons of darkness, each according to his guilt in God's vengeance. (1Qs 1:1–11—DSSE 72)

Another example of this is 1QS 4:5 which speaks of the necessity of having "great charity toward all the sons of truth." And CD 6:14–15 (DSSE 103) speaks of the necessity of separating oneself from "the sons of the Pit," i.e. the sons of darkness who are dominated by the evil spirits of Beliar. In the ceremony of initiation, the Levites curse all the men of the lot of Satan: "May there be no 'Peace'! for you in the mouth of those who hold fast to the Fathers!" (1QS 2:9—DSSE 73).

The other members of the sect are often referred to as "brothers" as can be seen from the following passage:

> They shall love each man his brother as himself; they shall succour the poor, the needy, and the stranger. A man shall seek his brother's well-being and shall not sin against his near kin. They shall keep from fornication according to the statute. They shall rebuke each man his brother according to the commandment and shall bear no rancor from one day to the next. (CD 6:20–7:3—DSSE 103)

In this text, the "brother" does not mean blood brother but rather one's co-religionist. In addition, we see here that the love is to be extended also to the "poor, the needy, and the stranger," thus giving evidence of this wider dimension at Qumran. But this does not negate the effect of the previous passages where there was clear evidence of the exclusion of some from the concerns of love. The review of some of the reasons for this exclusion give us insight into their conception of love as well as into the circumstances of the community.

As part of the instruction given to the initiate, the Master was also to

> instruct all the sons of light and teach them the nature of all the children of men according to the kind of spirit which they possess, the signs identifying their works during their lifetime, their visitation for chastisement, and the time of their reward." (1QS3—DSSE 75)

The Qumran community held that

> [God] has created man to govern the world, and has appointed for him two spirits in which to walk until the time of His visitation: the spirits of truth and falsehood. Those born of the truth spring from a fountain of light, but those born of falsehood spring from a source of darkness. All the children of righteousness are ruled by the prince of light and walk in the ways of light, but all the children of falsehood are ruled by the Angel of Darkness and walk in the ways of darkness. (1QS 3:17–21—DSSE 75–76)

> The Angel of Darkness leads all the children of righteousness astray . . . all his allotted spirits seek the overthrow of the sons of light. (1QS 3:13–15—DSSE 76)

Thus we see that, within the Qumran community, it is for fear of the contamination that could come about from the sons of darkness who are controlled by the spirit of darkness and deception that the members of the community are told to love only those who are sons of light! This community which seeks purity and steadfastness against the corruption of the world does not attend to the possible benefits of love for those outside of the community. In addition, it should be noted that the statement quoted above would seem to indicate that such hatred of the sinner was not to be unbounded but rather limited strictly by the guilt that he had before God. How this was to be conceived of or judged is difficult to determine, but it does make clear the grounds for such "hatred," and that it could admit of degrees.

But there may be another element to this restriction of love. We noted above the Deuteronomic context of the development of commandment in both the Old Testament and at Qumran. Commandment in this sense was directly related to the conditional understanding of covenant. In this conditional view of covenant, blessings and curses followed from the way one related to the obligations imposed by the covenant. Even God's love which is elsewhere expressed as "unconditional" is here spoken of as dependent upon one's fulfilling the obligations of the covenant.

Such a view of covenant was clearly in evidence at Qumran. As the initiate entered the covenant, he went through a ceremony of blessings and curses. After a recounting of the great deeds of God, the rebelliousness of the nation was recalled. This prepared for the initiates' confession of their own sins and their recognition of God's mercy toward them. Then the priests bless all the men of the lot of God. Thereupon the Levites curse all the men of the lot of Satan. To both the blessings and the curses, the initiates respond "Amen, Amen." (1QS 1–2—DSSE 72–73)

As for those who do not follow God:

> God's wrath and his zeal for his precepts shall consume him
> in everlasting destruction. All the curses of the Covenant
> shall cling to him and God will set him apart for evil. He
> shall be cut off from the midst of all the sons of light. . . .
> (1QS 2:15–16—DSSE 74)

In this context, what the member of the Qumran community is called upon to do is simply an echo of what God himself does to such a sinner! His lack of love is just as righteous as God's own failure to love the person who does not obey the commandments!

Love of One's Fellow Countryman

This is the meaning of the statement in Leviticus 19:18, at least within its present context. In its present context, the verse is a summary of a variety of rules directed at relations and responsibilities toward others. The beginning of v 18 is important: "Take no revenge and cherish no grudge against your fellow countrymen. You shall love your neighbor as yourself. I am the Lord."

Love of All Humanity

We have seen this extension of love previously in the passage quoted from TIss 7:6, where Issachar says: "I loved every human being as I love my children." And he encourages the reader to "walk with all mankind in sincerity of heart" (v 7).

Love of Enemies

We have seen love of blood relatives, of fellow members of the sect, even of all humanity, but there is evidence of one still wider boundary of love: one's enemies. There were various reasons given for this.

Non-retaliation in Old Testament thought was limited to one's own nation. However, in apocalyptic preaching it was based on the conviction that judgment belonged only to God. The community would be vindicated by God at the final judgment:

> I will pay to no man the reward of evil; I will pursue him with goodness. For judgement of all the living is with God and it is He who will render to man his reward. I will not envy in a spirit of wickedness, my soul shall not desire the riches of violence. I will not grapple with the men of perdition until the Day of Revenge, but my wrath shall not turn from the men of falsehood and I will not rejoice until judgement is made. I will bear no rancor against them that turn from transgression, but will have no pity on all who depart from the Way. I will offer no comfort to the smitten

until their way becomes perfect. (1QS 10:17–21—DSSE 90–91)

From the latter half of this passage we also see that the sectarian's hatred of the sinner may have had another purpose, to help turn the sinner back from his sin.

The discussion of love of enemies is given considerable attention in The Testaments of the Twelve Patriarchs, especially in the Testament of Joseph, where Joseph is presented as always loving the brothers who sold him into slavery. Several types of motives are given here. In one passage it is spoken of in terms of self-control which is pleasing to God (TJos 10:1–6). It is spoken of as being part of the fulfillment of the law, which was to be obeyed out of fear of the Lord and because thus would one be loved by God (TJos 11:1).

Such love is also spoken of simply as being "pleasing to God." The referent is clearly one's blood relatives, but the motive is interesting:

So you see, my children, how many things I endured in order not to bring my brothers into disgrace. You therefore love one another and in patient endurance conceal one another's shortcomings. God is delighted by harmony among brothers and by the intention of a kind heart that takes pleasure in goodness. (TJos 17:1–3)

Finally, in a passage pointed out by Perkins,[2] in The Testaments of the Twelve Patriarchs, love of enemies is encouraged with the promise that the one who does so will bring blessings upon himself. Thus in TJos, in a passage commonly taken to refer to the evil done to him by his brothers, Joseph says:

. . . if anyone wishes to do you harm, you should pray for him, along with doing good, and you will be rescued by the Lord from every evil. Indeed you can see that on account of my humility and patient endurance I took to myself a wife, the daughter of the priest of Heliopolis; a hundred talents of gold were given to me along with her, and my Lord caused them to be my servants. And he also gave me

mature beauty, more than those of mature beauty in Israel;
he preserved me until old age with strength and beauty.
(TJos 18:2–4)

Near the end of *Joseph and Aseneth,* Benjamin is about to kill
the pharaoh's son who has been wounded in battle, but he is stopped
by Levi.

By no means, brother, will you do this deed, because we
are men who worship God, and it does not befit a man who
worships God to repay evil for evil nor to trample underfoot
a fallen (man) nor to oppress his enemy till death. And
now, put your sword back into its place, and come, help
me, and we will heal him of his wound; and if he lives, he
will be our friend after this, and his father Pharaoh will like
our father (29:3–4).

Here there is a mixture of motivations: first, it is not right for a
man of God to kill a fallen enemy, and, second, that healing the
enemy will bring blessings upon themselves.

This excursion into the intertestamental literature shows that
there was abundant speculation on the matter of relations between
varying degrees of relatives, countrymen, strangers and enemies. This
enables us to situate more adequately the Johannine conception of
"love for one another" within its historical matrix.

NOTES

1. For example, TReu 6:10–11; TSim 4:7; TAsh 6:1.
2. Perkins, *Love Commands* 33.

BIBLIOGRAPHY

SOURCES

Aland, K. et al., *The Greek New Testament* (2nd ed.; New York: American Bible Society, 1968).

Charlesworth, J. H. (ed.), *The Old Testament Pseudepigrapha* (Vols. 1–2; Garden City: Doubleday, 1983–85).

de Jonge, M., *The Testaments of the Twelve Patriarchs. A Critical Edition of the Greek Text* (Leiden: E. J. Brill, 1978).

Lohse, E. (ed.), *Die Texte aus Qumran* (München: Kuesel, 1971).

Rahlfs, A. (ed.), *Septuaginta* (2 vols.; Stuttgart: Wurttembergische Bibelanstalt, 1965).

Robinson, J. M. (ed.), *The Nag Hammadi Library in English* (New York: Harper and Row, 1977).

Vermes, G., *The Dead Sea Scrolls in English* (2nd ed. Harmondsworth: Penguin, 1975).

REFERENCE WORKS

Bauer, W., Arndt, W. F., Gingrich, F. W., *A Greek-English Lexicon of the New Testament and Other Early Christian Literature* (Chicago: University of Chicago, 1957).

Blass, F., Debrunner, R., Funk, R. W., *A Greek Grammar of the New Testament and Other Early Christian Literature* (Chicago: University of Chicago, 1967).

Hatch, E., Redpath, H. A., *A Concordance to the Septuagint and Other Greek Versions of the Old Testament (Including the Apocryphal Books)* (Oxford: Clarendon, 1897) (Repr. Grand Rapids: Baker, 1983).

The Interpreter's Dictionary of the Bible. An Illustrated Encyclopedia, (New York: Abingdon Press, 1962).

Kittel, G., Friedrich, G. (eds.), *The Theological Dictionary of the New Testament* (7 vols.; Grand Rapids: Wm. B. Eerdmans, 1964–71).

Liddell, H. G., Scott, R., *A Greek-English Lexicon* (Oxford: Oxford University, 1940).

Metzger, B. et al, *A Textual Commentary on the Greek New Testament* (London: United Bible Societies, 1971).

Moulton, W. F., Geden, A. S., *A Concordance to the Greek Testament* (4th ed.; Edinburgh: Clark, 1963).

Strack, H. L., Billerbeck, P., *Kommentar zum Neuen Testament aus Talmud und Midrasch* (6 vols.; 3rd ed.; München: Beck, 1922–61).

Zerwick, M., *Biblical Greek* (Rome: Biblical Institute, 1963).

———, Grosvenor, M., *A Grammatical Analysis of the Greek New Testament* (Rome: Biblical Institute, 1974).

SECONDARY LITERATURE

Aune, D., *The Cultic Setting of Realized Eschatology in Early Christianity* (NovTSup 28; Leiden: Brill, 1963).

Barrett, C. K., *The Holy Spirit and the Gospel Tradition* (London: SPCK, 1975).

———, *The Gospel According to John* (2nd ed.; Philadelphia: Westminster, 1978).

———, "The Place of Eschatology in the Fourth Gospel," *ExpTim* 59 (1947–48) 302–05.

———, Christocentric or Theocentric? Observations on the Theological Method of the Fourth Gospel," in *La Notion biblique de Dieu BETL* 41 (1976) 361–76.

Barrosse, T., "The Relationship of Love to Faith in St. John," *TS* 18 (1957) 538–59.

Bauernfeind, O., "Die Fuerbitte angesichts der 'süende zum Tode,' " in *Von der Antike zum Christentum* (V. Schultze Festgabe; Stettin: Fischer and Schmidt, 1931) 43–54.

Beasley-Murray, G. R., *Baptism in the New Testament* (Exeter: Paternoster, 1962).

Becker, J., "Die Abschiedsreden Jesu im Johannesevangelium," *ZNW* 61 (1970) 215–46.

———, "Aufbau, Schichtung und theologiegeschichtliche Stellung des Gebetes in Johannes 17," *ZNW* 60 (1969) 56–83.

———, "Beobachtungen zum Dualismus in Johannesevangelium," *ZNW* 65 (1974) 71–87.

Berger, K., *Die Gesetzesauslegung Jesu. Teil I: Markus und Parallelen* (WMANT40; Neukirchen-Vluyn: Neukirchener, 1972).

Bergmeier, R., "Glaube als Werk? Die 'Werke Gottes' in Damaskusschrift II, 14–15 und Johannes 6, 28–29," *REVQ* 6 (1967) 253–60.

Bernard, J. H., *A Critical and Exegetical Commentary on the Gospel According to St. John* (Edinburg: Clark, 1928).

Bertram, "*ergon, ergazomai,*" *TDNT,* 4, 635–55.

Betz, O., *Der Paraklet: Fürsprecher im haretischen Spätjudentum, im Johannes-Evangelium und in neu gefundenen gnostischen Schriften* (Institutum Iudaicum 2; Leiden: E. J. Brill, 1963).

Blank, J., *Krisis. Untersuchungen zur johanneischen Christologie und Eschatologie* (Freiburg: Lambertus, 1964).

Bogart, J., *Orthodox and Heretical Perfectionism in the Johannine Community as Evident in the First Epistle of John* (SBLDS 33; Missoula: Scholars Press, 1977).

Boismard, M.-E., "La connaissance dans l'Alliance nouvelle d'après la Première Lettre de Saint Jean," *RB* 56 (1949) 365–91.

———, " 'Je ferai avec vous une alliance nouvelle' (Introduction à la Première Epitre de Saint Jean)," *LumVie* 8 (1953) 94–109.

———, "Le caractere adventice de Jn 12, 45–50," *Sacra Pagina* (ed. J. Coppens; Miscellanea Biblica. Congressus Internationalis Catholicus de Re Biblica; Vol. 2; Gembloux: Duculot, 1959) 189–92.

———, "Les citations targumiques dans le quatrième évangile," *RB* (1959) 374–78.

———, *Quatre hymnes baptismales dan la Première Epître de Pierre* (LD 30; Paris: Cerf, 1961).

———, "L'evolution du theme eschatologique dans les traditions johanniques, *RB* 68 (1961) 514–18.

———, *L'Évangile de Jean,* Vol. 3 of *Synopse des quatres Évangiles en francais* (Paris: Cerf, 1977).

————, "Un procédé rédactionnel dans le quatrième évangile: *La Wiederaufnahme*," in *L'Évangile de Jean: Sources, rédaction, théologie* (BETL; ed. M. de Jonge; Leuven: Gembloux, 1978) 235–41.

Bornkamm, G., "Der Paraklet im Johannes-Evangelium," in *Geschichte und Glaube*, Part I. *Gesammelte Aufsätse*, Vol. 3 (BEvT 48; Münich: Chr. Kaiser, 1968) 68–89.

Braun, F.-M., "La Réduction du Pluriel au Singulier dan l'Évangile et la Première Lettre de Jean," *NTS* 24 (1977) 40–67.

Braun, H., *Qumran und das Neue Testament* (2 Vols.; Tübingen: J.C.B. Mohr, 1966).

Brooke, A. E., *A Critical and Exegetical Commentary on the Johannine Epistles* (ICC; Edinburg: Clark, 1912).

Brown, R. E., *New Testament Essays* (Garden City: Doubleday, 1965).

————, *The Gospel According to John* (AB 29,29a; Garden City: Doubleday, 1966–70).

————, *The Epistles of John* (AB 30; Garden City: Doubleday, 1982).

————, *The Community of the Beloved Disciple* (New York: Paulist, 1979).

————, "The Paraclete in the Fourth Gospel," *NTS* 13 (1966–67) 113–32.

————, "The Kerygma of the Gospel according to St. John," *Int* 21 (1967) 387–400.

Bultmann, R., *The Gospel of John. A Commentary* (Philadelphia: Westminster, 1970).

————, *The Johannine Epistles* (Hermeneia; Philadelphia: Fortress, 1973).

————, *Theology of the New Testament* (Vols. 1–3; New York: Scribner's, 1955).

Burge, G., *The Anointed Community: The Holy Spirit in the Johannine Tradition* (Grand Rapids: Eerdmans, 1987).

Carrmignac, J., "Les dangers de l'eschatologie," *NTS* 17 (1971–72) 365–90.

Cavallin, H. C. C., *Life After Death: Paul's Argument for the Resurrection of the Dead in 1 Cor 15. Part I: An Enquiry into the Jewish Background* (Lund: Gleerup, 1974).

Charlesworth, J. H. (ed.) *John and Qumran* (London: G. Chapman, 1972).

Charlesworth, J. H. and Culpepper, R. A., "The Odes of Solomon and the Gospel of John," *CBQ* 35 (1973) 298–322.

Chmiel, J., *Lumière et charité d'après la Première Épitre de Saint Jean* (Rome: Gregorian University, 1971).

Collins, J. J., "Apocalyptic Eschatology and the Transcendence of Death," *CBQ* 36 (1974) 21–43.

————, "Jewish Apocalypses," *Semeia* 14 (1979) 21–59.

————, *The Apocalyptic Imagination* (New York: Crossroad, 1984).

Collins, R. F., " 'A New Commandment I Give To You, That You Love One Another . . .' (Jn 13:34)," *LavTheolPhil* 35 (1979) 235–61.

Cullmann, O., *Baptism in the New Testament* (SBT 1,1; London: SCM, 1950).

————, *The Christology of the New Testament* (Philadelphia: Westminster, 1963).

————, *1 Corinthians* (Hermeneia; Philadelphia: Fortress, 1975).

Culpepper, R. A., *The Johannine School. An Evaluation of the Johannine-School Hypothesis Based on an Investigation of the Nature of Ancient Schools* (SBLDS 26; Missoula: Scholars, 1975).

————, *The Anatomy of the Fourth Gospel: A Study in Literary Design* (Philadelphia: Fortress, 1983).

de la Potterie, I., *La vérité dans Saint Jean* (2 vols.; AnBib 73–74; Rome: Biblical Institute, 1977).

————, "Anointing of the Christian by Faith," *The Christian Lives by the Spirit,* I. de la Potterie and S. Lyonnet (Staten Island: Alba, 1971) 79–143.

de Jonge, M., *Jesus: Stranger from Heaven and Son of God* (SBLSBS 11: Missoula: Scholars, 1977).

Delcor, M., "Le vocabulaire juridique, cultuel et mystique de l'initiation dans la secte de Qumran," *Qumran-Probleme* (ed. H. Bardtke; Berlin: Akademie Verlag, 1963) 109–34.

Dodd, C. H., *The Interpretation of the Fourth Gospel* (Cambridge: Cambridge University, 1953).

————, "The First Epistle of John and the Fourth Gospel," *BJRL* 21 (1937) 129–56.

Eicholz, G., "Glaube und Liebe im I. Johannesbrief," *EvT* 4 (1937) 411–37.

Feuillet, A., "La morale chrétienne d'après Saint Jean," *EspVie* 83 (1973) 665–70.

————, "The Structure of First John: Comparison with the 4th Gospel," *BTB* 3 (1973) 194–216.

Forestell, T., *The Word of the Cross: Salvation as Revelation in the Fourth Gospel* (AnBib 57; Rome: Biblical Institute, 1974).

Fortna, R., *The Gospel of Signs* (SNTSMS 11; Cambridge: The University Press, 1970).

————, *The Fourth Gospel and Its Predecessor* (Philadelphia: Fortress, 1988).

Fuller, R. H., *The Foundations of New Testament Christology* (New York: Scribner, 1969).

———— (ed.), *Essays on the Love Commandment* (Philadelphia: Fortress, 1978).

Furnish, V., *The Love Command in the New Testament* (Nashville/New York: Abingdon, 1972).

Gowan, D. E., *Eschatology in the Old Testament* (Philadelphia: Fortress, 1986).

Grayston, K., *The Johannine Epistles* (NCB; Grand Rapids: Eerdmans, 1984).

Grether, O., *Name und Wort Gottes im Alten Testament* (Giessen: 1934).

Haenchen, E., *A Commentary on the Gospel of John* (Hermeneia; Philadelphia: Fortress, 1984).

Hahn, F., "Das biblische Verständnis des Heiligen Geistes. Soteriologische Funktion und 'Personalität' des Heiligen Geistes," in *Erfahrung und Theologie des heiligen Geistes* (ed. C. Heitmann and H. Muhlen; Hamburg: Agentur des Rauen Hauses, 1974) 131–50.

————, *The Titles of Jesus in Christology* (Lutterworth: London, 1969).

Harvey, A. E., *Jesus and the Constraints of History* (Philadelphia: Westminster, 1982).

Hauck, F., "*menein,*" *TDNT.*

Heise, J., *Bleiben. Menein in den johanneischen Schriften* (Tübingen: Mohr, 1967).

Herkenrath, J., "Sünde zum Tode," in *Aus Theologie und Philosophie* (ed. T. Steinbüchel and T. Müncher; F. Tillman Festschrift; Dusseldorf: Patmos, 1950) 119–38.

Holwerda, D. E., *The Holy Spirit and Eschatology in the Gospel of John. A Critique of Rudolf Bultmann's Present Eschatology* (Kampen: Kok, 1959).

Houlden, J. L., *The Johannine Epistles* (HNTC; New York: Harper and Row, 1973).

Humbert, A., "L'observance des commandements dan les écrits johanniques," in *Studia Moralia,* I (Rome: 1963), 187–219.

Joly, R., *Le vocabulaire chrétien del'amour est-il originel?* (Brussels: Université Libre, 1968).

Johnston, G., *The Spirit-Paraclete in the Gospel of John* (SNTSMS 12; Cambridge: Cambridge University, 1970).

Käsemann, E., *The Testament of Jesus* (Philadelphia: Fortress, 1968).

Klausner, J., *The Messianic Idea in Israel* (New York: Macmillan, 1955).

Kuhn, H. W., *Enderwartung und Gegenwärtiges Heil* (Studien zur Umwelt des NT 4; Göttingen: Vandenhoeck & Ruprecht, 1966).

Kysar, R., *The Fourth Evangelist and His Gospel. An Examination of Contemporary Scholarship* (Minneapolis: Augsburg, 1975).

Law, R., *The Tests of Life. A Study of the First Epistle of St. John* (Edinburgh: Clark, 1909).

Lazure, N., *Les valeurs morales de la théologie johannique. Evangile et Epitres* (EB; Paris: Gabalda, 1965).

Lohmeyer, E., "Probleme paulinischer Theologie, II, 'Gesetzeswerke'," *ZNW* 28 (1928) 177–207.

Mackenzie, J. L., "The Word of God in the Old Testament," *TS* (1960) 183–206.

MacRae, G. W., "Biblical News: Gnosis in Messina," *CBQ* 28 (1966) 322–33.

———, "The Fourth Gospel and 'Religionsgeschichte'," *CBQ* 32 (1970) 13–24.

———, "Nag Hammadi and the New Testament," *Gnosis. Festschrift für H. Jonas* (ed. B. Aland; Göttingen: Vandenhoeck und Ruprecht, 1978) 144–57.

———, "Theology and Irony in the Fourth Gospel," *The Word in the World: Essays in Honor of Frederick L. Moriarty, S.J.* (ed.

R. J. Clifford, G. W. MacRae; Cambridge, Mass.: Weston College Press, 1973) 83–96.

Malatesta, E., *Interiority and Covenant: A Study of einai en and menein en in the First Letter of Saint John* (AnBib 69; Rome: Biblical Institute, 1978).

Marshall, I. H., *The Epistles of John* (NICNT; Grand Rapids: Eerdmans, 1978).

Martyn, J. L., *History and Theology in the Fourth Gospel* (New York: Harper and Row, 1968).

————, "Clementine Recognitions 1, 33–71, Jewish Christianity, and the Fourth Gospel," *Festschrift für N.A. Dahl* (Oslo: Universitet, 1976).

————, "Glimpses into the History of the Johannine Community. From Its Origin Through the Period of Its Life in Which the Fourth Gospel Was Composed," *L'Évangile de Jean. Sources, Rédaction, Théologie* (BETL 44; Gembloux: Duculot, 1977) 149–75.

————, "Source Criticism and *Religionsgeschichte* in the Fourth Gospel," *Jesus and Man's Hope* (Vol. 1; Pittsburgh: Pittsburgh Theological Seminary, 1971) 247–73.

————, "We Have Found Elijah," *Jews, Greeks and Christians. Religious Cultures in Late Antiquity: Essays in Honor of William David Davies* (SJLA 21; Leiden: E.J. Brill, 1976) 180–219.

Mattill, A. J., "Johannine Communities Behind the Fourth Gospel: Georg Richter's Analysis," *TS* 38 (1977) 294–315.

Moran, W. L., "The Ancient Near Eastern Background of the Love of God in Deuteronomy," *CBQ* 25 (1963) 77–87.

Mowinkel, S., *He That Cometh* (New York: Abingdon, 1956).

Moule, C. F. D., *The Holy Spirit* (London: Mowbray, 1978).

Müller, U. B., "Die Bedeutung des Kreuzestodes Jesu im Johannesevangelium," *KD* 21 (1975) 49–71.

Nauck, W., *Die Tradition und der Charackter des ersten Johannesbriefes* (WUNT 3; Tübingen: Mohr, 1957).

Neirynk, F., "L'Epanalepsis et la critique littéraire. Á propos de l'évangile de Jean," *ETL* 56 (1980), 303–38.

Nickelsburg, G. W. E., *Resurrection, Immortality, and Eternal Life in Intertestamental Judaism* (Harvard Theological Studies xxvi; Cambridge: Harvard, 1972).

Nicolson, G., *Death as Departure: The Johannine Descent-Ascent Schema* (Chico: Scholars, 1983).

Nygren, A., *Agape and Eros* (2 vols; London: SPCK, 1932–37).

O'Connell, M. J., "The Concept of Commandment in the Old Testament," *TS* 21 (1960) 351–403.

Painter, J., "The 'Opponents' in 1 John," *NTS* 32 (1986) 48–71.

Pancaro, S., *The Law in the Fourth Gospel* (NovT Supp 42; Leiden: E.J. Brill, 1975).

Pelleteier, A., "Le vocabulaire du commandement dans le Pentateuque des LXX et dans le Nouveau Testament," *RSR* 41 (1953) 519–24.

Perkins, P., *The Johannine Epistles* (NTM; Wilmington: Glazier, 1979).

———, *Love Commands in the New Testament* (New York: Paulist, 1982).

———, *Resurrection: New Testament Witness and Contemporary Reflection* (New York: Doubleday, 1984).

Porsch, F., *Anwalt der Glaubenden. Das wirken des Geistes nach dem Zeugnis Johannesevangelium* (Stuttgart: Katholisches Bibelwerk, 1978).

———, *Pneuma und Wort. Ein Exegetischer Beitrag zur Pneumatologie des Johannesevangeliums* (FTS 16; Frankfurt: Knecht, 1974).

Preisker, H., "Jüdische Apokalyptik und hellenistischer Synkretismus im Johannes-Evangelium, dargelegt an dem Begriff 'Licht'," *TLZ* 77 (1952) 673–78.

Reynolds, S. M., "The Sin unto Death and Prayers for the Dead," *Reformation Review* 20 (1973) 130–39.

Richter, G., "Die Deutung des Kreuzestodes Jesu in der Leidensgeschichte des Johannesevangeliums," *Bibel und Leben* 9 (1968) 21–36, also in *Studien zum Johannesevangelium* (ed. J. Hainz; BU 13; Regensburg: F. Pustet, 1977) 58–73.

———, "Präsentische und futurische Eschatologie im 4. Evangelium," *Gegenwart und kommendes Reich: Schülergabe Anton Vögtle zum 65. Geburtstag* (ed. P. Fiedler, D. Zeller; Stuttgart: Katholisches Bibelwerk, 1975) 117–152 also in *Studien zum Johannesevangelium* (ed. J. Hainz; BU 13; Regensburg: F. Pustet, 1977) 346–82.

————, "Zum gemeindebildenden Element in den johanneischen Schriften," in *Studien zum Johannesevangelium* (ed. J. Hainz; BU 13; Regensburg: F. Pustet, 1977) 383–97.

Rigaux, B., *L'Antichrist et l'opposition au royaume messianique dans l'Ancien et le Nouveau Testament* (Gembloux: Duculot, 1932).

Ringgren, H., *The Faith of Qumran. Theology of the Dead Sea Scrolls* (Philadelphia: Fortress, 1963).

Schlier, H., "Vom Antichrist—Zum 13. Kapitel der Offenbarung Johannes," in *Die Zeit der Kirche* (Freiburg: Herder, 1956) 16–29.

Schmitt, J., "Simples remarques sur le fragment Jo. xx, 22–23," *Mélanges en l'honneur de Monseigneur Michel Andrieu* (Strasbourg: Strasbourg University, 1956) 415–23.

Schnackenburg, R., *The Gospel According to John* (Vols. 1–3; ET; New York: Seabury, 1968–82).

————, "Die situationsgelösten Redestücke in Joh 3," *ZNW* 49 (1958) 88–99.

————, *Die Johannesbriefe* (HTKNT 13; 5th ed.; Freiburg: Herder, 1975).

————, "Die johanneische Gemeinde und ihre Geisterfahrung," *Die Kirche des Anfangs. Festschrift Hein Schürmann zum 65. Geburtstag* (ed. R. Schnackenburg, J. Ernst, J. Wanke; Leipzig: St. Benno, 1977) 277–306.

Schrenk, G., "*entellomai, entolē,*" *TDNT,* 4, 544–56.

Segovia, F., "The Love and Hatred of Jesus and Johannine Sectarianism," *CBQ* 43 (1981), 258–72.

————, *Love Relationships in the Johannine Tradition* (SBLDS 58; Chico: Scholars Press, 1982).

————, "John 13 1–20, the Footwashing in the Johannine Tradition," *ZNW* 73 (1982) 31–51.

————, "John 15:18–16:4a: A First Addition to the Original Farewell Discourse?" *CBQ* 45 (1983) 219–30.

————, "The Structure, *Tendenz,* and *Sitz im Leben* of John 13: 31–14:31," *JBL* 104 (1985) 471–93.

Smalley, S. S., *1, 2, 3 John* (WBC; Waco: Word, 1984).

Smith, D. M., *The Composition and Order of the Fourth Gospel* (New Haven: Yale University Press, 1965).

————, "Johannine Christianity: Some Reflections on Its Character and Delineation," *NTS* 21 (1975) 222–48.

————, "God's Only Son. The Translation of John 3:16 in the Revised Standard Version," *JBL* 72 (1953) 213–19.

Spicq, C., *Agape in the New Testament* (3 vols.; St. Louis: Herder, 1966).

Thiering, B., "Inner and Outer Cleansing at Qumran as a Background to New Testament Baptism," *NTS* 26 (1979–80) 266–77.

Tomar, T., *Pasión y Resurrección en el IV Evangelio* (Salamanca: Universidad, 1976).

Trudinger, P., "Concerning Sins, Mortal and Otherwise. A Note on 1 John 5, 16–17," *Biblica* 52 (1971) 541–42.

van den Bussche, H., "La structure de Jean I–XII," in *L'Évangile de Jean*, Rescherches Bibliques 3 (1958), 61–109.

van der Ploeg, J., "Studies in Hebrew Law, I, The Terms," *CBQ* 12 (1950) 248–59.

————, "Eschatology in the Old Testament," *OTS* 17 (1972) 89–99.

van Dyke Parunak, H., "Oral Typesetting: Some Uses of Biblical Structure," *Biblica* 62 (1981) 153–68.

van Unnik, W. C., "De Verbinding *tauta eipōn* in het Evangelie van Johannes," *Ad Interim* (Kampen: J.J. Kok, n.d.) 61–73.

Vanhoye, A., "Notre Foi, oeuvre divine, d'après le quatrième Évangile," *NRT* 86 (1964) 337–54.

Vellanickal, M., *The Divine Sonship of Christians in the Johannine Writings* (Rome: Biblical Institute, 1977).

Vermes, G., *The Dead Sea Scrolls: Qumran in Perspective* (Philadelphia: Fortress, 2nd ed., 1977).

————, *Jesus the Jew* (Philadelphia: Fortress, 1981).

Volz, P., *Die Eschatologies der jüdischen Gemeinde im neutestamentlichen Zeitalter* (Hildescheim: Georg Olms, 1966 [1934]).

von Wahlde, U. C., *The Earliest Version of John's Gospel* (Wilmington: M. Glazier, 1989).

————, "A Redactional Technique in the Fourth Gospel," *CBQ* 38 (1976) 520–33.

————, "Faith and Works in Jn vi 28–29: Exegesis or Eisegesis?" *NovT* 22 (1980) 304–15.

————, "The Witnesses to Jesus in John 5:31–40 and Belief in the Fourth Gospel," *CBQ* 43 (1981) 385–404.

————, "*Wiederaufnahme* as a Marker of Redaction in Jn 6, 51–58," *Biblica* 64 (1983) 542–49.

————, "The Theological Foundation of the Presbyter's Argument in 2 Jn (vv 4–6)," *ZNW* (1985) 209–24.

Weiss, K., "Die 'Gnosis' im Hintergrund und im Spiegel der Johannesbriefe," in K.-W. Troeger, *Gnosis und Neues Testament* (Berlin: Evangelische Verlagsanstalt, 1973).

————, "Orthodoxie und Heterodoxie im 1. Johannesbrief," *ZNW* 58 (1967) 247–55.

Wellhausen, J., *Erweiterungen und Änderungen im vierten Evangelium* (Berlin: Reimer, 1907).

White, J. L., "New Testament Epistolary Literature in the Framework of Ancient Epistolography," *ANRW* II. 25.2 (Berlin: 1984) 1730–1756.

Windisch, H., *Die Katholischen Briefe* (HNT 15; 3rd ed; Tübingen, Mohr, 1951).

————, *The Spirit-Paraclete in the Fourth Gospel* (tr. J. W. Cox; Facet Books, Biblical Series 20; Philadelphia: Fortress, 1968).

Woll, D. B., *Johannine Christianity in Conflict* (SBLDS 60; Chico: Scholars Press, 1981).

Yates, R., "The Antichrist," *Evangelical Quarterly* 46 (1974) 42–50.

Author Index

Subject Index

Boldface *indicates major treatment.*

Abiding in (see "Remain in"), 87, 90, 105, 163, 167, 187n12, 210, 216
Additions (see redaction)
Agapan/philein, distinction between, **12,** 34, 34n12
Anointed, 125, 127, 143, **145–46,** 148, 159, 184, 186n9, 208, 217
Anthropology, **144–62, 162–169**
Antichrist, **160,** 191n43, 209
Apocalyptic worldview, 14, 121–22, 125, 135n41, 176, **183–85,** 191n43, 192n43, 195n66, 196,n74, 299, 230, 252
Atonement (see "expiatory death")

Baptism, 250–51, 258n28
as initiation, 262
with the Holy Spirit, 117, 133n27
Beginning (of Johannine tradition), **161–162,** 209, 213, 218, 250, 251

Begotten of God. (see "Born of God")
Being of God, 211
Belief, 13, 51, 64, 97, 116, 133n28, 152, 161, 201–202
correct and incorrect, 92, 168, 215, 221, 264
"in the name of", **51–52,** 54, 165
Beloved Disciple, 132n24
Born
of God, 62, 72n25,149–151, 163, 167, 184, 188n15, 188n22, 194n63, 206, 212, 221
of the devil, 151
"Both/And" position of author of 1 John, **144,** 146, 150–151, 157, 158, 167, 180, 186n3
Brother(s) (as designation of believer(s))
Love of, 106, 108, 113, 115, 169, 189, 214, 218, 255n5
Hatred of, 60, 211, 213

Child
of God, 66, 105, 147, 150, 158, 163, 165, 168, 181, 188n19, 218, 250
of the devil, 218

THEOLOGICAL INQUIRIES:

Serious studies on contemporary questions of Scripture, Systematics and Moral Theology. Also in the series: